THE COST OF PLEA BARGAINS

Reflections and Recommendations from the ABA Plea Bargain Task Force

Edited by
LUCIAN E. DERVAN, RUSSELL D. COVEY, THEA JOHNSON

AMERICAN BAR ASSOCIATION
Criminal Justice Section

Cover design by Carolina Martinez/ABA Design

Printed in the United States of America.

28 27 26 25 24   5 4 3 2 1

A catalog record for this book is available from the Library of Congress.

To my parents and to Anne, Dalton, and Adelaide
—LED

To my parents, Marjorie and Marvin Covey, and Julia, Noah, and Reuben
—RDC

To my father and to Geoff, Leo, and Max
—TBJ

Contents

Preface

Those who work and conduct research in the plea bargaining space know the realities of today's criminal justice system, the importance of confronting what it means to live in a system of pleas, and the deep need to offer concrete paths forward toward a more transparent, fair, and just system of adjudication. As discussed in the book, plea bargaining's history is complex, and efforts to bring attention to the problems of relying on bargained justice stretch deep into our history. But today, in a way never seen before, the legal community stands on the brink of real change. People are ready to discuss plea bargaining and work collaboratively toward meaningful reforms—prosecutors, defenders, judges, academics, and policymakers together. This fact is why it was imperative for the American Bar Association to convene a task force on plea bargaining in 2019, release a report in early 2023 containing principles unanimously agreed upon by task force members representing various corners of the criminal justice system, and adopt those principles as official ABA policy at the August 2023 ABA House of Delegates meeting.

This book tells the story of plea bargaining's rise, of the early roots of the movement to reform pleas, and of the work and recommendations of the ABA Plea Bargain Task Force. In addition to offering the reader the Task Force Report itself, this book also offers deeper insights into many of the concepts, concerns, and proposals raised in the report so that readers might better understand the basis for the report's recommendations and gain greater insights into the potential reforms referenced within its pages. We feel very fortunate to have served as the cochairs and reporter of the task force and to have had the opportunity to lead this work over the last several years. We hope that this book continues that work as a collection of materials that will inspire further discussion and lead to a better understanding of the plea bargaining system. We also hope that this work and the ideas contained within its pages will assist the movement to reform plea bargaining and lead us to a better future.

It is important to note at the outset that while the Task Force Report that appears at Chapter 2 represents the collective work of the entire task force that met for over three years and was unanimously adopted by the group, this book is a separate undertaking. For that reason, this work should not be interpreted as a supplemental report from the task force but, instead, as a separate work that offers greater detail and insights from some members of the group. It is also important to note that each author was invited to contribute their personal thoughts to this book and, therefore, the inclusion of those chapters in this work should not be construed as an endorsement of those concepts by other authors appearing herein or the editors. Rather, this book contains a diverse collection of thoughts that we hope will serve to continue our discussions as we wrestle with what comes next. Plea bargaining is a challenging area of law that desperately needs reform. The report of the task force is a significant and important step in that direction.

This book represents another vital element of that work by providing a platform for task force members to present their personal perspectives on plea bargaining in the wake of the task force's work and share additional knowledge about the system and its operation with a wider audience. This book also represents a resource for practitioners, academics, policymakers, students, the public, and others to dig deeper into the issue of plea bargaining and plea bargaining reform through the lens of each individual author and their unique perspectives within the criminal justice system. For this opportunity to engage in such a dialogue, we are thankful.

Plea bargaining's rise may be mostly complete, but our work crafting a plea system that is faithful to our aspirations for criminal justice is only just beginning. We hope this book serves to move us along that path.

Sincerely,

Lucian E. Dervan, Editor and Task Force Cochair
Russell D. Covey, Editor and Task Force Cochair
Thea Johnson, Editor and Task Force Reporter

CHAPTER 1

Fourteen Principles and a Path Forward for Plea Bargaining Reform

Editors

Plea bargaining accounts for almost 98 percent of federal convictions and 95 percent of state convictions in the United States. So prevalent is the American plea bargaining system that the U.S. Supreme Court wrote in 2012 that ours "is for the most part a system of pleas, not a system of trials."[1] Such dominance, however, has not always been the case. The American system of criminal law, in fact, was a system of trials at its inception, just as was the case with the English common law that served as its basis. But gradually, beginning in small and disparate ways in the late 18th and early 19th centuries, and then in broader and deeper ways in the late 19th and early 20th centuries, plea bargaining came to dominate. By 1970, the year the U.S. Supreme Court finally approved of the practice in *Brady v. United States*, upward of 90 percent of convictions were the result of pleas of guilty, and many of those were likely the result of bargains.[2]

The story of plea bargaining's rise to dominance is the story of an American invention growing in the shadows of the criminal justice system against a backdrop of common law precedent that rejected the use of threats of further punishment or promises of leniency to induce pleas of guilty. And, because it existed mostly in the shadows during its rise, plea bargaining came into existence without much oversight, regulation, or monitoring by the bar, the courts, or the legislatures. As a result, plea bargaining developed in different ways from one jurisdiction to another. During this hidden journey to dominance, jurisdictions also failed to establish guiding principles or guardrails to ensure that plea practices were appropriate and did not infringe on defendants' constitutional rights, particularly the right to trial found in the Sixth Amendment. But plea

1. Missouri v. Frye, 566 U.S. 134, 143–44 (2012).
2. Brady v. United States, 397 U.S. 742 (1970).

bargaining rose nonetheless and, as the numbers just given illustrate, eventually came to envelop the system it was created to assist.

In 2019, almost 50 years after the Supreme Court decision in *Brady*, the chair of the ABA Criminal Justice Section, Lucian Dervan, created a Plea Bargain Task Force. The reasons for the creation of the task force were numerous. As just noted, jurisdictions took varying approaches to bargains as the process developed over the years, some more faithful to the constitutional right to jury trial than others. Over time, the use of staggering sentencing differentials, often described as a trial penalty by defendants and their counsel, had also become more common. Further, by the late 2010s, a developing body of research had arisen that demonstrated that plea bargaining's innocence problem was large and significant. At the same time, data regarding the manner in which plea bargaining was exacerbating existing racial discrimination in the system was mounting. The hope was that the task force could collaboratively examine the system from the ground up, including the concerns just mentioned, and craft principles to guide the criminal justice community in the plea bargaining space—the types of guiding principles that had been so lacking during plea bargaining's shadowy rise to dominance. The letter to the newly formed group stated that the task force was to consider how plea bargaining has developed over time and what advantages and challenges have resulted. The letter also charged the group with considering the best path forward and potential solutions to the challenges identified by the group.

From the task force's inception, those working on the effort knew that the group had to be diverse to capture varying views of the plea bargaining system and identify innovative ideas about how the system should work. The task force, therefore, included representatives from various corners of the criminal justice system—the prosecution, the defense, the judiciary, the academy, various politically diverse advocacy groups, and the state and federal systems. During its duration, the task force regularly met to discuss the state of plea bargaining in America and collected and reviewed testimony from experts in the field and those impacted by the plea system, scholarly and legal reports on plea bargaining, state and federal rules of criminal procedure, and other materials. After almost four years, the members of the task force jointly created and unanimously endorsed 14 principles. The principles, which cover a host of topics such as the use of impermissibly coercive incentives, the use of pretrial detention in plea bargaining, the provision of adequate discovery before a defendant pleads guilty, and the collection of plea bargaining data by the courts, offer a vision of a plea bargaining system that is fairer, more transparent, and more just.

In releasing the 14 Principles, the task force also released a fulsome report discussing the principles, which is reproduced herein as Chapter 2. In the press release for the report launch, the ABA noted:

> The task force recommended several major steps that legislatures, lawyers, judges and court administrators can take to create a more fair and transparent plea bargaining system. "While the plea-bargaining process in the United States is broad and varied, the task force determined that it was vitally important to craft a single set of principles to guide plea practices generally," the report found. "These principles represent our conclusions about how plea bargaining should operate within our larger criminal justice system, a system based on the fundamental constitutional right to trial."

In August 2023, Professor Dervan, cochair of the task force, introduced Resolution 502 at the Annual Meeting of the ABA House of Delegates in Denver, Colorado. In his remarks, he said, "Our criminal justice system is a system of pleas[.] While there are many benefits from having such a plea system, there are also many troubling elements of plea bargaining that must be addressed[.] [The] 14 Principles [ ]create a path forward to a more transparent, fairer, and more just system of plea bargaining. It does this by encouraging an active docket of trials, by establishing principles to prevent coercive plea bargaining, and by encouraging more transparency and data collection related to plea bargaining."[3] Without any opposition, Resolution 502 was adopted by voice vote, and the 14 Principles reproduced next now stand as official ABA policy.

14 Principles from the Plea Bargain Task Force Report

Principle 1: A vibrant and active docket of criminal trials and pre- and post-trial litigation is essential to promote transparency, accountability, justice, and legitimacy in the criminal justice system.

Principle 2: Guilty pleas should not result from the use of impermissibly coercive incentives or incentives that overbear the will of the defendant.

Principle 3: In general, while some difference between the sentence offered prior to trial and the sentence received after trial is permissible, a substantial difference undermines the integrity of the criminal system and reflects a penalty for exercising one's right to trial. This differential, often referred to as the trial penalty, should be eliminated.

Principle 4: Charges should not be selected or amended with the purpose of creating a sentencing differential, sentencing enhancement, punishment or collateral consequence to induce a defendant to plead guilty or to punish defendants for exercising their rights, including the right to trial.

Principle 5: The criminal justice system should recognize that plea bargaining induces defendants to plead guilty for various reasons, some of which have little or nothing to do with factual and legal guilt. In the current system, innocent people sometimes plead guilty to crimes they did not commit.

Principle 6: A defendant should have a right to qualified counsel in any criminal adjudication before the defendant enters a guilty plea. Counsel should be afforded a meaningful opportunity to satisfy their duty to investigate the case without risk of penalty to their client.

Principle 7: There should be robust and transparent procedures at the plea phase to ensure that the defendant's plea is knowing and voluntary, free from impermissible coercion, and that the defendant understands the consequences of their decision to plead guilty.

Principle 8: The use of bail or pretrial detention to induce guilty pleas should be eliminated.

---

3. Lucian Dervan, Remarks at Annual Meeting 2023, ABA House of Delegates (Aug. 2023), https://www.americanbar.org/news/reporter_resources/annual-meeting-2023/house-of-delegates-resolutions/502/.

Principle 9: Defendants should receive all available discovery, including exculpatory materials, prior to entry of a guilty plea, and should have sufficient time to review such discovery before being required to accept or reject a plea offer.

Principle 10: Although guilty pleas necessarily involve the waiver of certain trial rights, there are rights that defendants should never be required to waive in a plea agreement.

Principle 11: An adequate understanding of the collateral consequences that may flow from a guilty plea is necessary to ensure the guilty plea is knowing and voluntary.

Principle 12: Law students, lawyers, and judges should receive training on the use and practice of plea bargaining consistent with the findings and recommendations of the ABA Criminal Justice Section Plea Bargain Task Force Report.

Principle 13: Court systems, sentencing commissions, and other criminal justice stakeholders, including prosecutor offices and public defenders, should collect data about the plea process and each individual plea, including the history of plea offers in a case. Data collection should be used to assess and monitor racial and other biases in the plea process.

Principle 14: At every stage of the criminal process, there should be robust oversight by all actors in the criminal system to monitor the plea process for accuracy and integrity, to ensure the system operates consistent with the Principles in this Report, and to promote transparency, accountability, justice, and legitimacy in the criminal system.

This book provides an opportunity to review the 14 Principles and Plea Bargain Task Force Report, contained in Chapter 2. The book then explores various issues related to plea bargaining and the report to add greater context to the task force's work. This begins at Chapter 3 with "The Historic Rise of Plea Bargaining." In this chapter, Lucian Dervan reveals that plea bargaining is a relatively modern American invention, not a common law practice with deep historic roots. While limited examples of bargains existed in the late 1700s and the 1800s, the use of plea bargaining more widely dates to the era of Prohibition and the necessity of clearing overwhelmed criminal dockets in the face of rampant overcriminalization in the early 1900s. This chapter includes discussion of several times in the mid-20th century when plea bargaining lay on the verge of ruin as the courts examined the practice with great skepticism. The chapter also considers the shadowy rise of plea bargaining and the resulting lack of oversight to give context for the task force's creation and the 14 Principles.

Following this introduction regarding the history of plea bargaining, the book introduces the history of the plea bargaining reform movement in Chapter 4, entitled "The Movement to Curtail Coercive Waivers." While, as discussed in Chapter 3, concern has existed regarding the role and development of plea bargaining in the United States since its earliest days in the 1800s, the last decade has seen a new and important focus on the realities of a system dominated by pleas. The Supreme Court, for example, noted only in 2012 that "criminal justice today is for the most part a system of pleas."[4] In this chapter, Norman Reimer tracks the history of the reform community's work in the plea bargaining space over the last decade and considers the impact of this work on the future of criminal justice reform. Reimer explores the major milestones and reports from the reform community in recent years, along with key findings from these endeavors about

4. Missouri v. Frye, 566 U.S. 134, 143–44 (2012).

the role and ramifications of modern plea bargaining. This chapter not only provides a historical record of groundbreaking reform work over the last ten years but also traces the evolution of the creation of a coalition of reform organizations that now stand on the cusp of significant and meaningful reform efforts in the plea space. Finally, the chapter considers the important role the task force, its report, and its 14 Principles will play in helping guide the work that is occurring as the reform community continues to increase its focus on making the plea system more just and fairer.

The book next explores much of the social science literature discussed in the Task Force Report. In Chapter 5, Vanessa Edkins, in "Plea Bargaining in the United States: Current and Future Contributions of Social Science," discusses the explosion of academic research regarding plea bargaining in recent years. This includes a number of new psychological studies exploring how the plea system functions and how decision-making occurs among its various actors. In her chapter, Edkins delves more deeply into the psychological research touched upon in the Task Force Report and explores what we have learned in recent years about the role of prosecutors, defense attorneys, and defendants in the plea system. Regarding prosecutors, the chapter considers various studies that identify factors that influence prosecutorial decision-making and the exercise of discretion in the plea system. This discussion includes works related to the role of evidence, pretrial detention, and implicit biases. In discussing the role of defense attorneys, the chapter examines various studies that shed light on how defense attorneys assess cases and make recommendations, along with discussion of the influence they have over defendants' decision-making. Finally, in a section describing research regarding defendants and the plea bargaining system, the chapter considers phenomena such as false pleas of guilty by the innocent and the manner in which plea incentives can become impermissibly coercive. This chapter offers a glimpse into the evolving world of academic research regarding plea bargaining that was relied upon by the task force as it crafted the 14 Principles. In concluding her chapter, Edkins reflects on the Task Force Report's desire to create a more transparent system in which more data is collected: "Moving plea bargaining out of the shadows will do more for advancing the research than any other reform we could suggest."

The book then offers more personal reflections on the plea bargaining system from several members of the task force. One of the main areas of focus for the Task Force Report was the elimination of the trial penalty, defined in the report as "the large differential between the pretrial plea offer and the sentence a defendant faces or receives after trial." In Chapter 6, "Practitioners' Nightmare/Reformers' Dream: The Tyranny of the Trial Penalty," Norman Reimer engages in a discussion of the trial penalty through the eyes of practitioners. The chapter begins this examination by offering several compelling examples of defendants who faced significantly longer sentences for exercising their constitutional right to trial and uses these examples to further explore the trial penalty. In addition to discussing the trial penalty in detail and considering its consequences, the chapter identifies and discusses various elements of the criminal system that led to and perpetuate the trial penalty. This analysis includes consideration of mandatory minimums, sentencing guidelines, unregulated prosecutorial discretion, and a lack of positive judicial intervention. The piece then explores the idea that plea bargaining represents a choice of efficiency over accuracy and presents thoughts on the impact of such a system on defense attorneys as they seek to serve their clients. In conclusion,

Reimer considers the ways in which the Task Force Report and its 14 Principles serve to address the trial penalty and assist practitioners in creating a more just and fairer system in which to operate.

We continue with the defense attorney perspective in Chapter 7, "A View from the Innocence Bar," by Adnan Sultan. This chapter assesses the practice of plea bargaining from the perspective of a public defender and an innocence lawyer. The author identifies the factors, pressures, and incentives that cause criminal defendants, regardless of guilt or innocence, to plead guilty. At the systemic level, this chapter identifies overcriminalization and underfunding of both defenders and prosecutors as major culprits of the coercive plea bargaining that leads innocent people to plead guilty. The chapter then highlights some of the key recommendations contained in the Task Force Report that might ameliorate the harshness of the current system and lessen the likelihood that innocent people will be compelled to plead guilty.

The book then continues to explore procedural concerns regarding the plea bargaining system and delves more deeply into potential solutions, some of which were introduced in the Task Force Report. This begins with Chapter 8 by Thea Johnson, entitled "The Problem of Fictional Pleas." The chapter examines how to address the issue of defendants pleading guilty to crimes they didn't commit to secure some benefit, like avoiding deportation, sex offender registration, or a mandatory minimum sentence. As the task force acknowledged in its report, this is a deeply complicated issue with no easy answers. Jumping off from this acknowledgment, the chapter traces the reasons for fictional pleas and what problems they pose for a criminal justice system already in a legitimacy crisis. The chapter then reflects on how the criminal justice community might approach reforming fictional pleas, drawing from many of the suggestions in the report. As noted in the chapter, the report was written with an eye to both the criminal justice system we currently have and the one we want to have. The knotty issue of how to address fictional pleas exemplifies the struggle between these two worlds.

This conversation on how to move toward a better criminal justice system is continued in Chapter 9 by Russell Covey, entitled "Plea Formalization." This chapter makes the case for transforming today's plea bargaining system, which is characterized by informality and ad hoc-ness, into a more formal process akin to other aspects of criminal procedure subject to far greater regulatory parameters. The starting point for formalizing plea bargaining would be to subject it to memorialization and filing requirements. Requiring all plea offers to be written and filed in court before they can be acted on is a crucial step on the road to making plea bargaining less lawless. The chapter discusses additional reforms that formalization might entail, including standardizing plea agreements, imposing formal limits on sentencing differentials, and abolishing the use of especially coercive bargaining chips such as offers of immediate release or removal of capital charges in exchange for guilty pleas. These tactics routinely cause innocent people to plead guilty.

The book then includes a chapter on plea reform by Clark Neily. In Chapter 10, entitled "Three Cures for Coercive Plea Bargaining," Neily discusses the coercive power of plea bargaining, focusing on the issue of innocent people pleading guilty to crimes they did not commit. The chapter points to three main mechanisms for inducing false guilty pleas: the increased exposure to punishment when a defendant goes to trial, the many ways that defendants suffer as they await trial (for instance, by being held in pretrial detention), and the ways in which the state undermines the quality of defense in this country. Neily then calls for a return to regular jury trials where the evidence can be tested and the government's behavior brought to light. The chapter makes several suggestions for how the criminal justice system can revive the jury trial and test the integrity of plea outcomes. Among these suggestions is instituting a trial lottery system, in which randomly assigned cases that were resolved by plea bargain would get the benefit of a full trial. As Neily writes, "[A] key virtue of trial lotteries would be to clarify whether illegitimate guilty pleas . . . are vanishingly rare, as some scholars contend, or instead fairly common[.]"Neily encourages us to view coercive plea bargaining as a sort of "cancer on America's criminal justice system" and treat it accordingly.

In Chapter 11, we conclude the book by offering some parting thoughts on where the movement to reform criminal justice goes next and the role of the Task Force Report and 14 Principles in that journey.

This book offers a lens into the world of plea bargaining, which is, in fact, the criminal justice system today. From its early days in New England townships to its rise to dominance in the 20th century, plea bargaining has always presented us with a challenge. Plea bargaining has many positive attributes. Bargains allow for finality for the system and its actors. Bargains also permit the system to collaboratively reward acceptance of responsibility and cooperation. Simultaneously, a system of bargains is ripe for abuse, and such abuses are well documented at this point. Plea bargaining also interrupts our system of trials, the system envisioned by our Founders and codified in both the Constitution and the Bill of Rights. Further, bargains have not only interrupted this system, but they have also led to the phenomenon of the vanishing trial in many jurisdictions. How does one weigh these benefits and challenges? How does a system obtain the benefits of the bargains without jeopardizing the fundamental rights at the center of the criminal justice system?

While this book is unable to answer all the questions posed by a system of pleas, this book does begin that discussion by focusing on the need for guardrails in the form of the 14 Principles. Through those principles and the insights and experiences documented herein, the system can find a path forward to both claim the benefits of plea bargaining and better protect against the abuses that such a system might invite.

CHAPTER 2

Plea Bargain Task Force Report

Plea Bargain
Task Force Report
AMERICANBARASSOCIATION
Criminal Justice Section

Contents

Acknowledgements

This Report was written by Thea Johnson, Associate Professor of Law, Rutgers Law School.

The Task Force acknowledges the extraordinary contributions to the work of the Task Force by Patrice Payne, Senior Staff Attorney at the American Bar Association's Criminal Justice Section. The Task Force also thanks Chelsea Fadio, Julie Pickett and Jenna Zawislak for their research assistance, Dale Rappaneau for editing work on the Report, Samuel Shopp for the design with assitance from Swafford & Sung on the production of the Report.

Disclaimer

Many of the recommendations included in this report were unanimously endorsed for publication by all current members of the American Bar Association's (ABA) Criminal Justice Section's Plea Bargain Task Force. Where a recommendation was not unanimously endorsed, it is noted.

The views expressed herein represent the opinions of the authors. They have not been reviewed or approved by the House of Delegates or the Board of Governors of the American Bar Association and, accordingly, should not be construed as representing the position of the Association or any of its entities.

The members of the Task Force participated in this project and the drafting of this Report in their personal capacities. Their participation and contributions to this Report should be considered as their personal views and not necessarily the views of their affiliated entities or institutions.

Introduction

The Plea Bargain Task Force formed in 2019 to address persistent criticisms of the plea bargain system in the United States.[1] Plea bargaining has become the primary way to resolve criminal cases. Indeed, some jurisdictions have not had a criminal trial in many years, resolving all their cases through negotiated resolutions.[2] For this reason, a critical examination of the modern plea system is necessary and important.

This Report comes after three years of work, during which the Task Force collected and reviewed testimony from experts in the field and those impacted by the plea system, scholarly and legal reports on plea bargaining, state and federal rules of criminal procedure, and other materials. What has become clear from this process is that plea bargaining is not one monolithic practice. It looks different depending on whether one is in state or federal court, a rural jurisdiction with few lawyers or an urban center with large prosecution and public defender offices. Even within the same courthouse, informal practices may differ between courtrooms and attorneys. Although these variations pose a challenge for the development of any one-size-fits-all set of recommendations to reform plea bargaining practices, this Report identifies and addresses numerous concerns with plea bargaining that are common to a wide variety of jurisdictions. The Report then provides guidance to jurisdictions on how to meet those challenges while also promoting justice, transparency, and fairness.

There are many purported benefits of plea bargaining in the current criminal justice system. Nearly all jurisdictions have limited resources and plea bargaining provides a mechanism to efficiently resolve cases. By preserving resources this way, jurisdictions are able to direct greater resources to investigations and cases that proceed to trial. Additionally, plea bargaining provides a mechanism to incentivize defendants to cooperate with the government or to accept responsibility for their criminal conduct. A plea also provides a clear and certain resolution to a case, which offers finality for the defendant, the victim, the courts, and the community. Furthermore, defendants use the plea process to avoid some of the most severe aspects of the criminal system.

In moderation, many of these benefits make sense. But as the Task Force discovered, too often these benefits have become the driving force of criminal adjudication at the cost of more fundamental values. For instance, according to the testimony the Task Force collected, at times, efficiency and finality trump truth-seeking. Furthermore, many benefits of plea bargaining are, when viewed in a different light, a means to mitigate the excessive harshness of the modern American criminal system. In this sense, plea bargaining is not so much providing a benefit as it is a safety valve for quotidian injustice.

Moreover, the Task Force reviewed substantial evidence that defendants—including innocent defendants—are sometimes coerced into taking pleas and surrendering their right to trial. This happens for a number of reasons. For instance, mandatory sentencing laws often make the risks of taking a case to trial intolerable, and in some cases, prosecutors understand and exploit these fears to induce defendants to plead guilty in cases where they otherwise would prefer to exercise their constitutional right to have the case decided by a jury. Similarly, mandatory collateral consequences, including the threat of deportation, push defendants to accept pleas in cases they might otherwise fight at trial.

The Task Force also discovered that the integrity of the criminal system is negatively affected by the sheer number of cases resolved by pleas. For example, police and government misconduct often goes unchecked because so few defendants proceed to pre-trial hearings where such misconduct is litigated. The reality that so few pretrial matters are litigated leads prosecutors to be less critical of their witnesses and less willing to scrutinize the strength of their cases, knowing that they won't be held accountable at trial. Defense lawyers, similarly, are less likely to properly investigate cases, knowing their clients will almost certainly take a plea. Plea bargaining creates perverse incentives across the system for lawyers and judges who focus on disposition rates and getting through cases quickly rather than resolving cases justly. Furthermore, the loss of trials in favor of plea bargains is a profound loss for civic engagement. Jury trials provide critical oversight to the criminal system, and juries remain one of the only ways for citizens to shape how prosecutors enforce laws. The voice of the community is almost entirely lost in a system dominated by pleas.

More troubling still, the Task Force heard many ways in which plea bargaining promotes and exacerbates existing racial inequality in the criminal system. The Task Force collected testimony from experts in the field who demonstrated that throughout the plea process similarly situated defendants of color fare worse than white defendants.[3] Black defendants in drug cases, for instance, are less likely to receive favorable plea offers that avoid mandatory minimum sentences and, as a result, receive higher sentences for the same charges as white defendants.[4] The same is true for gun cases, in which Black defendants are more often subjected to charge stacking—a technique that allows prosecutors to pile on many charges, increasing the likely sentence after trial and the government's leverage during plea negotiations - than white defendants.[5] In fact, across all charges the Task Force found evidence of significant racial disparities in prosecutorial decisions to drop or reduce charges. For example, white defendants who face initial felony charges are less likely than Black defendants to be convicted of a felony, and white defendants facing misdemeanor charges are more likely than Black defendants to have their cases dismissed or resolved without incarceration.[6]

In addition, since plea bargaining is affected by other areas of the criminal system that are themselves inflected with racial bias, plea practice is shaped by racism in ways often not reflected in data regarding initial charges and sentences. For instance, Black defendants are more likely to be held in pretrial detention, which in turn increases the likelihood that they will plead guilty.[7] But the prevalence of guilty pleas has made it more unlikely that racial bias in policing will be discovered. After all, the primary ways a defendant might unearth a police officer's bias—through pre-trial litigation or demands for impeachment information at a trial—have been nearly eliminated because of the ascendance of plea bargaining.[8]

The Plea Bargain Task Force was convened under the auspices of the American Bar Association's Criminal Justice Section and was made up of a wide and diverse group of lawyers, judges, academics, those serving as prosecutors and defenders, and representatives from a broad spectrum of advocacy groups. Its membership consisted of the following individuals:*

Lucian E. Dervan (Co-Chair), Professor of Law, Belmont University College of Law, and Founding Director of the Plea Bargaining Institute

Russell Covey (Co-Chair), Professor of Law, Georgia State University College of Law

Thea Johnson (Reporter), Associate Professor of Law, Rutgers Law School

Hon. Kimberly Esmond Adams, Judge, Superior Court of Fulton County, Georgia

Derwyn Bunton, Chief Legal Officer, Southern Poverty Law Center, (formerly Chief District Defender, Orleans Public Defenders)

Vanessa Edkins, Director of Quantitative Research, Gartner, Inc.; Professor Emeritus, Psychology, Florida Institute of Technology

A. J. Kramer, Federal Public Defender for the District of Columbia

Jenny Kim, Partner, The Gober Group

Marc Levin, Chief Policy Counsel, Council on Criminal Justice

Clark Neily, Senior Vice President for Legal Studies, CATO Institute

Norman L. Reimer, Former Global CEO, Fair Trials; Former Executive Director, National Assocation of Criminal Defense Lawyers

Rebecca Shaeffer, Legal Director (Americas), Fair Trials

Adnan Sultan, Senior Staff Attorney, The Innocence Project

Jonathan Wroblewski, Director of the Office of Policy and Legislation, Criminal Division, U.S. Department of Justice

*The Hon. Billy McDermott served on the task force as the representative from the National District Attorneys Association (NDAA) until March 2021. During that time, he was Deputy States Attorney, Wicomico County, MD. Hon. McDermott left the taskforce in March 2021 as a result of having been appointed to the federal bench. Though Mr. McDermott participated in many of the discussions that led up to the creation of the task force report, he neither reviewed nor approved this final report. We acknowledge here, however, his important contributions to the project and the task force's findings and recommendations.

The Principles

While the plea bargaining process in the United States is broad and varied, the Task Force determined that it was vitally important to craft a single set of principles to guide plea practices generally. Those principles, which guide the Report's more specific observations and recommendations, are listed below. These principles should be shared widely with members of the criminal justice community so that they might influence behavior and decision-making moving forward. These principles represent our conclusions about how plea bargaining should operate within our larger criminal justice system, a system based on the fundamental Constitutional right to trial.

Principle 1

A vibrant and active docket of criminal trials and pre- and post-trial litigation is essential to promote transparency, accountability, justice, and legitimacy in the criminal justice system.

Principle 2

Guilty pleas should not result from the use of impermissibly coercive incentives or incentives that overbear the will of the defendant.

Principle 3

In general, while some difference between the sentence offered prior to trial and the sentence received after trial is permissible, a substantial difference undermines the integrity of the criminal system and reflects a penalty for exercising one's right to trial. This differential, often referred to as the trial penalty, should be eliminated.

Principle 4

Charges should not be selected or amended with the purpose of creating a sentencing differential, sentencing enhancement, punishment or collateral consequence to induce a defendant to plead guilty or to punish defendants for exercising their rights, including the right to trial.

Principle 5

The criminal justice system should recognize that plea bargaining induces defendants to plead guilty for various reasons, some of which have little or nothing to do with factual and legal guilt. In the current system, innocent people sometimes plead guilty to crimes they did not commit.

Principle 6

A defendant should have a right to qualified counsel in any criminal adjudication before the defendant enters a guilty plea. Counsel should be afforded a meaningful opportunity to satisfy their duty to investigate the case without risk of penalty to their client.

Principle 7

There should be robust and transparent procedures at the plea phase to ensure that the defendant's plea is knowing and voluntary, free from impermissible coercion, and that the defendant understands the consequences of their decision to plead guilty.

Principle 8

The use of bail or pretrial detention to induce guilty pleas should be eliminated.

10 Plea Bargain Task Force Report

Principle 9

Defendants should receive all available discovery, including exculpatory materials, prior to entry of a guilty plea, and should have sufficient time to review such discovery before being required to accept or reject a plea offer.

Principle 10

Although guilty pleas necessarily involve the waiver of certain trial rights, there are rights that defendants should never be required to waive in a plea agreement.

Principle 11

An adequate understanding of the collateral consequences that may flow from a guilty plea is necessary to ensure the guilty plea is knowing and voluntary.

Principle 12

Law students, lawyers, and judges should receive training on the use and practice of plea bargaining consistent with the findings and recommendations of this Report.

Principle 13

Court systems, sentencing commissions, and other criminal justice stakeholders, including prosecutor offices and public defenders, should collect data about the plea process and each individual plea, including the history of plea offers in a case. Data collection should be used to assess and monitor racial and other biases in the plea process.

Principle 14

At every stage of the criminal process, there should be robust oversight by all actors in the criminal system to monitor the plea process for accuracy and integrity, to ensure the system operates consistent with the Principles in this Report, and to promote transparency, accountability, justice, and legitimacy in the criminal system.

THE REPORT

Terminology:

A few notes about terminology are important to understand this Report. A **plea bargain** is an agreement struck between the prosecutor and the defendant about the resolution of the defendant's criminal case. Often, plea agreements contain some promise as to both the charges of conviction and the final sentence that the defendant will face. Defendants commonly agree to plead to certain criminal charges with the understanding that a judge will make the final decision as to sentencing. In those situations, a prosecutor may agree to make a sentencing recommendation to the judge.

One of the most common forms of plea bargaining is known as **charge bargaining**. A defendant is presented with an initial set of charges at the time of arraignment. In charge bargaining, the prosecutor and defense counsel will negotiate over those charges, generally agreeing that the defendant will plead guilty to some lesser charge that often carries a lower maximum or presumptive sentence, or no mandatory minimum sentence when compared with the initial charges. In other instances, the prosecution will elect to bring additional charges, including charges that may carry a mandatory minimum sentence, if the defendant refuses to accept an initial plea offer. The parties might also engage in **sentencing bargaining**, where they agree that the prosecutor will recommend or the judge will impose a particular sentence or sentencing range that reflects a discount from the potential sentence faced by the defendant. In addition, the parties may also engage in **fact bargaining,** where they negotiate over the set of facts that will form the basis of the charge. For instance, it is common in drug cases for the parties to agree that the defendant will only plead guilty to a charge associated with a certain quantity of drugs, even though the prosecutor may have evidence indicating that a higher quantity of drugs was provable.

Guilty pleas are not always the product of plea bargains, but the exact terms of a guilty plea are typically negotiated through plea bargaining. The federal government has estimated that approximately seventy-five percent of guilty pleas in the federal system are induced by some negotiation between the parties.[9] It is critical to note, however, that a defendant always has the option to plead guilty without negotiating a plea beforehand. Depending on the jurisdiction, defendants may plead to the entire indictment or to the top charge they are facing, leaving determination of sentence to the judge's discretion. In misdemeanor cases, it is common for a defendant to accept a guilty plea and the sentence of the judge without any plea bargaining with the government.

Typically, the defendant pleads guilty at a **plea hearing** following a **plea colloquy** in which the judge asks the defendant a series of questions to determine whether the defendant's plea is **knowing and voluntary**, as required by the U.S. Constitution. The plea colloquy may also involve the development of a factual record to support the charges. At the colloquy, the judge may also ask the defendant if they understand any potential consequences of the conviction, including immigration consequences. Once a defendant has formally entered a plea, they may be sentenced.

How to Read this Report:

Although plea practices vary among jurisdictions, one common thread in every criminal courtroom across the country is the deep entrenchment of plea bargaining in the daily administration of criminal justice. Plea bargaining touches every element of criminal practice, including discovery, sentencing, collateral consequences, and procedural rights. This Report identifies general problems with the plea system and provides recommendations for reform and guidance to criminal justice stakeholders seeking to improve their plea-bargaining systems and practices.

However, because plea bargaining has become so engrained in the fabric of the criminal system, any attempt to reform plea bargaining will create ripple effects throughout the system. Throughout this Report the Task Force acknowledges those ripple effects. For instance, this Report identifies the problem of disparate plea outcomes for similarly situated defendants. Any effort to regulate plea outcomes to make them more uniform poses a risk that certain defendants will face harsher sentences than they do now. Many, including some members of this Task Force, would view as misguided a "correction" to disparate outcomes that increased all sentences. Yet, permitting such uneven outcomes of similarly situated defendants to continue or allowing defendants to be punished for exercising a constitutional right is also misguided, and, as this Report will document, the time for reform of the plea-bargaining system is now. As such, we provide here some guidance for how this Report should be read to avoid perverse outcomes that may stem from gradual implementation of reform.

First, the Task Force prepared this Report with an eye toward the criminal justice system we would like to see, rather than account for all potential ripples that might flow from our recommendations in the world that exists now. The Task Force acknowledges that increasing transparency, accountability, and fairness in the plea arena may negatively affect some defendants, victims, or other stakeholders. Nonetheless, these Principles reflect values too often ignored in our current system, and this Report should be read with an understanding that its primary purpose is to promote transparency, accountability, justice, and legitimacy in the criminal justice system as a whole.

Second, the recommendations in this Report assume the good faith of prosecutors and other system actors who are acting in service of justice. The Report should not be read as suggesting that these actors be prevented from exercising their vision of justice. This Report was written with the hope and expectation that relevant stakeholders follow its recommendations in good faith and with a continued eye towards justice, but it was also written to provide parameters to guide and encourage good faith behavior by judges, lawyers, and legislators.

Third, we recognize that many problems addressed in this Report do not stem directly from the practice of plea bargaining itself, but rather are manifestations of problems in other parts of the criminal justice system, such as overly harsh sentencing rules or one-size-fits-all collateral consequences that impose unjust or intolerable conditions on individual defendants. Problems and imbalances in these other areas inevitably manifest in plea bargaining practice, and so this Report addresses facets of the criminal justice system beyond the plea process itself. In this same vein, we seek to address multiple audiences in this Report with the goal of educating legislators, judges, lawyers, law students, and the public about how to improve our plea-bargaining system. This means our recommendations may run along multiple paths. For instance, we recommend changes to the law for legislators to implement while also making recommendations to lawyers and judges on how to improve plea practice in the absence of any changes to the law.

Fourth, although many of these recommendations seemingly require a greater allocation of resources to the criminal system, we think a fairer and more legitimate criminal justice system is well worth the investment. For too long efficiency has been a driving factor behind the modern plea process. Efficiency has a role to play in criminal law policymaking, but it should not be the primary goal of that policy. Rather, the goal should be a criminal justice system where defendants are guaranteed due process, victims receive justice, and the rule of law can flourish.

Principle One

A vibrant and active docket of criminal trials and pre- and post-trial litigation is essential to promote transparency, accountability, justice, and legitimacy in the criminal justice system.

The public jury trial is among the greatest strengths of the American criminal justice system. The purpose of a trial by jury is to ensure the government proves its case beyond a reasonable doubt—the highest standard of proof available under the law—before members of the accused's community. Trials provide developed factual and legal records for appellate review. They serve as a check on the system both through community participation and through the judicial review process. In other words, the public jury trial promotes fundamental values of transparency, accountability, justice, and legitimacy. Moreover, the right to a jury trial is a prominent feature of the U.S. Constitution. It is the only right acknowledged both in the body of the Constitution and in the Bill of Rights. For these reasons, this Report starts from the premise that **trials are essential to a healthy criminal justice system and central to our system of justice**.

Unfortunately, trials have become rare legal artifacts in most U.S. jurisdictions—and even nonexistent in others.[10] Plea bargaining has replaced the public jury trial, and this is problematic for many reasons.

First, the Sixth Amendment guarantees a right to an open, public trial in criminal cases. Plea bargains provide no adequate constitutional substitute. Even though guilty pleas are taken publicly, the negotiation over the terms of those pleas happens in courtroom hallways or through phone calls between attorneys, without oversight from the judge, the public, or the media. There rarely is any community participation in this negotiation process. Instead, it is left to the parties themselves to negotiate an outcome and present it to the judge. The judge may act as a check on the process by either accepting or rejecting the plea, but the negotiation of the plea happens entirely off the record. Furthermore, appellate review of plea bargaining is limited and as a result, countless potential legal issues present in the cases are never addressed or resolved by the courts on the merits. The state of the law atrophies when plea bargains replace trials, as do the trial skills and knowledge of attorneys who no longer try cases but rather negotiate resolutions. Further, civil engagement through jury service is weakened or lost as jury trials disappear.[11]

By definition, defendants waive many constitutional rights when they plead guilty to a criminal offense. The act of pleading guilty necessarily means relinquishing the right to a jury trial and the right to confront adverse witnesses. It may also entail loss of the opportunity to challenge evidence that was procured in violation of the Constitution. And depending on the law of the jurisdiction, it may also relieve the prosecutor of the duty to turn over discovery in the case. There may be many sensible reasons for a defendant to forgo these rights in exchange for a negotiated resolution to the case, nonetheless, a guilty plea comes with far fewer protections—constitutional or otherwise—than a trial, and much is lost in a system that relies almost entirely on guilty pleas.

Finally, a common critique is that a **system of pleas hides police misconduct**. There are various ways that police misconduct can be identified and investigated in the criminal and civil systems, but the primary remedy for police misconduct in the court system is the exclusionary rule, which prohibits the state from using evidence it obtained by violating the defendant's constitutional rights. Challenges to police misconduct are typically resolved through pretrial litigation, but the death of the trial has also increasingly meant the death of pretrial litigation, including those hearings that would bring to light police misconduct. Trial and pretrial litigation are essential for holding police and other state actors accountable, and plea bargaining has eroded these systems of accountability.

Of course, the trial system is not perfect, but the procedural rules and safeguards attached to trial help to promote transparency, accountability, justice, and legitimacy in the criminal justice system. As such, The Task Force starts this Report by reaffirming the central role that trials—and the attendant rights that accompany them—play in a fair criminal justice system.

Although it is difficult - and beyond the Task Force's mandate - to identify an "optimal" number of trials that should occur in a healthy criminal justice system, there is a strong consensus among members of the Task Force that the current trend toward ever fewer trials is deleterious to the ability of the criminal justice system to perform its basic functions and must be reversed. Every jurisdiction should devote thought to whether a sufficient number of trials are being conducted to ensure robust community participation and oversight through jury service, maintain the trial skills of prosecutors, defense attorneys, judges, law enforcement officers, and others so as to preserve the ability of any individual to exercise their right to trial, and to ensure that criminal charges are resolved in ways that are fair, consistent, and that reflect justice.

Principle Two

Guilty pleas should not result from the use of impermissibly coercive incentives or incentives that overbear the will of the defendant.

All too frequently, as evidence collected by the Task Force indicates, plea bargaining coerces people to plead guilty. Of course, some level of coercion is inherent in the plea system. Once the state arrests a person and charges them with a crime, the state has power over that person. Sometimes the state exercises that inherent power, however, in ways that impermissibly coerce defendants to plead guilty. For instance, the state may induce the defendant to plead guilty with incentives that make it irrational for even an innocent person to turn down the deal. Such offers are inherently coercive. Mandatory minimum sentencing laws in particular, which are available in all jurisdictions, give prosecutors tremendous power in plea bargaining. A prosecutor may choose to charge a defendant with an offense or set of offenses that carries a mandatory minimum sentence if the defendant refuses to accept the current plea offer on the table. Under certain circumstances, this behavior may coerce a defendant to plead guilty rather than pursue their right to trial and risk a mandatory minimum sentence as a result.

The Task Force collected other examples of impermissible coercion as well, like prosecutors threatening to indict a defendant's child to discourage the defendant from pursuing trial,[12] or "wiring" pleas in such a way that one defendant's fate rested in the hands of a co-defendant.[13] In at least one jurisdiction, a prosecutor refused to make favorable plea deals with women in child abuse cases unless they agreed to sterilization.[14] These are just some of the extreme examples we found of coercive plea bargaining.

A primary purpose of this Report is to identify and discourage the use of these coercive tactics. Chief among them is the practice of imposing harsher sentences on those who are convicted after exercising their right to trial. Although **a modest reduction in sentence is justified in some cases resolved through guilty pleas because a defendant accepts responsibility, sentences should not be punitively inflated simply because a defendant exercised a fundamental right**. Defendants also should not be punished for exercising their pretrial rights, including the right to seek pretrial release, the right to discovery, the right to investigate the case, and the right to file pretrial motions.

1. Sentence reductions for acceptance of responsibility not limited to trial

To ensure defendants are not punished for exercising their trial rights, **where a defendant accepts responsibility after conviction at trial, the same or similar reductions should be available even when the defendant testified at trial, if the defendant satisfies the requirements for receiving such reduction. Mere denial of guilt should not be a basis for a sentence enhancement. The standards for receiving an acceptance of responsibility reduction of sentence should be transparent, available to the defendant, and applied consistently to all defendants**.

2. Abolition or avoidance of mandatory minimum sentence provisions

Mandatory minimum sentencing provisions pose an extremely high risk of misuse in plea bargaining practice, a point made repeatedly by witnesses testifying before the Task Force.[15] When a defendant is charged with a crime carrying a mandatory minimum sentence, the promise of a greatly reduced sentence through plea bargaining often pressures defendants into abandoning their rights or even their legitimate claims of innocence. Many members of the Task Force believe that, because they risk overbearing the will of the defendant, **mandatory minimum sentences should be abolished.** This recommendation is consistent with ABA policy that calls for the elimination of mandatory minimum sentences in criminal cases.[16] Other members of the Task Force, while concerned about some of the negative consequences associated with mandatory minimums, do not support a complete and total ban on such sentences.

While many members of the Task Force strongly encourage legislators to reduce or abandon mandatory minimums, all members agree that **where mandatory minimums remain in statutory form, they should not be used to induce pleas of guilt through the plea bargaining process.** This is especially true in cases or enforcement areas where prosecutors have been regularly willing to offer defendants plea bargains that do not trigger mandatory minimum sentences.

3. Establishment of safety-valve authority

Judges also have an important

role to play in safeguarding against coercion in plea bargaining. This Report encourages legislators to give power back to judges to regulate the boundaries of plea bargaining. Many members of the Task Force would encourage legislation that gives **judges the authority to depart from any existing mandatory minimums, and further would encourage them to do so in the interests of justice, including to avoid a substantial differential between the trial sentence and any lesser sentence offered as part of a plea bargain**. As we make clear below in subsection 5 of this Principle, this would require that plea negotiations be transparent and recorded, which would allow judges to compare post-trial sentencing recommendations from the government to pre-trial offers in the same case.

4. Prohibition on using threat of capital punishment to induce guilty pleas

In addition, **the threat of capital punishment or life without the possibility of parole should never be used to induce a plea of guilty. Such tactics are inherently coercive.** The National Registry of Exonerations includes individuals who pleaded guilty to avoid being sentenced to death, and were later exonerated.[17] The Task Force calls on local bar associations and the ABA to provide formal ethical guidance to prosecutors that makes clear that threatening the imposition of the death penalty for the purpose of inducing a guilty plea is unethical.

5. Plea offers must be in writing and filed with the court

To ensure that trial judges and reviewing courts have a full and accurate record of the plea negotiations, **all plea offers, whether accepted or not, should be in writing and filed with the court prior to sentencing or dismissal of the case**. In Principle Thirteen, this Report further highlights the need for plea bargains to be memorialized. This practice promotes transparency, which is sorely lacking in the plea practice of many jurisdictions.

Principle Three

In general, while some difference between the sentence offered prior to trial and the sentence received after trial is permissible, a substantial difference undermines the integrity of the criminal system and constitutes a penalty for exercising one's right to trial. This differential, often referred to as the trial penalty, should be eliminated.

The trial penalty is the large differential between the pretrial plea offer and the sentence a defendant faces or receives after trial. A recent comprehensive report on the trial penalty by the National Association of Criminal Defense Lawyers (NACDL) reveals the scope of the problem.[18] As the NACDL Trial Penalty report documents, in federal felony cases there is on average a seven-year difference between the sentence after trial and the sentence after a plea,[19] meaning a defendant's sentence after a plea is on average seven years shorter than the sentence resulting from trial. In drug trafficking cases, the average difference between the trial sentence and the plea sentence is nine years. Evidence gathered by the Task Force points to this difference in sentencing as having a powerfully coercive impact on the defendant's decision to plead guilty or proceed to trial because going to trial involves the risk of a drastically longer sentence. Even innocent defendants may make the rational choice to avoid the risk of a large post-trial sentence when a much lower sentence is on the table.

1. Abolition of mandatory minimum sentences will help combat the trial penalty

Mandatory minimum sentences are a significant source of the trial penalty. As such, **we reiterate our call here for legislators to repeal mandatory minimum sentences and for prosecutors to avoid, where possible, using statutes that carry mandatory minimum sentences.**

2. Strict limitations on sentencing differentials

Regardless of whether mandatory minimum sentences are repealed, states can implement procedural rules or policy changes that limit the trial penalty. The Task Force recommends that all jurisdictions adopt policies that limit the size of sentencing differentials to ensure that **the difference between the sentence offered prior to trial and the sentence received after trial is reasonable and non-coercive.** The Task Force has chosen not to recommend a specific point at which a sentencing differential becomes unreasonable and coercive. Rather, the Task Force believes that each jurisdiction should engage in a deliberative and considered analysis of this issue to determine what they believe constitutes a reasonable and non-coercive differential between the pretrial offer and the post-trial sentence. This analysis goes hand-in-hand with our suggestion in Principle One that jurisdictions aim to meaningfully increase their trial rates. Several scholars have identified potential fixed differentials.[20] Jurisdictions may differ in where they draw the line, but drawing a line in the first place provides guidance to lawyers and judges on the appropriate boundaries for plea bargaining. **These policies should be in writing, easily accessible, and evenly applied to similarly situated defendants.** In addition, **the reasons why a defendant receives a plea offer that includes any reduction in sentencing outcome or exposure should be articulated, documented, and consistent with this Report.**

This Report seeks to empower the primary players in the plea bargaining process—judges, prosecutors, and defense attorneys—to shift the culture and norms around plea bargaining to ensure fair outcomes and processes. As such, **all stakeholders are responsible for monitoring the system and ensuring that defendants are not subject to a trial penalty.** In Principle Fourteen, we make several suggestions for how stakeholders can both monitor and audit the plea system to promote accurate and fair results. In Principle Thirteen, we encourage court systems to collect data on several aspects of plea bargaining, including sentence offers and final sentences within the same case. With this information, we encourage stakeholders to monitor how the trial penalty operates in their jurisdictions and to implement formal or informal policies that lessen its impact. We also make several suggestions in Principle Four for how stakeholders can better regulate the plea process to limit such differentials and other forms of coercion.

Principle Four

Charges should not be selected or amended with the purpose of creating a sentencing differential, sentencing enhancement, punishment or collateral consequence to induce a defendant to plead guilty or to punish defendants for exercising their rights, including the right to trial.

While prosecutorial discretion is a fundamental tenet of our criminal justice system, the legal system must find ways to regularize the charging process and closely monitor prosecutorial charging decisions. Perhaps no single decision has more of an impact on the scope and context of later plea negotiations than the selection of charges at the outset of the case.

1. Prosecutors have an ethical duty to refrain from charging for the purpose of obtaining tactical bargaining advantages.

Prosecutors have an ethical responsibility to select charges solely based on their duty to see that justice is done. **Charges should never be selected, amended, or enhanced solely or even partially for the purpose of enhancing leverage in plea bargaining, or for creating significant sentencing differentials between plea and trial outcomes.**

2. Charging oversight

Since the initial charging decision is so critical, to the extent practicable, **prosecutors' offices should centralize the initial charging decision with highly experienced prosecutors.** Many jurisdictions currently treat initial charging decisions as an opportunity for new prosecutors to learn the ropes. However, we encourage prosecutors to see the initial charging decisions as one of the most critical stages of the criminal process, one that should be handled with great care and reflection.

3. Written charging policies

Charging prosecutors must make an early and careful assessment of each case, and demand that police and investigators provide complete information available at the time of the charging decision before the initial charge is filed. **Charging decisions should be based on written policies that are publicly accessible, evenly applied, and that include non-prosecution and diversionary options where appropriate.** Further, **prosecutorial screening must include sufficient training, oversight, and other internal enforcement mechanisms to ensure reasonable uniformity in charging.**

4. Charging in the interest of justice

The prosecutorial mindset should not focus on what the prosecutor can charge, but rather what the prosecutor should charge in light of the evidence and interests of justice. We understand the interests of justice is not a defined concept and that different prosecutors will have different conclusions about what qualifies as falling within it. But the Task Force believes that when prosecutors ask critical questions early in the charging process, it will result in fairer charging.

Further, consistent with Standard 3-4.3 (Minimum Requirements for Filing and Maintaining Criminal Charges) of the ABA Standards for the Prosecution Function, **a prosecutor should seek or file criminal charges *only if* the prosecutor reasonably believes the charges are supported by probable cause, admissible evidence will sufficiently support conviction beyond a reasonable doubt, and the decision to charge is in the interests of justice.**

5. Substantial limitations on amending charges after commencement of plea bargaining

Based on the Task Force's fact-finding efforts, it appears that some prosecutors will threaten to amend charging documents by adding charges to induce the defendant to plead guilty. This practice is coercive. The Task Force makes this finding despite the fact that this practice has been held to be constitutional by the Supreme Court. In *Bordenkircher v. Hayes*, a 1978 Supreme Court case, a prosecutor made an initial offer of five years of incarceration to a defendant in a check forgery case.[21] The prosecutor told the defendant that if he rejected the offer, the state would then seek additional charges that carried a mandatory life sentence. The defendant rejected the offer, the state amended the charges, and the defendant was sentenced to life after a trial. The Supreme Court upheld the prosecutor's action as constitutional, finding that as long as the amended charges are properly chargeable and the defendant has been advised by competent counsel, such behavior by the prosecutor does not violate the Constitution.[22] As the Court noted, it "has necessarily accepted as constitutionally legitimate the simple reality that the prosecutor's interest at the bargaining table is to persuade the defendant to forgo his right to plead not guilty," even by adding much more serious charges than the prosecutor initially thought were warranted for the case.[23] We reject the logic of *Bordenkircher*. Our ethical understanding of plea bargaining has evolved substantially since the 1970s. Standards reflected in this Report are higher than those required by law. And we encourage litigation that would cause the Court to reexamine such precedents.

Further, to avoid such coercion, once an initial charging decision has been made after the careful process outlined above, **charges should be amended only based on material changes in the available proof or in the interests of justice.** The Task Force is not suggesting that charges cannot ever change at a later point in the case; the discovery of new evidence may make new charges appropriate. But prosecutors should only amend charges for a reason consistent with Standard 3-4.3, and such decisions should never seek to punish a defendant for refusing to accept an early offer.

To ensure that charge bargaining does not become a coercive tool, **oversight is especially critical whenever prosecutors seek to amend charges after formal or informal plea bargaining discussions have commenced.** Ideally, when a prosecutor seeks to amend the charges brought against a defendant, including as part of a plea offer, that decision should be approved by the supervisory prosecutor overseeing charging. In considering whether to approve the amended charges, the supervisory attorney must reexamine (1) whether the original charges were brought to induce a defendant to plead guilty by creating a sentencing differential between those charges and the plea offer, (2) whether the amended charges are being brought to punish a defendant for exercising their right to trial, and (3) whether the charges that will be brought at trial are consistent with Standard 3-4.3 (Minimum Requirements for Filing and Maintaining Criminal Charges) and Standard 3-4.4 (Discretion in Filing, Declining, Maintaining, and Dismissing Criminal Charges) of the ABA Standards for the Prosecution Function. Charges should only be amended if there is a substantial change in the available proof from the time of the initial charges or if a prohibited consideration contributed to the original charges. The supervisor's determinations and reasons for the determinations should be placed in writing and maintained in official records of the office.

The Task Force hopes that such rigorous screening will also eliminate another common problem identified by critics of plea bargaining—namely, the use of plea bargaining to resolve cases that ought to be dismissed. **Prosecutors should dismiss weak cases rather than seek to resolve them through plea bargaining.** Prosecutors should not fear dismissals, and the Task Force discourages any policies or practices within prosecutors' offices that deter line prosecutors from dismissing weak cases.[24]

6. Data collection

Finally, consistent with Principle Thirteen, **rigorous data collection should be part of the initial charging practice as well as any decisions to amend the initial charges. The data should be periodically analyzed and made available to the public.** This collection, analysis, and distribution of data will increase transparency and provide outside oversight to prosecutors' charging decisions.

Principle Five

The criminal justice system should recognize that plea bargaining induces defendants to plead guilty for various reasons, some of which have little or nothing to do with factual and legal guilt. In the current system, innocent people sometimes plead guilty to crimes they did not commit.

It is an unfortunate but undeniable fact that in some cases innocent people plead guilty to crimes they did not commit.[25] A study of DNA exonerations conducted by the Innocence Project found that 11% of exonerated individuals had pleaded guilty.[26] While it is difficult for a variety of reasons to estimate the number of innocent people who have pleaded guilty, most studies likely undercount wrongful convictions.[27] **The Task Force recognizes the many compelling reasons an innocent person may plead guilty, but we also acknowledge that such a phenomenon is antithetical to a fair criminal justice system.** One primary purpose of this Report is to suggest and encourage reforms that decrease the pressure innocent defendants feel to plead guilty and increase the likelihood that their cases are dismissed or fully litigated through the trial and appellate process.

While other Principles address additional risk factors and solutions to the problem of innocent people pleading guilty, we note here three specific concerns about plea bargaining's innocence problem. First, **the Task Force is concerned about the particular pressure on innocent people to plead guilty in misdemeanor court**, where cases are processed quickly and innocent defendants are often presented with plea offers that are difficult to refuse. For instance, prosecutors in misdemeanor courts may make early "exploding offers," which are one-time deals that are very good compared to the likely alternative, or they may offer a plea with a recommendation of time served but simultaneously seek the imposition of bail if the offer is rejected. In both scenarios, the innocent defendant must choose between continuing to fight the case (sometimes while being held pretrial) or pleading guilty to terminate the prosecution and potentially obtain release from custody. Further, misdemeanor defendants in many parts of the country are not provided counsel to assist with making these decisions.[28] For these reasons, to avoid as much as possible the risk that innocent people will plead guilty, all recommendations in this Report should be read to apply to misdemeanor courtrooms as much as felony ones.

Second, as jurisdictions work to make it less likely that innocent people plead guilty, the Task Force recommends ending barriers to post-conviction review and relief for innocence claims brought by individuals who pled guilty. Many states have rules that make it impossible for a defendant who accepted a guilty plea to challenge their conviction based on new evidence of their innocence. Other jurisdictions bar defendants from seeking DNA testing if they pleaded guilty. Because we know that innocent people plead guilty, **defendants should have access to all available mechanisms for post-conviction review of innocence claims, regardless of the method of conviction.** We do not believe this will open the floodgates of post-conviction litigation. Defendants seeking review based on new evidence or other reasons must still satisfy any legal standard currently in place in the jurisdiction in which they bring the claim. But states should not bar defendants from making such claims in the first place. Furthermore, many defendants benefit from plea bargaining and therefore will be unlikely to risk forfeiting that benefit by having the full charges and potential sentence reinstated. Ultimately, we cannot tolerate a system where innocent people are convicted and incarcerated with no form of relief.

Third, because the evidence in cases where the defendant is innocent is often weak or questionable, these types of cases also tend to garner the most significant sentencing differentials that create overwhelming incentives for these individuals to plead guilty to something they have not done. Consistent with Principle Three, all jurisdictions should adopt policies that limit the size of sentencing differentials to ensure that the difference between the sentence offered prior to trial and the sentence received after trial is reasonable and non-coercive. Such limitations will greatly reduce the risk that innocent defendants will falsely plead guilty

Finally, we note that when innocent people plead guilty to crimes they did not commit, it leaves the victim's interests unvindicated and may create a meaningful public safety risk. Once a suspect has agreed to falsely plead guilty, enforcement authorities typically close their investigation under the mistaken belief that the true perpetrator has been apprehended. With the investigation closed and the wrong person behind bars, the true perpetrator may reoffend. In addition to acknowledging that innocent people plead guilty, therefore, we should also acknowledge the detriments to and potential risks to victims and society when this happens.

Principle Six

A defendant should have a right to qualified counsel in any criminal adjudication before the defendant enters a guilty plea. Counsel should be afforded a meaningful opportunity to satisfy their duty to investigate the case without risk of penalty to their client.

As a constitutional matter, defendants are entitled to counsel in criminal cases whenever they are subjected to incarceration.[29] But that leaves many defendants without a clear right to counsel—particularly in misdemeanor cases. Across the country, but especially in rural areas, defendants make the decision to plead guilty without the benefit of counsel. Often these decisions carry grave consequences, such as the imposition of serious fines or fees, collateral consequences, or immigration consequences. For this reason, the Task Force recommends that **jurisdictions provide counsel to defendants in any criminal adjudications, including felonies, misdemeanors, and violations that carry potential criminal sanctions, regardless of whether the defendant is subjected to incarceration**. At the very least, **defendants should not accept a plea offer without consulting counsel or formally waiving their right to counsel**.

In line with Principle Eleven, **defense attorneys have a duty to ascertain reasonably identifiable collateral consequences, including immigration consequences, that apply to their clients, and to notify and discuss such consequences with their clients prior to the entry of any guilty plea.** This consultation should go beyond the strictures of *Padilla v. Kentucky*, which require defense attorneys to advise clients about the clear deportation consequences of their conviction.

Defense counsel should have access to immigration and civil attorneys to assist them in understanding which non-criminal consequences apply and how those consequences will apply to an individual client.

The Task Force understands these recommendations may require significant resource allocations for jurisdictions, many of which are already under-resourced. However, if jurisdictions adopt our recommendations in Principle Eleven, including limiting the number and type of collateral consequences, and our recommendations in Principle Four that encourage prosecutors to engage in more early screening of cases to lead to a greater number of dismissals, there should be fewer cases to contend with overall. Of course, the Task Force understands that some of these recommendations will come up against resource constraints in the current system. As such, it is important to note that compliance with these recommendations should not prevent defendants who wish to plead guilty from resolving their cases through guilty pleas. This Report aims to identify practical policy changes that will improve the overall functioning of our criminal justice system, but nothing in this Report should be read as preventing defendants from resolving their cases by plea bargain if they want to, even if they do so without counsel.

Principle Seven

There should be robust and transparent procedures at the plea phase to ensure that the defendant's plea is knowing and voluntary, free from impermissible coercion, and that the defendant understands the consequences of their decision to plead guilty.

As a constitutional matter, a plea may only be accepted if it is entered knowingly and voluntarily. Unfortunately, in the current system guilty pleas are often entered quickly and with little appreciation by the judge or lawyers for whether the defendant did indeed understand the nature and consequences of pleading guilty. Current practices also often fail to identify or root out actual sources of coercion. As such, this Principle seeks to enhance procedures as they stand now. As with much of this Report, these recommendations are as much about changing legal culture as they are about changing policy.

Federal Rule of Criminal Procedure 11, and similar state rules, should require a searching inquiry by the judge to ensure the defendant is knowingly and voluntarily pleading guilty. The federal rules of criminal procedure, and most state procedural rules, require that prior to accepting a guilty plea, the Court must engage in a colloquy with the defendant to ensure that the defendant understands the legal rights they will waive upon entry of a guilty plea and the consequences of so doing. Courts are also typically required to establish that there is a factual basis for the plea. As numerous practitioners report, however, these plea colloquies almost always are treated as tightly scripted and largely ceremonial events, often consisting entirely of leading, yes-no questions asked by the judge. Although yes-no questions may sometimes be appropriate for ensuring the plea is voluntary, deeper questioning may at times be required. For instance, during the colloquy, if the defendant evinces confusion when the judge asks whether the defendant understands that she could be deported as a result of the crime, it is up to the judge as much as the defense attorney to determine whether the defendant truly understands that deportation consequences may result from her plea. Furthermore, it may be appropriate for the judge to ask more searching questions of the government as well to determine that the government's actions are not coercive. In the current system, nearly all scrutiny at the plea colloquy is on the defendant, but the Task Force encourages judges to scrutinize the actions of the prosecutor as well before accepting a plea.[30]

Indeed, **all participants in a plea proceeding—judge, defense attorney, and prosecutor—are responsible for ensuring the plea is knowing and voluntary, and that there is a sufficient factual basis to establish it.** For instance, prosecutors can contribute to this effort by slowing down their recitation of the charges and facts. Both judges and attorneys should avoid using complicated language that may confuse a lay audience, and they should encourage the defendant to ask questions. We understand that this will slow the pace of court, but it is a constitutional requirement that defendants waive their rights knowingly and voluntarily, and all parties have a responsibility to ensure that when defendants decide to waive their constitutional rights, they do so in line with constitutional standards.

Promoting transparent and open procedures also benefits the victims of crime. Victims should not feel excluded from or confused by the adversarial process; rather, they should understand the plea process and how the parties reached the agreement. It is critical to the integrity of the system that victims feel that they have access to the justice system, including a meaningful understanding of the plea process

We acknowledge that people plead guilty for many reasons beyond guilt.[31] For instance, defendants denied pretrial release might decide to plead guilty in exchange for a sentence of time-served or probation rather than remain incarcerated, unable to work or take care of children. Defendants may also plead guilty to avoid a mandatory minimum sentence after trial or to escape immigration or collateral consequences.[32] Defendants have pleaded guilty to avoid their children and other family members being prosecuted for crimes.[33] The Task Force heard from practitioners that judges in certain jurisdictions ask defendants whether they are pleading guilty because they are guilty and for no other reason. Some members of the Task Force are concerned that such a question perpetuates the self-validating nature of the current system and ignores that people plead guilty for reasons other than guilt. Because of the myriad of reasons that people plead guilty, some members of the Task Force would discourage judges from asking this question.

Furthermore, the Task Force believes that a full factual record is an important component of the plea colloquy to ensure a factual basis supports the charges and defendants have notice of the state's evidence against them. At the same time, the Task Force understands that sometimes defendants plead guilty to crimes they did not commit or to crimes that may not even exist. For instance, the Task Force found examples of defendants pleading guilty to attempted reckless crimes—which are legal impossibilities in most jurisdictions—to secure the benefits of the plea. The Task Force also found examples of defendants pleading guilty to crimes that both the defendant and the prosecutor agree that they did not commit to avoid a mandatory minimum sentence or collateral consequence associated with the charge that accurately matched their behavior.[34] Although most states technically ban baseless pleas by statute,[35] there is good evidence that lawyers in many local jurisdictions engaged in some form of bargaining that involves baseless or fictional pleas. In an ideal world, such factually and legally baseless pleas would not exist. But the Task Force recognizes that these sorts of pleas are often the only way for a defendant to avoid unusually harsh consequences, such as deportation from the country, which neither the defense attorney nor prosecutor believe serve as appropriate punishment or the interests of justice. Because of this, the Task Force hesitates to suggest that jurisdictions limit or ban such pleas. Some members of the Task Force, however, believe that factually or legally baseless pleas should be eliminated.

The issue of factually and legally baseless pleas is a symptom of broader problems with the criminal justice system. These pleas are usually motivated by the wish to avoid mandatory minimum sentences or mandatory collateral consequences that attach to a particular charge. As noted elsewhere in this Report, many though not all members of the Task Force call upon legislatures to eliminate both mandatory minimum sentences and collateral consequences that are not specifically tailored to the offense of conviction. Among the many benefits of this reform would be a reduced need for false pleas. But until those fixes are made, the Task Force does not suggest that courts limit the ability of the parties to negotiate "creatively,"[36] even while the Task Force acknowledges its deep discomfort with factually and legally baseless pleas.

Principle Eight

The use of bail or pretrial detention to induce guilty pleas should be eliminated.

The threat or imposition of pretrial detention may coerce a defendant, including an innocent one, into pleading guilty. Defendants in pretrial detention are more likely to plead guilty and to do so earlier in their case than those awaiting trial from home.[37] Further, defendants in pretrial detention have other significant barriers to fighting their cases effectively, including less access to counsel. Pretrial detention also poses a risk to a defendant's physical and psychological health—a reality made clear during the COVID-19 pandemic as jails and prisons became viral hotspots. Incarcerated people got sick from or were killed by COVID-19 at much higher rates than the general population.[38] Furthermore, like so many aspects of the criminal system, pretrial detention is disproportionately imposed on non-white defendants compared to white defendants.

As a primary matter, **prosecutors should never use pretrial detention to induce guilty pleas.** Every jurisdiction has its own procedural rules regarding pretrial detention and bail. We do not make formal suggestions about what standards any particular jurisdiction should adopt. Instead, we encourage prosecutors in their recommendations and judges in their bail decisions to hew closely to the rules of procedure in their jurisdiction and only impose pretrial detention when absolutely necessary under the rules. For the most part, defendants should be released on their own recognizance without onerous restrictions to continue to fight their cases from home. In rare cases where release on recognizance is not appropriate, all parties—defense counsel, prosecutor, and judge—should seek the least restrictive pretrial conditions for the defendant.

In addition, **prosecutors should not request bail in cases where they would otherwise recommend time served or its equivalent. There should be a formal presumption of release when a plea offer has been made that includes a time served offer or its equivalent.** Such presumptions avoid the risk that prosecutors or judges will punish defendants for refusing to accept offers early in the case. Whether someone enters a plea or not should play no role in the decision to detain them pretrial.

We note that these recommendations align with formal American Bar Association policy. In Resolution 112C, the House of Delegates of the ABA urged both local and state governments to favor the release of defendants upon their own recognizance or unsecured bond and to make bail and release determinations "based upon individualized, evidence-based assessments that use objective verifiable release criteria that do not have a discriminatory or disparate impact based on race, ethnicity, religion, socio-economic status, disability, sexual orientation, or gender identification."[39]

Principle Nine

Defendants should receive all available discovery, including exculpatory materials, prior to entry of a guilty plea, and should have sufficient time to review such discovery before being required to accept or reject a plea offer.

The Constitution requires that a guilty plea be made voluntarily and knowingly. To ensure defendants take pleas knowingly, they should be allowed to review the evidence against them in the state's possession. In addition, the Supreme Court made clear in *Brady v. United States* that before trial defendants should receive any evidence in the state's possession that tends to exculpate them.[40] Unfortunately, defendants are often denied discovery, including exculpatory evidence, before they make the decision to plead guilty. Pleading without discovery is particularly common in misdemeanor cases, but even in serious felony cases, defendants often make life-altering decisions without any sense of the evidence against them. In addition, there are examples of prosecutors withholding evidence of actual innocence from defendants who pleaded guilty.[41]

To promote the integrity of guilty pleas and ensure that such pleas are constitutionally sound, defendants should receive and have time to review all available discovery, including both inculpatory and exculpatory information. This includes all legally available materials in the prosecutor's possession and control. Admittedly, legal limitations prevent what a prosecutor can share with the defendant. For instance, grand jury minutes may be sealed before an indictment, or a prosecutor may move to keep witness names under seal for safety reasons. But any legally available discovery in the prosecutor's possession *at the time of the plea offer* should be provided to defendants before they decide to plead guilty.

The Task Force understands that there exists a broad universe of potential evidence in any case, some of which may not be in the state's possession before trial. This is particularly true for early-stage criminal cases in which the prosecutors themselves may have a limited understanding of the evidence. Still, even in these instances, evidence in the prosecutor's possession or readily available to them should be provided to the defendant before the court accepts a plea. Furthermore, if prosecutor offices only charge after careful screening, as recommended in Principle Four, prosecutors will be well-positioned to understand the universe of evidence that exists early in the case, even while others may require significant investigation.

We make a special note here to reaffirm that defendants should receive any and all *Brady* material in the prosecutor's possession. **Prosecutors have a legal and ethical duty to consistently review their files for *Brady* material and provide it to defendants as soon as possible—both before and after a defendant agrees to enter a guilty plea.** The prosecutor's duty to turn over *Brady* information is a continuous and sacred obligation. As the Supreme Court noted in *Berger v. United States*, "A prosecutor has a duty to refrain from improper methods calculated to produce a wrongful conviction . . . [While he] may strike hard blows, he is not at liberty to strike foul ones."[42] Prosecutors strike foul blows when they hide exculpatory material.

Defendants must also have sufficient time to review discovery materials with counsel. A defendant may choose to waive the right to review discovery and plead guilty without such review, but **the right to receive *Brady* material should never be waivable.** Any waiver of other discovery rights must be done knowingly and voluntarily—meaning, the judge must determine that defendants freely chose to waive their right to review discovery material and were not influenced by prosecutorial pressure to plead guilty. If defendants request time to review the discovery materials, they should not be punished for that choice by, for instance, the withdrawal of plea offers. No plea offer should be contingent on the defendant's waiver of the right to review discovery. The Task Force does not attempt to specify a particular amount of time that a defendant should be entitled to review discovery materials, but various states, like New York, have successfully established discovery schedules that seek to ensure that defendants retain the opportunity to review discovery prior to making critical plea decisions.[43]

Principle Ten

Although guilty pleas necessarily involve the waiver of certain trial rights, there are rights that defendants should never be required to waive in a plea agreement.

To plead guilty a defendant must necessarily waive some essential trial rights. Such waivers include the right to a jury, right to cross-examine witnesses at trial, and the right to testify in one's own defense. The nature of a guilty plea is that the defendant agrees to forgo trial and the rights that necessarily accompany it.

But, as the Task Force heard from numerous witnesses, prosecutors across jurisdictions often demand waivers that go well beyond these basic trial rights. For instance, prosecutors in some cases have demanded that defendants, as part of a guilty plea, waive ineffective assistance of counsel claims, future requests for compassionate release, the right to appeal, the right to request future sealing of their criminal conviction, and the right to *Brady* material, among others.[44] These waivers have nothing to do with trial, and they can and do lead to injustices. For instance, if a defendant pleaded guilty because of their lawyer's incompetence but waived the right to make future ineffective assistance of counsel claims, they cannot challenge their lawyer's poor performance, even if that poor performance is what led to the faulty plea in the first place.[45] Defendants forced to give up compassionate release claims to secure a plea bargain might be kept in prison even if they are gravely ill and would otherwise be eligible for such relief. The Task Force cannot see how these waivers are an appropriate part of the choice of process - plea or trial - that a defendant accepts.

All waivers, beyond those trial rights which must be waived as part of the guilty plea, should be presumptively disfavored. Furthermore, certain rights are so fundamental to the integrity of the criminal system that they should never be waived pursuant to a plea agreement. For that reason, **the Task Force concludes that the following rights should never be waived as part of a guilty plea: ineffective assistance of counsel, *Brady* compliance, innocence claims, Freedom of Information Act (FOIA) claims, compassionate release, the right to challenge sentencing errors, challenges to the constitutionality of the statute of conviction, and the right to appeal or seek post-conviction review related to the above.**

In addition, we make a special note that **defendants should not be required to waive the right to challenge governmental misconduct to receive the benefit of a plea.** The Task Force is particularly concerned with the use of such waivers to hide police misconduct such as illegal searches, Miranda violations, or coercive interrogation practices. Motions to suppress evidence under the Fourth and Fifth Amendments do not merely serve an evidentiary purpose; they also serve a broader societal purpose. Like a trial, public pre-trial hearings on police and government conduct promotes the integrity of the criminal justice system. Bad behavior is brought to light and addressed through the courts or other means, while the discovery that police or government actors acted appropriately strengthens public trust in the system. If a defendant proceeds to a pre-trial hearing and loses, the prosecutor's offer to the defendant should not increase merely because the defendant exercised their right to a pre-trial hearing. Plea offers should only get worse, if at all, because of the unanticipated discovery of new evidence that suggests additional criminal conduct occurred or that puts the defendant's conduct in substantially more culpable light.

Principle Eleven

An adequate understanding of the collateral consequences that may flow from a guilty plea is necessary to ensure the guilty plea is knowing and voluntary.

A current look at the National Inventory of Collateral Consequences reveals over 40,000 possible collateral consequences that may result from criminal convictions.[46] These consequences range from mandatory sex offender registration to the inability to obtain certain professional licenses. In addition, immigration consequences for noncitizens frequently flow from criminal convictions. For instance, nearly every drug conviction, with only a few exceptions, requires deportation.[47]

The Task Force is particularly concerned about the frequent disconnect between the nature of collateral consequences and the type of crime for which the defendant is convicted. In many states, conviction of *any* felony will prohibit a person from ever working at a variety of jobs, such as in funeral services or as a dietician, among other professional fields.[48] Additionally, the state imposes many collateral consequences that have no connection to crime at all—most profoundly, exclusion from all jury service and denial of the right to vote. Because of the number and scope of collateral consequences, it is nearly impossible for a defendant to be fully informed of all potential collateral consequences that may flow from a conviction.

As a primary matter, then, **collateral consequence reform should be a legislative priority.** Collateral consequences—particularly those that are mandatory—have a corrupting influence on the criminal system, encouraging false pleas and other manipulations of the plea process. As such, **there should be meaningful legislative efforts to reduce the number of collateral consequences. In addition, legislators should ensure that when collateral consequences apply, they are both substantively and temporally related to the offense.** In other words, it should make sense for the collateral consequence to apply given the nature of the conviction, and that the collateral consequence, like most punishments, follows the conviction and has a set end point.

Further, many non-legislative bodies, like licensing boards and employers, are responsible for the imposition of collateral consequences. We encourage those bodies to reconsider any mandatory collateral consequences that are not necessary for keeping the public safe. For example, while the Task Force understands why state licensing boards responsible for teachers and childcare workers would exclude defendants convicted of crimes against children, it is less clear why a defendant with any felony conviction cannot, as noted above, be a dietician or funeral director.

While legislators and other relevant groups work to undo the current regime of collateral consequences, **other criminal justice actors, like defense lawyers, prosecutors, and judges, should share responsibility for informing defendants of relevant collateral consequences.** Defense attorneys, at minimum, should review potential collateral consequences with a client before the client accepts a plea. The Task Force also encourages prosecutors and judges to see themselves as playing a role in ensuring a defendant understands collateral consequences—particularly immigration consequences—before accepting a plea. Judges, for instance, should perform a more searching inquiry as part of the plea colloquy, including into any immigration consequences. Judges often rely on defense attorneys to explain the consequences of a plea to a defendant, but when a defendant expresses confusion and asks for clarification, judges should see it as their role to describe the potential consequences a defendant might face.

Similarly, prosecutors should be mindful of which collateral consequences attach to a particular charge and consider collateral consequences in charging decisions to determine if the decision to charge is in the interests of justice, as required by the ABA Standards for the Prosecution Function. Further, in the many jurisdictions where defendants do not have access to a lawyer in misdemeanor cases, prosecutors should be aware of the relevant collateral consequences for each charge and inform defendants of such consequences when presenting a plea offer.

The Task Force recognizes that this training of defense attorneys, prosecutors, and judges will require a significant allocation of resources, but dedicating resources to making these stakeholders knowledgeable about collateral consequences is a worthy effort. That said, our ultimate hope is that legislatures and licensing boards decrease the number and scope of such consequences, which lead to unjust results and manipulations of the plea process.

Principle Twelve

Law students, lawyers, and judges should receive training on the practice and use of plea bargaining consistent with the findings and recommendations of this Report.

The Task Force heard from many stakeholders who wanted more guidance and training on ethical plea practices. The American Bar Association provides Criminal Justice Standards for Pleas of Guilty, but those standards mostly focus on establishing the basis for the guilty plea and the lawyers' responsibilities at the time of a guilty plea. These standards are valuable, but they do not address the broader context in which plea bargaining takes place. As such, we encourage law students, lawyers, and judges to receive training on the use of plea bargaining consistent with the findings and recommendations of this Report.

Although this Report speaks to many audiences, judges and lawyers carry out the day-to-day work of plea bargaining. We hope that training in line with this Report will encourage judges and lawyers to think more deeply about their obligations at plea bargaining and consider where they should challenge current practices and norms.

Further, we hope that if jurisdictions commit to this training, particularly for judges, it will translate into clearer guidelines for plea practice and a decrease in disparate outcomes for similarly situated defendants. As the Task Force heard while gathering evidence, even judges within the same courthouse may handle plea practice very differently, with each judge creating rules for how and why a plea may proceed. As one judge described it to the Task Force, there are widely divergent judicial philosophies operating behind the scenes, and attorneys and defendants must navigate a system with no clear dictate on plea bargaining.[49] This means that similarly situated defendants in the same county, arrested on the same day, may have dissimilar experiences when taking a plea for no other reason than the identity of the judge on the bench that day. Although the Task Force does not believe that plea practice must be uniform among courtrooms, some consistency is important to ensure that similarly situated defendants are treated fairly.

Finally, the Task Force believes that training law students is critical to creating the cultural change these Principles intend to inspire. With few exceptions, law school curricula for future criminal attorneys focuses heavily on trials, trial advocacy, and the rules of criminal procedure, which have little to do with plea practice. We hope law schools will take seriously the need to educate their students—especially those intending to practice criminal law—about the role of plea bargaining in the criminal system. Many law schools are currently engaged in thinking about how to incorporate criminal justice reform into their criminal law curriculum and this Report is an important contribution to that project. The American Bar Association, in collaboration with law schools, advocacy organizations, local bar associations and others, should seek out platforms and mechanisms for this training. The members of this Task Force are committed to participating in future training efforts.

Principle Thirteen

Court systems, sentencing commissions, and other criminal justice stakeholders, including prosecutor offices and public defenders, should collect data about the plea process and each individual plea, including the history of plea offers in a case. Data collection should be used to assess and monitor racial and other biases in the plea process.

A common critique of the modern plea bargain system is how little we know about it. The Task Force collected evidence about the shrouded nature of the plea process.[50] Sometimes the system is not even transparent to the very defendants whose fate is being negotiated.[51] Indeed, defendants rarely participate in the negotiation process. Rather, defendants rely on their attorneys to accurately interpret and/or anticipate the nature of the charges, possible sentence, potential collateral consequences, offers made by the state, and the particular rules (and temperament) of the judge presiding over their case. We rely on defense counsel to explain all of this to defendants in terms they can understand so they can make informed plea decisions. When a defendant has an ineffective defense attorney, much of what is hidden from the public is also hidden from the defendant. This, of course, is true for victims as well, who are often excluded from the plea process and have no idea how and why a plea was negotiated and decided on.[52] Greater transparency would help defendants and crime victims alike better understand what is happening in their cases, and help lawyers provide more accurate advice about the merits of particular plea offers and relevant court or jurisdiction-specific tendencies that may inform the merits of the offer.

This pronounced lack of data about the plea system also means that it is difficult for scholars and policy makers to study and improve the system. Besides the final sentence and charges, very little about the process is ever formally recorded. Data regarding any prior offers—and whether and why they got better or worse—are rarely collected outside of the lawyers' files (if even there). Sometimes even the final charge and sentence will not make its way into any database that would allow for the collection and comparison of this basic data. Further, as the Task Force heard during expert testimony, sometimes deals or promises are made off-the-record that then may be forgotten or not honored once the parties are on the record.[53] This lack of data makes it difficult to measure the full impact of plea bargaining, or many of its features, such as the prevalence of the false pleas discussed in Principle Seven.

The Task Force notes that the evidence collected about plea bargaining paints a particularly troubling picture about how defendants of color fare compared to white defendants. The Task Force took testimony from experts that demonstrated that Black defendants are more likely to receive harsh plea outcomes than similarly situated white defendants. As Juval Scott, the Federal Defender for the Western District of Virginia, noted in her testimony, at least part of the problem with studying and understanding the full extent of racial disparities during the plea process is that we often only understand the final sentence in a case, but not how that sentence *came to be* in the first place.[54]

The criminal justice system, including the plea process, should be transparent and accessible to the public. As such, it is critical that plea bargaining be brought out of the shadows. One way to achieve this is for stakeholders to put more information about each individual plea on the record.[55] **Plea agreements should be in writing and placed on the record.** There may be cases where a plea should be kept confidential, but the general rule should require recording pleas. This information should include, at a minimum, prior plea offers, but may also include the reasons an offer got better or worse. Information on individual cases should be used to create broader databases of information to help researchers and policy makers study and improve plea bargaining. To this end, **plea offers, charging decisions, and sentencing outcomes should be recorded in a digital database that is searchable and available to prosecutors, defense counsel, and judges. It should also be made publicly available so that academics can survey and summarize the data,** which will have salutary effects for the criminal justice system. For instance, better data collection and analysis gives sentencing judges a more complete record of the plea negotiations to make sure that the final plea or trial sentence are not the result of the defendant being punished for exercising certain pre-trial or trial rights. As this Report notes in Principle Three, better data can help judges stay alert to any possible trial penalties.

Many of these suggestions echo a recent resolution by the American Bar Association that urges all prosecutors to "regularly collect, analyze, and produce timely reports that include the crimes charged; the defendant's [] race, gender and zip code; prosecutorial recommendations as to pretrial release and the court's decision on pretrial release; the disposition of each charge including plea offers and sentence[, and to] make data publicly available and easily accessible[.]"[56] We would extend this obligation to other criminal justice stakeholders, like court systems and public defender offices, consistent with attorney-client privilege.

As with many of the proposals in this Report, the Task Force understands that the recommendations require additional work for already overworked lawyers, judges and clerks in our criminal courts. Despite these realities, the Task Force sees data collection about plea bargains as a particularly worthy effort, given that plea bargaining remains, in many ways, a black box. The Task Force is encouraged to see that many local jurisdictions have already begun collecting this data. For instance, the Ohio court system began requiring judges to collect this data for study.[57] The Wilson Center at Duke Law School partnered with North Carolina district attorneys to collect and study data about the plea process.[58] These experiments show that data collection is feasible and that models exist for court systems, public defenders, and prosecutor offices to start their own data collection and analysis efforts.

Principle Fourteen

At every stage of the criminal process, there should be robust oversight by all actors in the criminal system to monitor the plea process for accuracy and integrity, to ensure the system operates consistent with the Principles in this Report, and to promote transparency, accountability, justice, and legitimacy in the criminal system.

This Report has detailed several broad Principles and targeted suggestions that we hope individual stakeholders, court systems, and state legislatures will adopt. But we also encourage these groups to go beyond merely adopting the Principles and to think more broadly about mechanisms that can ensure the Principles are used in practice. To this end, **jurisdictions should establish mechanisms to monitor the plea process from charging decision to disposition, as well as implement an audit process to test the validity and integrity of guilty pleas**. In other fields, like medicine, it is considered essential to have regular forms of oversight in place to protect the public. The criminal justice system, whether at the federal or state level, is a public institution meant to serve a public good, including promoting and maintaining public safety and imposing punishment on wrongdoers. Unfortunately, the system sometimes falls short of this ideal. To understand how and why it does, mechanisms for monitoring and oversight must be created and implemented.

Many of the suggestions throughout this Report should provide some initial guidance for establishing such monitoring systems, but the Task Force encourages courts, public defenders, and prosecutor offices to create organization-specific checks on existing structures and policies. In addition, these stakeholders should implement a system of audits to select and test the accuracy and integrity of guilty pleas.[59] Such audits would seek to determine, in a select set of cases, if coercive methods, like the threat of a large trial penalty, were used to secure a guilty plea, or whether the defense attorney adequately investigated the case, or if the judge confirmed that the plea was knowing and voluntary. By auditing a set of cases post-conviction to ensure these probative questions are answered, stakeholders might better promote integrity and fairness in all cases.

ACTION ITEMS

The primary job of the Task Force was to identify and explain the critiques of the modern plea system. As such, although we offer broad suggestions throughout the Report for ways to reform the plea system, we have not made proposals for specific reforms. In addition, we have hesitated to make specific policy or legal proposals because, as noted in the Introduction, the plea system in this country differs widely depending on the jurisdiction. Certain reforms may make sense in one place, but not another. Having said that, we offer here some possible suggestions for broad areas of reform that interested stakeholders, spurred by this Report, might pursue.

Many of the problems identified in this Report require changes to laws, rules of procedure or regulations. We have recommended the elimination of mandatory minimums and mandatory collateral consequences, but lawmakers might also consider ways to protect defendants from coercive plea practices, as by limiting the trial penalty through statute. Further, states could modify their rules of procedure to ensure a more robust plea colloquy. In addition, regardless of whether the Supreme Court revisits its precedent on plea bargaining practices, state courts are welcome to interpret the state constitutions as providing greater protections to defendants during plea bargaining than the federal Constitution.

Other problems we have identified could be resolved through the adoption of ethical rules that provide guidance and boundaries for the behavior of judges and lawyers. Many of our entreaties to legal stakeholders in the pages of this Report could be easily translated into ethical rules or advice handed down by the American Bar Association, local state bar associations or state judges.

We also encourage court systems, prosecutors and public defender offices to adopt formal policies that put into writing the recommendations of this Report. Formal policies will provide guidance, but also encourage the culture change we hope this Report will inspire.

APPENDIX A: TASK FORCE MEMBERS

Lucian E. Dervan (Co-Chair), Professor of Law, Belmont University College of Law

Lucian E. Dervan is a Professor of Law and Director of Criminal Justice Studies at Belmont University College of Law in Nashville, Tennessee. He is also the Founding Director of the Plea Bargaining Institute, an entity he created in partnership with Fair Trials. His research and writing focus on plea bargaining, white collar crime, and international criminal law. In addition to his books and articles, he is the founder and author of *The Plea Bargaining Blog.* Dervan currently serves on the ABA Board of Governors. He is also the founder and Chair of the ABA Global White Collar Crime Institute and is a member of the American Bar Foundation. Dervan previously served as Chair of the ABA Commission on the American Jury and Chair of the ABA Criminal Justice Section. Prior to joining the academy, Dervan served as a law clerk to the Honorable Phyllis A. Kravitch of the United States Court of Appeals for the Eleventh Circuit. He also practiced law with King & Spalding LLP and Ford & Harrison LLP.

Russell Covey (Co-Chair), Professor of Law, Georgia State University College of Law

Russell Covey is a Professor of Law at Georgia State University College of Law, teaching criminal law and procedure. In addition to publishing many book chapters and articles in his field, Covey is the co-editor of The Wrongful Convictions Reader (Carolina Press 2018). He has filed amicus briefs on behalf of the National Association of Criminal Defense Lawyers. Covey's recent work study police misconduct and the effects of jailhouse informants as causes of wrongful convictions.

Thea Johnson (Reporter), Association Professor of Law, Rutgers Law School

Thea Johnson is an Associate Professor of Law at Rutgers Law School. Her scholarship focuses on the ways that stakeholders manipulate the plea process and stretch ethical boundaries to achieve particular outcomes. She has won several awards for her scholarship, including the 2022 Greg Lastowka Award for scholarly excellence at Rutgers. Prior to joining Rutgers Law, Johnson was an Associate Professor of Law at the University of Maine School of Law, a Thomas C. Grey Fellow at Stanford Law School, and a public defender in New York City.

Hon. Kimberly Esmond Adams, Superior Court of Fulton County

Hon. Kimberly Esmond Adams began her service as a judge on the Superior Court of Fulton County in the Atlanta Judicial Circuit in 2009 and has been re-elected without opposition for three successive terms. Prior to her election, Adams served as Chief Senior Assistant District Attorney in the Office of the Fulton County District Attorney following an employment defense practice with a national labor and employment boutique. A highly-regarded bar leader and community servant, Judge Adams has held numerous leadership positions and received various notable awards and accolades. She currently serves as Chair of the Judicial Council of the National Bar Association and previously served as President of the Georgia Association of Black Women Attorneys (GABWA), Chair of the Judicial Section of the Gate City Bar Association, and Board Chair for *Forever Family*, an organization that provides support and services to children with incarcerated parents. She also was invited to the White House in 2012 to participate in a summit on parental incarceration. Judge Adams holds membership in the American Judges Association and the National Association of Women Judges as well as diverse community and civic groups.

Derwyn Bunton, Chief Legal Officer, Southern Poverty Law Center (formerly, Chief District Defender, Orleans Public Defenders)

Derwyn Bunton is the Chief Legal Officer for the Southern Poverty Law Center. He was formerly the Chief District Defender for Orleans Parish (New Orleans) Louisiana leading the Orleans Public Defender's Office. Before his role at OPD, Bunton was the Executive Director of Juvenile Regional Services and an Associate Director of the Juvenile Justice Project of Louisiana. Bunton is the Board's President of the Fair Fight Initiative, which works to end mass incarceration and support victims of systemic injustice.

Vanessa Edkins, Director of Quantitative Research, Gartner Inc.; Professor Emeritus of Psychology, Florida Institute of Technology

Vanessa Edkins is the Director of Quantitative Research at Gartner, Inc. She is also Professor Emeritus of Psychology at Florida Institute of Technology, where she previously served as the Department Head of the School of Psychology. She has published many works, including the book, ***A System of Pleas: Social Science's Contribution to the Real Legal System***. Her work has been cited in the ***Wall Street Journal***, ***The Economist*** and in congressional testimony. In addition to her publications, Edkins has been a part of the Steering Committee on an NSF Research Coordination Network grant which examines plea bargaining from multiple fields of study.

A. J. Kramer, Federal Public Defender for the District of Columbia

A. J. Kramer has been the Federal Public Defender for the District of Columbia since 1990. Prior to his position in DC, he was the Chief Assistant Public Defender in Sacramento, California and an Assistant Federal Public Defender in San Francisco, California. He is a permanent faculty member of the National Criminal Defense College in Macon, Georgia. Kramer is Fellow of the American College of Trial Lawyers and a member of the Department of Defense Advisory Committee on the Investigation, Prosecution, and Defense of Sexual Assault Cases in the military.

Jenny Kim, Partner, The Gober Group

Jenny Kim is a partner at The Gober Group. Prior to this position, she served as Vice President of Operations and General Counsel for the Philanthropy Roundtable and also as Deputy General Counsel and Vice President, Public Policy for Koch Companies Public Sector, LLC. She is also a board member of the Due Process Institute and The Just Trust for Action.

Marc Levin, Chief Policy Counsel, Council on Criminal Justice

Marc Levin is the Chief Policy Counsel for the Council on Criminal Justice. He began the Texas Public Policy Foundation's criminal justice program in 2005. Levin serves as Senior Advisor for the Right on Crime initiative which he developed the concept for in 2010. He has testified on criminal justice policy before Congress as well as state legislatures. Levin has published policy papers, articles, book chapters and op-eds. He also presented at the national Criminal Justice Association 2020 Virtual Forum on Criminal Justice.

Clark Neily, Senior Vice President for Legal Studies, CATO Institute

Clark Neily is Senior Vice President for Legal Studies at the CATO Institute. Neily was a senior attorney and constitutional litigator at the Institute for Justice and Director of the Institute's Center for Judicial Engagement. He is an adjunct professor at George Mason's Antonin Scalia School of Law. He is also the author of *Terms of Engagement: How Our Courts Should Enforce the Constitution's Promise of Limited Government.*

Norman L. Reimer, Former Global CEO, Fair Trials; Former Executive Director, National Assocation of Criminal Defense Lawyers

Norman Reimer was the global Chief Executive Officer of Fair Trials. Prior to that Reimer served as the Executive Director of the National Association of Criminal Defense Lawyers for 15 years. During his tenure there he established the John Adams Project with the American Civil Liberties Union to represent the accused at Guantanamo and led a collaboration to establish Clemency Project 2014, which procured 894 presidential commutations. During his career as a defense attorney, Reimer was involved in many landmark decisions in search and seizure, habeas corpus and international extradition law. He has also had a hand in amicus briefs before both state courts and the United States Supreme Court.

Rebecca Shaeffer, Legal Director (Americas), Fair Trials

Rebecca Shaeffer serves as Legal Director (Americas) for Fair Trials. She is a member of the Steering Committee for an International Protocol on Non-Coercive Investigative Interviewing, which developed the Mendez Principles. Shaeffer also leads advocacy on the development and enforcement of criminal procedural safeguards. Shaeffer is the lead author of recent reports on areas such as global plea bargaining and pre-trial decision making.

Adnan Sultan, Senior Staff Attorney, The Innocence Project

Adnan Sultan is a staff attorney at The Innocence Project, where he works nationwide to litigate post-conviction cases. Part of his work at the Innocence Project is instructing law students at the Innocence Project clinic at Cardozo School of Law in New York City. Prior to his position at the Innocence project, Sultan worked as a staff attorney at the Bronx Defenders and was a member of the Bronx Defenders' Forensic Practice Group.

Jonathan Wroblewski, Director of the Office of Policy and Legislation, U.S. Department of Justice

Jonathan Wroblewski has served as the Principal Deputy Assistant Attorney General, head of the Office of Legal Policy and the Criminal Division's Director of the Office of Policy and Legislation during his time at the US Department of Justice. In his position for the criminal division, Wroblewski has served as a member of the United States Sentencing Commission, on the Federal Judicial Conference's Advisory Committee on the Criminal Rules and on the American Bar Association's Criminal Justice Council. He is also the Director of Harvard Law School's Semester in Washington Program.

APPENDIX B: TESTIMONY

The Task Force invited experts and relevant stakeholders to present oral testimony to the task force on two separate dates in 2019 and 2021. In addition, the Task Force issued a call for additional written commentary on plea bargaining. Those who gave oral testimony or submitted written testimony for the Task Force are included in this Appendix.

ORAL TESTIMONY:

Professor Zamir Ben-Dan, Assistant Professor of Law at Temple Law School, September 26, 2021

Professor Carlos Berdejó, Professor of Law at Loyola Law School, November 15, 2019

Justin Brooks, Director & Co-Founder of the California Innocence Project, November 15, 2019

Patricia Cummings, Supervisor of the Conviction Integrity and Special Investigations Unit of the Philadelphia District Attorney's Office, November 15, 2019

Hon. Michael P. Donnelly, Justice of the Supreme Court of Ohio, November 15, 2019

Professor Vida Johnson, Associate Professor of Law at Georgetown University Law Center, September 26, 2021

Martín A. Sabelli, Former President of the National Association of Criminal Defense Lawyers, November 15, 2019

Juval Scott, Federal Public Defender for the Western District of Virginia, September 26, 2021

Somil Trivedi, Senior Staff Attorney in the Criminal Law Reform Project at the American Civil Liberties Union, November 15, 2019

Professor Jenia I. Turner, Professor of Law at SMU Dedman School of Law, November 15, 2019

WRITTEN TESTIMONY:

Scott E. Leemon, Criminal Defense Attorney, New York, March 31, 2021

William Otis, Adjunct Professor of Law at Georgetown University Law Center, March 24, 2021

William Ring, County Attorney for the Coconino County Attorney's Office, April 8, 2021

Anna Roberts, Professor of Law at Brooklyn Law School, April 15, 2021

Dr. Nancy Lynn Rogers, Neurosurgeon, July 15, 2021

David W. Shapiro, Partner at The Norton Law Firm, April 5, 2021

Christopher Slobogin, Professor of Law at Vanderbilt Law School, March 24, 2021

Kenneth Wine, Attorney at Law, President of the Criminal Trial Lawyers Association of Northern California, April 5, 2021

ENDNOTES

1 The Plea Bargaining Task Force was created by then ABA Criminal Justice Section Chair Lucian E. Dervan. Professor Dervan created three task forces in his role as Chair – the Plea Bargaining Task Force, the Women in Criminal Justice Task Force, and the Corporate Criminal Liability Task Force.

2 Studies by the Pew Research Center show of nearly 80,000 defendants who faced charges in the federal system in fiscal year 2018, fewer than 2% went to trial and only 320 of those that did win an acquittal. Eight percent of the cases were dismissed, and the other 90% were resolved through guilty pleas. This trial rate represents a significant decline from even recent precedent. For instance, in 1998, 7% of cases went to trial. The number of trials has decreased, even while the number of cases charged in federal courts has "increased substantially." John Gramlich, *Only 2% Of Federal Criminal Defendants Go To Trial, And Most Who Do Are Found Guilty*. The Pew Research Center, June 11, 2019. Trials are vanishingly rare in state criminal systems as well. In the last decade, states like New York, Pennsylvania and Texas have all had trial rates of less than 3%. Some jurisdictions in the country report not having had a criminal trial in years. Jeffrey Q. Smith & Grant R. MacQueen, *Going, Going, But Not Quite Gone: Trials Continue to Decline in the Federal and State Courts. Does It Matter?*, 101 Judicature 4, 32-34 (2017); *See also* The National Association of Criminal Defense Lawyers, *Vanishing Trials*, https://www.nacdl.org/Landing/Vanishing-Trials (showing that in fiscal year 2018, 90% of federal criminal cases ended in guilty pleas, 8% of cases were dismissed, and only 2% went to trial); Benjamin Weiser, *Trial by Jury, a Hallowed American Right, Is Vanishing*, N.Y. Times, Aug. 7, 2016. In addition, there were no criminal trials in Santa Cruz County in Arizona from 2010 until at least 2012. Marisa Gerber, *No Criminal Trials Held in Santa Cruz County Since 2010*, Nogales Int'l, Nov. 21, 2012.

3 The Task Force has decided to capitalize Black, but not white when referring to racial groups. In making this decision, we follow the lead of several organizations and publications which argue that the two terms carry different meanings when used to describe racial or ethnic groups. Mike Lewis, *Why We Capitalize "Black" (and not "white")*, Columbia Journalism Rev., June 16, 2020; Nancy Coleman, *Why We're Capitalizing Black*, N.Y. Times, July 5, 2022.

4 Testimony of Juval Scott; Samuel R. Gross, Maurice Possley, & Klara Stephens, *Race and Wrongful Convictions in the United States*, Nat'l Reg. of Exonerations 1, 16 (2017), lhttps://www.law.umich.edu/special/exoneration/Documents/Race_and_Wrongful_Convictions.pdf (finding that Black people are five times more likely to go to prison for drug possession than white people, and Black people are twelve times more likely to be wrongly convicted of drug crimes); *One War. Two Races. Bias Reigns in Florida's War on Drugs.*, Herald Tribune, Dec. 12, 2016 (finding that Black people make up 46% of felony drug convictions in Florida since 2004, despite only making up 17% of the population of the state); Elizabeth Hilton, *An Unjust Burden: The Disparate Treatment of Black American in the Criminal Justice System*, Vera Inst. of Just. 6 (May 2018) ("the risk of incarceration in the federal system for someone who uses drugs monthly and is [B]lack is more than seven times that of his or her white counterpart."). For a comprehensive list of the studies on racial disparities in the criminal system, *see also*, Radley Balko, *There's Overwhelming Evidence That the Criminal Justice System Is Racist. Here's The Proof*, The Wash. Post, Jun. 10, 2020.

5 Testimony of Juval Scott; *See also*, Josh Salman, Emily Le Coz & Elizabeth Johnson, *Florida's Broken Sentencing System: Designed For Fairness, It Fails To Account For Prejudice*, Herald Tribune, Dec. 12, 2016 (discussing that, on average, Black defendants received longer sentences in Florida than white defendants for the same or similar crimes).

6 Testimony of Carlos Berdejó; Carlos Berdejó, *Criminalizing Race: Racial Disparities in Plea Bargaining*, 59 B.C. L. Rev. 1187, 1191 (2018); *See also*, Gene Demby, *Study Reveals Worse Outcomes For Black And Latino Defendants*, NPR, July 17, 2014 (discussing a 2014 study in Manhattan which found that Black defendants were 19% more likely to be offered plea deals that included jail time than other defendants); Sonja B. Starr & M. Marit Rehavi, *Mandatory Sentencing and Racial Disparity: Assessing the Role or Prosecutors and the Effects of Booker*, 123 Yale L. J. 1, 7 (2013) (discussing a 2013 study that showed that federal prosecutors are almost twice as likely to bring charges carrying mandatory minimums against Black defendants compared to white defendants charged with similar crimes).

7 Testimony of Professor Zamir Ben-Dan.

8 Testimony of Professor Vida Johnson.

9 During oral arguments in *Class v. United States*, the assistant solicitor general, arguing for the government, noted that approximately 25% of pleas in the federal system are "open pleas" that do not involve any promises from the government in exchange for the defendant's guilty plea. As such, the remaining 75% of plea agreements involve favorable treatment or an exchange. Transcript of Oral Arg. at 61–62, *Class v. United States*, 138 S. Ct. 798 (2018) (No. 16-424).

10 *See supra* note 2.

11 Fewer trials also mean fewer citizen jurors. Americans are much less likely to be called for jury service than a decade ago, even while most Americans believe it is a critical part of being a good citizen. In 2006, over 71,000 people were selected to serve as jurors in federal trials compared with 43,000 in 2016. The last available statistics for state courts shows that about 15% of adults are summoned for jury service each year, with only about 5% of those who are called actually serving on a jury. John Gramlich, ***Jury Duty is Rare, but Most Americans See it as Part of Good Citizenship***, The Pew Research Center, August 24, 2017. The right to a jury is enshrined in the Constitution. As the Supreme Court wrote in 2019, "[o]ther than voting, serving on a jury is the most substantial opportunity that most citizens have to participate in the democratic process." ***Flowers v. Mississippi***, 139 S. Ct. 2228, 2238 (2019). And yet, fewer and fewer Americans will ever experience jury service.

12 In ***U.S. v. Seng Cheng Yong***, federal prosecutors in Las Vegas offered to drop charges against a defendant's son if he agreed to plead guilty rather than pursuing his right to trial. At the time of the plea, the prosecutors were aware of pervasive law enforcement misconduct during the investigation. They did not disclose this misconduct to the defendant, who decided to take the plea. On appeal, the Ninth Circuit conceded that "the Government does not deny using the charges against [defendant's son] as a bargaining chip in its plea negotiations with Yong." The Ninth Circuit upheld defendant's guilty plea because the government had probable cause to charge the defendant's son. Charges against other defendants in the case, who proceeded to trial, were eventually dismissed because of the law enforcement misconduct. ***U.S. v. Seng Cheng Yong***, 926 F.3d 582 (9th Cir. 2019). Throughout the United States there are examples of prosecutors using family members as bargaining chips during the negotiation of a plea. The Second Circuit upheld a plea where the government told the defendant that it would only agree to a favorable plea bargain for his wife if he agreed to plead guilty. ***United States v. Marquez***, 909 F.2d 738 (2d Cir. 1990). In another case, the government agreed to forgo the death penalty for a defendant if his brother, who was also a co-defendant, promised to plead guilty. To put it another way, one brother was able to save another brother from the death penalty, but only by giving up his right to trial. ***United States v. Vest***, 125 F.3d 676 (8th Cir. 1997).

13 Federal prosecutors in United States District Court for the District of Columbia offered two co-defendants what is known as a "wired" plea. The plea, which came with a likely sentence of between two and six years, required both defendants to accept the terms of the offer. One defendant readily agreed to the plea; the other defendant, as a result of ineffective assistance of counsel, did not. The prosecutors took the plea off the table and proceeded to trial, where both defendants were given sentences of over twenty years. The Court of Appeals overturned the sentence of the defendant with the ineffective lawyer, allowing him to get the benefit of the initial plea deal. The sentence of the defendant who was willing to take the initial "wired" plea deal had his sentence upheld, even though it was, at least, fifteen years longer than the initial deal that the prosecutors believed was a just resolution to the case. ***United States v. Knight***, No. 19-3016, (D.C. Cir. 2020).

14 In Tennessee, a prosecutor would only offer a favorable plea to mothers in certain abuse and neglect cases who agreed to sterilization. Although the chief prosecutor later disavowed the policy, a Nashville prosecutor made sterilization and required use of birth control part of the negotiation process in at least four cases. Shelia Burke, *Tennessee Prosecutor Fired Over Plea Bargains Involving Female Sterilization*, Associated Press, April 1, 2015.

15 Testimony of Somil Trivedi, Martín Sabelli, and Justin Brooks; Written testimony of David Shapiro and Kenneth Wine.

16 ABA Resolution 10B passed the American Bar Association House of Delegates on August 15, 2017. The measure "opposes mandatory minimum sentences in any criminal case, and urges Congress and state legislatures to repeal existing criminal laws requiring minimum sentences." *ABA Opposes Mandatory Minimum Sentences*, Aug. 15, 2017, available at https://www.americanbar.org/news/abanews/aba-news-archives/2017/08/aba_opposes_mandator/.

17 Almost three-quarters of homicide exonerees who pled guilty were convicted of murder (44/61). It appears that the great majority did so to avoid the risk of execution. All but two were prosecuted in death penalty states, and 70% had falsely confessed (31/44), which greatly increases the risk of conviction. They all avoided the death penalty, but the sentences they did receive were stiff: fourteen were sentenced to life or life without parole, the rest got sentences that averaged twenty-two years. National Registry of Exonerations, ***Innocents Who Plead Guilty***, November 2015, available at https://www.law.umich.edu/special/exoneration/Documents/NRE.Guilty.Plea.Article1.pdf.

18 **National Association of Criminal Defense Lawyers,** The Trial Penalty: The Sixth Amendment Right to Trial on the Verge of Extinxtion

and How to Save It, July 10, 2018, available at https://www.nacdl.org/DocumentTrialPenaltySixthAmendmentRighttoTrialNearExtinct.
19 *Id.*

20 The idea of fixing the plea to trial sentencing differential is not new. The Editors of the Yale Law Journal proposed a "specific discount rate" as early as 1972. Note, *Restructuring the Plea Bargaining*, 82 Yale L. J. 286 (1972). See also, James Vorenberg, *Decent Restraint of Prosecutorial Power*, 94 Harv. L. Rev. 1521, 1560-61 (1980) (proposing "a relatively modest, prescribed sentencing concession of ten to twenty percent of the sentence received for a guilty plea."), Mirko Bagaric et. al., *Plea Bargaining: From Patent Unfairness to Transparent Justice*, 84 Mo. L. Rev. 1 (2019) ("The size of the discount should be up to thirty percent."); Darryl Brown, Free Market Criminal Justice (2016), at 108 (reporting that the "Criminal Justice Act of 2003 ... authorized sentence discounts" that were limited to "a one-third reduction from the post-trial sentence"); Stephanos Bibas, *Plea Bargaining Outside the Shadow of Trial*, 117 Harv. L. Rev. 2463, 2488 (2004) (explaining that the Guidelines initially prescribed "a three-level discount (on average, 35%) for guilty pleas in serious federal cases regardless of the chance of acquittal," which was subsequently modified to an automatic two-level reduction with the possibility of a third upon motion by the government). In his article, *Fixed Justice: Reforming Plea Bargaining with Plea-Based Ceilings*, Russell D. Covey offers several suggestions for how fixed discounts can work in practice to achieve fairer results in the criminal system. 82 Tul. L. Rev. 1237 (2008).

21 *Bordenkircher v. Hayes*, 434 U.S. 357, 363-65 (1978).

22 *Id.*

23 *Id.*, at 364.

24 This suggestion is in line with the ABA Criminal Justice Standards for the Prosecution Function, which encourages prosecutors not to file or to dismiss charges for a variety of reasons, including a lack of evidence for the charges or a prosecutor's doubt about the guilt of the accused. *Minimum Requirements for Filing and Maintain Criminal Charges*, Standard § 3-4.3 (2017).

25 *See* Andrew Pardieck, Lucian E. Dervan, and Vanessa Edkins, *The Global Rise of False Testimony for False Pleas*, 44 Fordham Int'l L. J. 469 (2020) (discussing false pleas of guilty and false testimony in support of such pleas); Lucian E. Dervan, and Vanessa Edkins, *The Innocent Defendant's Dilemma: An Innovative Empirical Study of Plea Bargaining's Innocence Problem*, 103 J. Crim. L. & Criminology 1 (2013) (discussing the phenomenon of false pleas of guilty by the innocent).

26 Glinda S. Cooper, Vanessa Meterok & Prahelika Gadtaula, *Innocents Who Plead Guilty: An Analysis of Patterns in DNA Exoneration Cases*, 31 Fed. Sent. R. 215, 234 (2019).

27 Written Testimony of Professor Anna Roberts (pointing to her work, *Convictions as Guilt*, 88 Fordham L. Rev. 2501, 2533 (2020)), which persuasively argues that estimates of the proportion of people "with convictions who are 'wrongfully convicted' or 'innocent' undercount in a variety of ways," as by "excluding those who lacked representation, incentive, written record, knowledge, or the correct procedural vehicle to get recognition that their conviction was wrongful.").

28 *See, e.g.*, National Association of Criminal Defense Lawyers, *Three-Minute Justice: Haste and Waste in Florida's Misdemeanor Courts*, at 15, July 2011, available at https://www.nacdl.org/Document/ThreeMinuteJusticeFloridasBrokenMisdemeanorCourts (finding in a study of Florida misdemeanor courts that 66% of defendants appeared at arraignment without counsel).

29 *Argersinger v. Hamlin*, 407 U.S. 25, 38 (1971).

30 Testimony of Somil Trivedi.

31 *See* Lucian E. Dervan, *Class v. United States: Bargained Justice and a System of Efficiencies*, 2017-2018 Cato Supreme Court Rev. 113 (2018) (discussing the various "determinative issues" that lead a defendant to plead guilty).

32 *Padilla v. Kentucky*, 559 U.S. 356, 368 (2010) (acknowledging that defendants plead guilty to avoid immigration consequences).

33 *See supra* note 12.

34 Thea Johnson, *Fictional Pleas*, Ind. L. J. 855, 861 (2019) (finding that defendants plead guilty to crimes that both the defendant and the prosecutor agree that they did not commit to avoid a mandatory minimum sentence).

35 Tina M. Zottoli, Tarika Daftary-Kapur, Vanessa A. Edkins, Allison D. Redlick, Christian M. King, Lucian E. Dervan, Elizabeth Tahan, *State of the States: A Survey of Statutory Law, Regulations and Court Rules Pertaining to Guilty Pleas Across the United States*, 37 Behav. Sci. & Law 388, 414 (2019) ("The majority of states (42), Washington, DC, and the federal government explicitly disallow baseless pleas. Commonly, the language dictates that that the courts must establish or find a factual basis for any guilty plea. Three states are explicit about a factual basis requirement only for specific cases, such as pleas of guilty to charges that may result in incarceration (Montana) or pleas of not guilty by reason of insanity (New York and Louisiana); Louisiana otherwise requires only that the attorney be satisfied that there is a factual or strategic basis for the plea. Idaho mentions baseless pleas only insofar as to restrict their use in juvenile proceedings, with no mention of adult proceedings. Some states, however, do not expressly require a factual basis, and two states (Colorado and South Dakota) expressly allow baseless pleas, with certain restrictions. For example, in Colorado, as long as the defendant understands the plea agreement, he or she can waive the establishment of a factual basis for the guilty plea; South Dakota allows the same for defendants who plead nolo contendere. We screened 335 cases for this topic. Most of the relevant cases dealt with adequate sources of proof for establishing the factual basis for the plea . . . , and whether the circumstances rose to the level of an injustice that would require[.]")

36 *Padilla*, 559 U.S. at 373.

37 *Vanessa A. Edkins* and Lucian E. Dervan, ***Freedom Now or a Future Later: Pitting the Lasting Implications of Collateral Consequences against Pretrial Detention in Decisions to Plead Guilty***, 24 *Psych, Pub Pol'y, & Law 204 (2018) (revealing that the* rate of innocent individuals who pleaded guilty in a psychological study tripled where defendants were held pretrial).

38 Neal Marquez, Julia A. Ward, Kalind Parish, *COVID-19 Incidence and Mortality in Federal and State Prisons Compared with the US Population, April 5, 2020, to April 3, 2021,* JAMA 326(18) (2021).

39 American Bar Association, Resolution 112C (2017), available at https://www.americanbar.org/content/dam/aba/directories/policy/annual-2017/2017-am-112c.pdf.

40 *Brady v. Maryland*, 373 U.S. 83 (1963)

41 Susan R. Klein et al., *Waiving the Criminal Justice System: An Empirical and Constitutional Analysis*, 52 Am. Crim. L. Rev. 73, 76 (2015) (outlining the many typical waivers at plea bargaining, including the waiver of *Brady* material, FOIA and DNA); Carrie Johnson, *Justice Department Ends Limiting Compassionate Release in Plea Deals After NPR Story*, NPR, March 11, 2022.

42 *Berger v. United States*, 295 U.S. 78, 88 (1935).

43 The Center for Court Innovation, *Discovery Reform in New York: Major Legislative Provisions*, at 3 (May 2019), https://www.courtinnovation.org/sites/default/files/media/document/2019/Discovery-NYS_Full.pdf ("Defendants will no longer be required to consider a plea offer without knowledge of the evidence against them.")

44 Klein, *Waiving the Criminal Justice System, supra note* 41, at 76 ("As we transformed from an adversary process where guilt was determined by trial to an administrative process where guilt and penalties are determined by negotiation, many prosecutors began demanding waiver of all constitutional criminal procedure rights, not just the trial and investigative-related ones inherent in replacing the trial with the plea.").

45 Some state bar associations have held that it is unethical for a prosecutor to require a waiver of ineffective assistance of counsel at the guilty plea. *Kansas Bar: Unethical to Negotiate IAC Waiver in Plea Deal*, Bloomberg Law, April 19, 2017 (noting that nineteen states have addressed the issue with all but two saying the practice is unethical).

46 CSG Justice Center, *The National Inventory of Collateral Consequences of Conviction*, available at https://csgjusticecenter.org.

47 Immigration and Nationality Act (INA) § 237(a)(2)(B)(i), 8 U.S.C. § 1227(a)(2)(B)(i) (2012), gives the general grounds for drug deportability. Essentially, if a noncitizen after admission is convicted of a violation or conspiracy or attempt to violate a law related to a controlled substance, he is deportable. Controlled substance is defined under 21 U.S.C. § 802(5)-(6) (2012) as "a drug or other substance, or immediate precursor," included in schedule I, II, III, IV, or V of the Federal Controlled Substances Act. These laws essentially mean that possession-only offenses, including marijuana possession (under thirty grams), are considered deportable.

48 *See supra* note 46.

49 Testimony of Hon. Michael P. Donnelly.

50 Testimony of Professor Jenia I. Turner; *See also*, Jenia I. Turner, *Transparency at Plea Bargaining*, Notre Dame L. Rev. 972 (2021).

51 Testimony of Hon. Michael P. Donnelly.

52 *Id.*

53 Hon. Michael P. Donnelly, *Sentencing by Ambush: An Insider's Perspective on Plea Bargaining Reform*, 54 Akron L. Rev. 222, 229 (2021).

54 Testimony of Juval Scott.

55 Many of these suggestions come from the testimony and research of Professor Jenia I. Turner.

56 American Bar Association, Resolution 504 and Report, available at https://www.americanbar.org/content/dam/aba/administrative/news/2021/08/annual-meeting-resolutions/504.pdf

57 Laura A. Bischoff, *Ohio Court Data Project Promises to Bring Transparency, Improve Justice in Felony Cases*, The Columbus Dispatch (Oct. 4, 2021), https://www.dispatch.com/story/news/2021/10/04/ohio-sentencing-data-platform-tested-improve-court-transparency/5992267001/.

58 The Wilson Center for Science and Justice at Duke Law has been working with prosecutors to create plea tracking checklists and models that allow for the collection of data about the negotiation of pleas. *Wilson Center Project Takes Unprecedented Look into Plea Negotiations*, July 15, 2021, available at https://wcsj.law.duke.edu/2021/07/wilson-center-project-takes-unprecedented-look-into-plea-negotiations/. In Ohio, there is a judge-led effort to create uniform codes for sentencing that will allow judges to collect data on sentencing and enter it in a state-wide database. Ohio Sentencing Data Platform, available at https://www.ohiosentencingdata.info. Both efforts are meant to increase the transparency and fairness of the plea and sentencing process.

59 Although it is beyond the scope of the Report, we encourage stakeholders with an interest in reform and auditing structures to explore many bold ideas in this area. For instance, some scholars have suggested implementing a "trial lottery," which randomly subjects certain cases that were resolved by plea to a jury trial. Kiel Brennan-Marquez, Darryl K. Brown, & Stephen E. Henderson, *The Trial Lottery*, 56 Wake Forest L. Rev. 1 (2021); Other scholars and advocates recommend a "second look" policy or law that would allow judges, after a reasonable time, to look at a defendant's sentence and determine whether it was fair or should be adjusted. Particularly in cases where defendants went to trial and received a harsher sentence than the plea offer, such "second look" policies could provide a remedy to a prior injustice. Nazgol Ghandnoosh, *A Second Look at Injustice*, The Sentencing Project, May 12, 2021, available at https://www.sentencingproject.org/publications/a-second-look-at-injustice/. Clark Neily, a member of the Task Force, has suggested several fixes for the modern plea system, including independent Plea Integrity Units, which would be responsible for reviewing and monitoring plea systems; a trial audit that would include potential professional consequences for prosecutors; and informing juries of their right to nullify as a way to reinvigorate the jury system. Clark Neily, *A Distant Mirror: American-Style Plea Bargaining Through the Eyes of a Foreign Tribunal*, 27 Geo. Mason L. Rev. 719, 741-47 (2020).

CHAPTER 3

The Historic Rise of Plea Bargaining

Lucian E. Dervan

As the Plea Bargain Task Force began its review of modern plea bargaining practices, the group did not lose sight of the significance of the history of plea bargaining's rise to dominance. Far from having deep common law roots or a storied history of careful crafting and implementation, modern-day plea bargaining is actually a relatively modern American invention. While limited examples of bargains exist in the late 1700s and the 1800s, the use of plea bargaining more widely dates to the era of Prohibition and the necessity of clearing overwhelmed criminal dockets in the face of rampant overcriminalization in the early 1900s. From these early roots, plea bargaining rose to dominate the criminal system, though it did so mainly in the shadows without the oversight, regulation, or monitoring one might expect of a phenomenon of such significance. This chapter will explore the history of plea bargaining and, in so doing, explain why plea bargaining remained in the shadows for so long and why the work of the task force in creating the 14 Principles to guide our use of bargains is both necessary and timely.

The Early Era of Bargains

Today, plea bargaining accounts for close to 98 percent of federal convictions and around 95 percent of state convictions.[1] But just a century or two ago, the mere idea of using offers of leniency or threats of punishment to induce a plea of guilty in court would have been met not only with skepticism but also with revulsion.

An illustration of the early common law view on incentives to "confess," whether in court or in a police station, is the 1783 English case of *Rex v. Warickshall.* In *Warickshall,* the suspect was alleged to have received stolen goods and was brought to the police station for questioning. In return for a "promise of favor," the suspect confessed to the crime. In reviewing the matter, the British court struck down the statement as

1. *See* U.S. SENT'G COMM'N SOURCEBOOK (U.S. SENT'G COMM'N 2022); Padilla v. Kentucky, 559 U.S. 356, 372 (2010).

having been improperly coerced. According to the court, "[A] confession forced from the mind by the flattery of hope, or by the torture of fear, comes in so questionable a shape . . . that no credit ought to be given to it."[2] This is an important statement highlighting the significance placed by the common law on free and voluntary confessions to ensure the information received is reliable. The common law saw the jury trial, rather than offers of leniency or threats of punishment to induce a confession, as the most reliable method of ascertaining guilt or innocence.

A similar view of the significance of jury trials and a rejection of coercive incentives to confess and bypass trial are found in early American law. The right to a jury trial in criminal cases, for example, is the only right enumerated in both the Bill of Rights and the unamended text of the Constitution.[3] This was not merely a procedural tool in the newly established country's criminal justice system; the trial by jury was considered fundamental to maintaining a just system of law. Thomas Jefferson wrote, "I consider trial by jury as the only anchor ever yet imagined by man, by which a government can be held to the principles of its constitution."[4]

The embrace of jury trials and suspicion of pleas of guilty as a mechanism of adjudication can be seen in early American criminal case law as well. For example, consider the 1804 Massachusetts Supreme Court case of *Commonwealth v. Battis*.[5] The defendant in the case was charged with the rape and murder of a 13-year-old girl in Dedham, Massachusetts. After his apprehension, Battis appeared in court and attempted to plead guilty. The court, however, refused to accept the plea and remanded Battis to jail to reconsider his decision. Later, the defendant was brought back to court and once again attempted to plead guilty. The court remained skeptical of the decision to waive the right to a jury trial but, after thorough questioning, determined that there had been no "tampering with him, either by promises, persuasions, or hopes of pardon, if he would plead guilty." Having satisfied itself that there had been no promise of leniency in return for waiving the constitutional right to trial, the court accepted the plea. Historically, cases such as *Battis* demonstrate the significance of the right to a jury trial in the early American criminal justice system and the reluctance of courts to accept guilty pleas for fear the "confessions" were not voluntary. As the court noted in *Warickshall*, the common law demanded that confessions not result from the "flattery of hope, or by the torture of fear."[6]

The importance of voluntary pleas of guilty, free from the coercive forces of offers of leniency and threats of further punishment, is also found in U.S. Supreme Court precedent from the 19th century. In the case of *Bram v. United States*, for example, the Supreme Court considered whether a defendant's confession was lawful. In examining

2. Rex v. Warickshall, 168 Eng. Rep. 234, 235 (1783).

3. Clark Neily & Somil Trivedi, *The Unconstitutional Convictions You Don't Know About*, CATO INST. (Dec. 12, 2021), https://www.cato.org/commentary/unconstitutional-convictions-you-dont-know-about#:~:text=These%20include%20Kevin%20Strickland%2C%20a,misconduct%20by%20the%20federal%20government.

4. *Id.*

5. Commonwealth v. Battis, 1 Mass. 95, 95 (1804); *see also* Hallinger v. Davis, 146 U.S. 314, 324 (1892) (affirming, for the first time, a defendant's right to plead guilty if voluntary; the case involved a lower court reluctant to allow a plea of guilty to the charges in the case).

6. Rex v. Warickshall, 168 Eng. Rep. 234, 235 (1783).

the issue, the Court embraced the notion that confessions must be offered freely and voluntarily. Further, the Court went on to consider the role of incentives to confess and adopted language reminiscent of the earlier British common law. According to the Court in *Bram*, the "true test of admissibility is that the confession is made freely, voluntarily and without compulsion or inducement of any sort."[7]

Despite such strong common law precedent from both England and the United States, various forms of plea bargaining began to appear sporadically in the United States shortly after the founding period. For example, in his book *Plea Bargaining's Triumph*, Professor George Fisher documents discrete examples of charge bargaining in Middlesex County, Massachusetts, liquor law prosecutions during the late 1700s.[8] Further, in his book *Pleading Out*, Professor Dan Canon documents the use of plea bargaining in Massachusetts and eventually New England in the mid-1800s. As an example of the unsettled nature of the practice, however, Professor Canon also provides an example of a Boston prosecutor at the time who was criminally charged for offering such bargains.[9]

Though these examples demonstrate that forms of plea bargaining were beginning to evolve as early as the late 1700s and that such practices were beginning to increase in frequency and geographic reach in the 1800s, many courts remained concerned about the practice and its impact on defendants' fundamental right to trial. Appellate opinions extremely critical of the practice, for example, can be found in the late 1800s, particularly in the period following the American Civil War. In one case, the court said, "When there is reason to believe that the plea has been entered through inadvertence . . . and mainly from the hope that the punishment to which the accused would otherwise be exposed may thereby be mitigated, the Court should be indulgent in permitting the plea to be withdrawn."[10] In another case from this era, the court put a sharper edge on its commentary. Plea bargaining, the court said, "[is] hardly, if at all, distinguishable in principle from a direct sale of justice."[11]

Plea Bargaining Finds a Foothold

Despite the common law language from cases such as *Warickshall*, *Battis*, and *Bram* and the additional statements from appellate courts examining early pleas in the post–Civil War period, plea bargaining continued to bubble up in the trenches of the criminal justice system on its slow rise to dominance. While various factors likely led to the rise of plea bargaining in various parts of the United States during the late 19th and early 20th centuries, the practice began to take root in the 1920s and 1930s for at least two reasons.[12]

First, at the turn of the 20th century, those with nefarious purposes embraced the concept of pleading guilty to fashion a system of bribery within American courts. As

7. Bram v. United States, 168 U.S. 532, 584 (1897).

8. George Fisher, Plea Bargaining's Triumph: A History of Plea Bargaining in America 21 (2003).

9. Dan Canon, Pleading Out 16–17 (2022).

10. People v. McCrory, 41 Cal. 458, 462 (1871).

11. Wright v. Rindskopf, 43 Wis. 344, 354 (1877).

12. Fisher, *supra* note 8, at 6.

Albert Alschuler documents in his research on early plea bargaining practices, judges, prosecutors, and defenders would accept bribes from defendants seeking to "resolve" their cases without a jury trial. In Chicago, for example, "fixers" would stand in front of the courthouse to manage payments from the defendants who benefited from their willingness to forgo a trial in favor of a plea of guilty.[13] According to Professor Alschuler, "The gap between [] judicial denunciations of plea bargaining [in the late 19th century] and the practices of many urban courts at the turn of the century and thereafter was apparently extreme. In these courts, striking political corruption apparently contributed to a flourishing practice of plea bargaining."[14] This, of course, is not actually plea bargaining as that term has come to be understood. But this piece of American criminal justice history is an interesting reminder of the relative newness of plea bargaining as a recognized and approved form of case resolution and the manner in which the power of the criminal justice system has been used to coerce in different ways over the span of American history.

Second, and more pivotal in tracing the rise of plea bargaining into a widely utilized and dominant mechanism of criminal adjudication, is the growth of overcriminalization in the early part of the 20th century. Particularly as the United States entered the era of Prohibition, the American court system became overwhelmed as dockets swelled and resources failed to meet demand. Rather than respond by increasing the number of courts, prosecutors, and defense counsel, public officials began searching for a way to make the criminal justice system more efficient. The answer, many decided, was to begin to embrace the practice that had, up until this time, been rejected by the courts as impermissibly coercive—plea bargaining.

In 1931, as overcriminalization continued to overburden the criminal justice system, President Herbert Hoover convened the Wickersham Commission to examine crime in America. The commission's report made specific reference to plea bargaining as a mechanism for addressing the court system's ills.

> [F]ederal prosecutions under the Prohibition Act terminated in 1930 had become nearly eight times as many as the total of all pending federal prosecutions in 1914. In a number of urban districts the enforcement agencies maintain that the only practicable way of meeting this situation with the existing machinery of federal courts . . . is for the United States Attorneys to make bargains with defendants or their counsel whereby defendants plead guilty to minor offenses and escape with light penalties. . . .
>
> Lawyers everywhere deplore, as one of the most serious effects of prohibition, the change in the general attitude toward the federal courts. . . . [T]he huge volume of liquor prosecutions . . . has injured their dignity, impaired their efficiency, and endangered the wholesome respect for them which once obtained.[15]

---

13. *See* Albert W. Alschuler, *Plea Bargaining and Its History*, 29 COLUM. L. REV. 1 (1979); *see also* Lucian E. Dervan, *Bargained Justice: Plea Bargaining's Innocence Problem and the* Brady *Safety-Valve*, 2012 UTAH L. REV. 51.

14. *See* Alschuler, *supra* note 13, at 24.

15. NAT'L COMM'N ON LAW OBSERVANCE & ENFORCEMENT, REPORT ON THE ENFORCEMENT OF THE PROHIBITION LAWS OF THE UNITED STATES 56 (1931) (quoted in Alschuler, *supra* note 13, at 32); *see also* FISHER, *supra* note 8, at 210–12.

There is limited data to explore how the need for more efficiency in the criminal justice system in the early 20th century impacted the growth of plea bargaining, but data is available regarding the rate of guilty pleas generally. Between the early 20th century and 1925, pleas of guilty in the federal criminal justice system rose from 50 percent to 90 percent of convictions.[16] Based on the comments from the Wickersham Commission, it is likely that much of this growth represented not just pleas of guilty, but pleas of guilty in return for bargains.

Interestingly, while it appears that practitioners and policymakers in the early 20th century had decided to abandon the concerns expressed by courts dating back to the 1700s regarding the manner in which offers of leniency or threats of punishment might reduce the accuracy and reliability of criminal adjudications, the U.S. courts had not yet made this leap. In fact, as late as the 1960s, it is believed that the U.S. Supreme Court was on the cusp of ruling that the by-then relatively common practice of plea bargaining was, in fact, unconstitutionally coercive. In 1958, for example, the case of *Shelton v. United States* made its way to the Supreme Court.[17] The defendant in the matter, Shelton, had pleaded guilty to one count of interstate transportation of stolen vehicles in return for a promise from the prosecution to both recommend a reduced sentence on the single charge and dismiss any remaining charges. In today's environment of bargained justice, few would raise an eyebrow at such a deal. Yet, in 1958, such actions in direct contravention of the language in cases such as *Warickshall*, *Battis*, *Bram*, *McCrory*, and *Wright* were of unknown constitutionality.

Despite pleading guilty, Shelton consistently maintained his innocence and eventually asked that his plea be set aside as involuntary and coerced. And the U.S. Court of Appeals for the Fifth Circuit agreed and wrote:

> There is no doubt, indeed it is practically conceded, that the appellant pleaded guilty in reliance on the promise of the Assistant United States Attorney that he would receive a sentence of only one year. The court, before accepting the plea, did not ascertain that it was in truth and in fact a voluntary plea not induced by such promise. It necessarily follows that the judgment of conviction must be set aside and the plea of guilty vacated.[18]

The Fifth Circuit then went on to channel the judgments from the post–Civil War era when it added, "Justice and liberty are not the subjects of bargaining and barter."[19] The panel decision, however, was later overturned en banc, and the case was appealed to the Supreme Court. The justices, though, were denied the opportunity to weigh in on the constitutionality of plea bargaining because the government filed an admission of error and removed the case from consideration. Of the decision to remove the case from the Supreme Court's purview, Professor Albert Alschuler in his review of the history of plea bargaining speculated that

16. *See* Dervan, *supra* note 13, at 59.

17. *See* Shelton v. United States, 242 F.2d 101 (5th Cir.), *judgment set aside*, 246 F.2d 571 (5th Cir. 1957) (en banc), *rev'd per curiam on confession of error*, 356 U.S. 26 (1958).

18. *Shelton*, 242 F.2d at 113.

19. *Id.*

> the Solicitor General (or perhaps some other official in the Justice Department) may have assessed the probable votes of individual Supreme Court Justices, may have sensed a substantial likelihood that the Court would hold the practice of plea bargaining unlawful, and may have sought to foreclose this ruling through a confession of error on narrow and disingenuous grounds.[20]

That plea bargaining's fate lay in the balance a mere 60 years ago in the *Shelton* case is a stark reminder that the phenomenon that has come to dominate our criminal procedure is a relatively new American invention. This was also not the only close call for plea bargaining's future during this era. Ten years later, which was only 50 years ago, another case made its way to the Court, and this time the justices were able to render a decision, though a limited one at that.

In 1966, Charles Jackson was indicted for kidnapping resulting in injury to the victim under 18 U.S.C. § 1201(a).[21] This statute differentiated between the maximum punishment available to those who pleaded guilty and those who put the government to the burden of a trial. Pursuant to the language of the statute, only defendants who proceeded to trial could receive the death penalty, while those who pleaded guilty could not receive more than life in prison. In examining the statute, the lower court found the sentencing differential unconstitutional because it made the "risk of death" the "price for asserting the right to jury trial."[22] On appeal, the U.S. Supreme Court agreed.

> It is no answer . . . that federal trial judges may be relied upon to reject coerced pleas of guilty and involuntary waivers of jury trials. For the evil in the federal statute is not that it necessarily coerces guilty pleas and jury waivers but simply that it needlessly encourages them. A procedure need not be inherently coercive in order that it be held to impose an impermissible burden upon the assertion of a constitutional right. Thus the fact that the [statute] tends to discourage defendants from insisting upon their innocence and demanding trial by jury hardly implies that every defendant who enters a guilty plea to a charge under the [statute] does so involuntarily. The power to reject coerced guilty pleas and involuntary jury waivers might alleviate, but it cannot totally eliminate, the constitutional infirmity in the capital punishment provision of the [statute].[23]

While this case involved a statute containing a sentencing incentive to plead guilty, rather than a plea bargain from the prosecutor with such a promise of leniency, the implications of this Supreme Court decision are clear. While reiterating that defendants are free to plead guilty voluntarily, the Court attacked the concept of a system that discourages defendants from asserting their right to trial by imposing more severe punishments on those who refuse to plead guilty. The distance from this pronouncement regarding a statute to a complete abolishment of plea bargaining was negligible. Yet plea bargaining exists in our criminal justice system today, and that is because just two

20. Alschuler, *supra* note 13, at 37.
21. United States v. Jackson, 390 U.S. 570 (1968).
22. *Id.* at 571.
23. *Id.* at 583.

years after *Jackson*, in *Brady v. United States*, the Supreme Court suddenly turned the precedents of the previous centuries on their heads.[24]

The *Brady* Decision and the Birth of Modern Plea Bargaining

The *Brady* case involved a defendant who asserted that he had pleaded guilty only to avoid the possibility of receiving the death penalty and who requested that his plea be withdrawn. Given the large size of the incentives in the matter, many believed that the Court would strike down the plea because it clearly resulted from the "flattery of hope" and the "torture of fear." Contrary to such opinions, however, the Court ruled that plea bargains, including pleas in the face of the death penalty, were lawful. The Court continued by reiterating that pleas must be voluntary and, therefore, incentives that overbear the will of the defendant would not be permitted. While the decision of the Court in *Brady* is contrary to the common law tradition and the precedent established in the centuries leading up to the case, the Supreme Court appears to have had little other choice in 1970. By the time the Court directly took up the issue of plea bargaining, 90 percent of cases in the United States were being resolved through pleas of guilty. It is hard to imagine what a system struggling even to bring the remaining matters to trial would have done had plea bargaining been ruled unconstitutional. Trials themselves were also taking longer and requiring more resources by 1970 because of the previous decade's due process revolution. According to one study, the length of criminal trials almost doubled from the beginning to the end of the 1960s.[25] The Court, therefore, also hoped that the *Brady* decision would assist in freeing up resources for what it described as "real disputes" that now required more time to litigate.

Another important element of the *Brady* decision was the Court's belief that in adopting plea bargaining it was adopting an inherently reliable procedure that would create incentives for guilty defendants to plead guilty while simultaneously freeing up resources for the trials of the innocent. In the *Brady* decision, the Court said, "[W]e would have serious doubts about this case if the encouragements of guilty pleas by offers of leniency substantially increased the likelihood that defendants, advised by competent counsel, would falsely condemn themselves. But our view is to the contrary . . . ."[26] This unsupported assumption that the creation of a plea bargaining system was unlikely to lead innocent defendants to falsely plead guilty appeared in subsequent cases as well. In the 1975 case of *Menna v. New York*, the Court said, "[A] counseled plea of guilty is an admission of factual guilt so reliable that, where voluntary and intelligent, it quite validly removes the issue of factual guilt from the case."[27] Again in the 1985 case of *Hill v. Lockhart*, the Court, quoting language from the U.S. Court of Appeals for the Seventh Circuit, said, "[T]he concern that unfair procedures may have resulted in the conviction

---

24. Brady v. United States, 397 U.S. 742 (1970).

25. *See* Alschuler, *supra* note 13, at 38.

26. Brady v. United States, 397 U.S. 742, 758 (1970); *see also* Dervan, *supra* note 13, at 51 (examining the "*Brady* safety-valve").

27. Menna v. New York, 423 U.S. 61, 62 n.2 (1975).

of an innocent defendant is only rarely raised by a petition to set aside a guilty plea."[28] More recently, the concept of the reliability of pleas of guilty was echoed in a 2017 dissent in the case of *Lee v. United States*, where Justice Thomas wrote, "In any event, the Court in *Hill* recognized that guilty pleas are themselves generally reliable."[29] Unfortunately, as the Task Force Report points out, the Supreme Court was wrong in *Brady* when it assumed that plea bargaining would not have an innocence problem, and Justice Thomas is wrong in believing it now.

A 2015 report from the National Registry of Exonerations sheds light on the significance of the false plea issue and the inherently unreliable nature of confessions in the context of plea bargaining. The report, entitled "Innocents Who Plead Guilty," notes that of the first 1,700 exonerees in the database, 15 percent had pleaded guilty to an offense they had not committed.[30] In recent years, the percentage of exonerations involving individuals who falsely pleaded guilty to something they did not do has increased. By the end of 2022, the National Registry of Exonerations had 3,284 exonerations within its data set. Of that number, 25 percent involved a false plea of guilty.[31] The data regarding false pleas of guilty in cases where no actual crime occurred also paints a troubling picture regarding the role of bargained justice in leading innocent defendants to falsely plead guilty. According to the National Registry of Exonerations, more than 40 percent of exonerations in the data set now involve "no-crime exonerations," which are exonerations where the exoneree was convicted of a crime that never actually occurred. In this category, a staggering 48 percent of the cases involved false pleas of guilty by the innocent.

While we might all like to believe, as the Supreme Court has indicated in past rulings, that innocent people will always fight at trial, the psychological evidence is quite to the contrary. As Dr. Vanessa Edkins describes in her chapter herein on the psychology of plea decision-making, people plead guilty for various reasons, some of which have little or nothing to do with actual guilt. The importance of recognizing this reality of modern plea bargaining led the Plea Bargain Task Force to draft Principle 5, recognizing that in "the current system, innocent people sometimes plead guilty to crimes they did not commit."[32] This is an important statement as we consider the history of plea bargaining's rise, the justifications underlying the Supreme Court's seminal decision to permit bargained justice in 1970, and how we might best proceed forward in a system of pleas. This principle also reminds us that the Supreme Court in *Brady* and in many of its progeny relied on a false assumption regarding the reliability of plea bargaining. The Supreme Court in 1970 forgot the lessons of the *Warickshall* case from almost two hundred years earlier—"[A] confession forced from the mind by the flattery of hope, or by the torture of fear, comes in so questionable a shape . . . that no credit ought to be given to it."[33] In looking to the future, therefore, we should not feel constrained by the

28. Hill v. Lockhart, 474 U.S. 52, 58 (1985).

29. Lee v. United States, 137 S. Ct. 1958, 1973 (2017) (Thomas, J., dissenting).

30. *See* Nat'l Registry of Exonerations, Innocents Who Plead Guilty (Nov. 24, 2015).

31. *See* Nat'l Registry of Exonerations, The National Registry of Exonerations 2022 Annual Report 11 (May 8, 2023).

32. *See* ABA Crim. Just. Section, 2023 Plea Bargain Task Force Report; ABA Resol. 502, ABA House of Delegates (passed Aug. 7, 2023).

33. Rex v. Warickshall, 168 Eng. Rep. 234, 235 (1783).

erroneous precedent of the past. Rather, we should look at plea bargaining with a fresh perspective and utilize the 14 Principles to create a new path forward.

Finally, there was also another important aspect of the Court's *Brady* decision worthy of consideration. By acknowledging the role plea bargaining had come to play in the American criminal justice system and bringing this practice into the light, the Court created an opportunity for the once-shadowy practice to be better examined, regulated, and monitored. The sentiment from *Brady* that plea bargaining should be brought into the light was further expressed by the Court eight years later in the *Bordenkircher v. Hayes* opinion. *Bordenkircher* involved a defendant who was charged with forgery, which carried a two- to ten-year sentence. The prosecution eventually offered the defendant a plea bargain for five years of imprisonment but threatened the defendant by stating that if he proceeded to trial, he would be charged as a habitual offender and sentenced to life in prison. Bordenkircher rejected the deal, was convicted of the more serious offense, and received the promised sentence of life in prison. In a manner similar to *Brady*, the *Bordenkircher* Court permitted the behavior to stand. Regarding the benefits of permitting plea bargaining, even a reprehensible example such as found in this case, the Court stated, "[A] rigid constitutional rule that would prohibit a prosecutor from acting forthrightly in his dealings with the defense could only invite unhealthy subterfuge that would drive the practice of plea bargaining back into the shadows from which it has so recently emerged."[34] Unfortunately, while some may have hoped that decisions such as *Brady* and *Bordenkircher* would create an opportunity for careful examination, regulation, and monitoring of plea bargaining practices and the creation of a more just and transparent criminal justice system, the actual results fell woefully short of any such expectations. As discussed in the Task Force Report, over 50 years after *Brady* we find ourselves in a criminal justice system where plea practices remain largely unchecked, where plea practices vary widely from jurisdiction to jurisdiction, and where impermissibly coercive incentives that overbear the will of the defendant in violation of *Brady* persist. The 14 Principles developed by the Task Force seek to address these concerns and provide a viable path forward to achieve many of these unrealized goals.

The Post-*Brady* World and the Future of Plea Bargaining

After *Brady*, limited attempts were made to regulate and proscribe the appropriate limits of plea bargaining as had been made possible by the Court's recognition of plea bargaining as an available avenue of adjudication. For example, Federal Rule of Criminal Procedure 11, which had existed since 1944 to create a mechanism for pleading guilty, was expanded to include specific provisions related to plea bargaining. The Advisory Committee notes from 1974, just four years after *Brady*, offer a glimpse into those amendments and contain language reminiscent of the Supreme Court's own aspirations.

> The [1974] amendments to rule 11 are designed to achieve two principal objectives:
>
> > (1) Subdivision (c) prescribes the advice which the court must give to insure that the defendant who pleads guilty has made an informed plea.

34. Bordenkircher v. Hayes, 434 U.S. 357, 365 (1978).

> (2) Subdivision (e) provides a plea agreement procedure designed to give recognition to the propriety of plea discussions; to bring the existence of a plea agreement out into the open in court; and to provide methods for court acceptance or rejection of a plea agreement.

The Supreme Court also continued to rule in plea bargaining cases, particularly during the 1970s, though those rulings did little or nothing to lay down appropriate guidelines for the operation of the system, rein in the use of impermissibly coercive incentives, or acknowledge or address the innocence issue discussed earlier. In the *Alford* ruling of 1970, for example, the Court permitted defendants to plead guilty while maintaining their innocence.[35] Rather than creating the system of pleas envisioned by the *Brady* court, the *Alford* decision has gone on to be a vehicle for sweeping miscarriages of justice and serves as a mechanism for creating impermissibly coercive incentives that have likely resulted in countless innocent people going to prison.

In the early 2000s, the Supreme Court began to examine plea bargaining with renewed interest and a more developed understanding of the role of plea bargaining in the American criminal justice system. In 2012, for example, the Court in *Missouri v. Frye* finally acknowledged the important role of plea bargaining.

> Because ours "is for the most part a system of pleas, not a system of trials," it is insufficient simply to point to the guarantee of a fair trial as a backstop that inoculates any errors in the pretrial process. "To a large extent . . . horse trading [between prosecutor and defense counsel] determines who goes to jail and for how long. That is what plea bargaining is. It is not some adjunct to the criminal justice system; it is the criminal justice system."[36]

During this period, the Court also began to create additional procedural protections related to the plea bargaining process. In *Frye*, for example, the Court determined that plea bargaining is a "critical stage" of a criminal prosecution and, therefore, the Sixth Amendment right to effective assistance of counsel applies. In a case from two years earlier, *Padilla v. Kentucky*, the Court ruled that the Sixth Amendment requires criminal defense attorneys to advise their clients when the clients' decision to plead guilty might result in deportation.[37] Finally, in a 2017 decision, the Court ruled that a defendant retained the right to challenge the constitutionality of their statute of conviction even after pleading guilty where they did not expressly waive that right.[38] These cases signal that we are in a period of reassessment regarding our system of pleas. And, hopefully, this reassessment by the courts will be done without the errors of the past and with the insights that modern research, experience, and perspective can offer.

As we reflect on the history of plea bargaining from its early offshoots in various locations in the United States in the 18th and 19th centuries to its rise to dominance beginning in the period of overcriminalization at the turn of the 20th century, we must recognize that throughout much of that history, plea bargaining operated in

---

35. North Carolina v. Alford, 400 U.S. 25 (1970).

36. Missouri v. Frye, 566 U.S. 134, 143–44 (2012) (internal citations omitted); *see also* Lafler v. Cooper, 566 U.S. 156 (2012).

37. Padilla v. Kentucky, 559 U.S. 356 (2010).

38. Class v. United States, 582 U.S. — (2017).

the shadows. Even when the Supreme Court brought bargained justice into the light in 1970, it remained relatively unregulated, unobserved, and unmonitored. That has now begun to change. As discussed by Norman Reimer in his chapter herein on the history of the reform movement around plea bargaining, people and organizations focused on criminal justice reform efforts are now taking note of the system of pleas that results in 95 to 98 percent of convictions in America. And it is into this space that the work of the ABA Plea Bargain Task Force steps.

As courts, legislatures, ethics commissions, bar associations, advocacy organizations, prosecutor and defender offices, and others begin to examine plea bargaining anew and craft their opinions, statutes, rules, and policies, there must be a set of guiding principles to lead us in that work. It is our conviction that the 14 Principles from the task force offer such a path forward and will help lead us to a fairer, more just, and more transparent system of criminal justice. As we look back on the history of plea bargaining, we hope that this will be a turning point at which we begin to regulate the plea bargaining system in a way that is informed by a more fulsome understanding of plea bargaining's history.

CHAPTER 4

The Movement to Curtail Coercive Waivers

Norman L. Reimer

The Rise of the Trial Penalty Reform Movement

The ABA Plea Bargain Task Force Report, which is the focus of this publication, represents a critical turning point in a reform movement that has been slowly but surely gaining steam for a decade. The fact that the largest and most influential bar association in the world has recognized that plea bargaining has evolved to present an existential threat to justice is itself a breakthrough of enormous importance. The elevation of this issue will undoubtedly inject new energy into the reform movement, but it must be seen as both the culmination of efforts that have been a decade or more in the making and a complement to several exciting new initiatives that provide genuine hope that meaningful reform is possible. In this chapter, we consider some of the works that preceded the creation of the Plea Bargain Task Force and explore where the movement to reform our system of pleas might go with the task force's seminal report in hand.

Milestone Reform Events

Individuals have been sounding the alarm about the dangers inherent in a system reliant on plea bargaining since the advent of the earliest bargains in the 1800s. As one court noted in 1877, "[Plea bargaining is] hardly, if at all, distinguishable in principle from a direct sale of justice."[1] While concerns such as those expressed by the courts in the 1800s have existed for centuries now, plea bargaining was, in many respects, ignored as it grew and eventually came to dominate during the 1900s. But this began to change in a significant way in the last decade as a growing realization developed regarding just how pervasive plea bargaining has become and the necessity of closely scrutinizing a

1. Wright v. Rindskopf, 43 Wis. 344, 354 (1877).

system in which almost everyone pleads. The Supreme Court itself wrote in 2012 that "criminal justice today is for the most part a system of pleas, not a system of trials."[2] And academics during this period also began to explore and challenge the plea bargaining system in new and innovative ways, with one researcher writing in 2012, "[T]he constitutionality of modern day plea bargaining is in great doubt."[3] Importantly, the reform community also began to look more closely at plea bargaining during the 2010s and started to lend their considerable resources, expertise, and voices to the issue.

An Offer You Can't Refuse

Perhaps the first major project emanating from the reform community was the 2013 publication by Human Rights Watch (HRW) of *An Offer You Can't Refuse: How U.S. Federal Prosecutors Force Drug Defendants to Plead Guilty.*[4] The report, which was researched and authored by Jamie Fellner, then senior advisor in the U.S. program of HRW, lays bare the problem in gut-wrenching detail. It depicts an array of representative human tragedies; explains how federal prosecutors unabashedly manipulate a panoply of statutes, including many that prescribe mandatory minimums; employ unbridled discretion to coerce guilty pleas from those accused of controlled substance offenses; and viciously punish those who assert fundamental rights. The report provides the basic definition of the trial penalty and succinctly identifies its source:

> The trial penalty is the price prosecutors make defendants pay for exercising their right to trial.
>
> * * *
>
> Prosecutors have discretion, largely unreviewable by judges, as to what charges to bring, what promises or threats to make in plea bargaining, and whether to carry out those threats if the defendant does not plead. . . . When prosecutors choose to pursue charges carrying mandatory penalties and the defendant is convicted, judges must impose the sentences. Prosecutors, in effect, sentence convicted defendants by the charges they bring.[5]

---

2. Lafler v. Cooper, 566 U.S. 156, 169–70 (2012); *see also* Missouri v. Frye, 566 U.S. 134 (2012). During this time there was also exponential growth in the study of plea bargaining in the field of law and psychology. *See, e.g.*, Lucian Dervan & Vanessa Edkins, *The Innocent Defendant's Dilemma: An Innovative Empirical Study of Plea Bargaining's Innocence Problem*, 103 J. CRIM. L. & CRIMINOL. 1 (2013); Tina M. Zottoli et al., *Plea Discounts, Time Pressures, and False-Guilty Pleas in Youth and Adults Who Pleaded Guilty to Felonies in New York City*, 22(3) PSYCH. PUB. POL'Y & L. 250 (2016); Allison D. Redlich, Miko M. Wilford & Shawn Bushway, *Understanding Guilty Pleas through the Lens of Social Science*, 23 PSYCH. PUB. POL'Y & L. 458, 458 (2017); Allison D. Redlich, Stephanos Bibas, Vanessa A. Edkins & Stephanie Madon, *The Psychology of Defendant Plea Decision Making*, 72 AM. PSYCH. 339, 342 (2017); Kelsey S. Henderson & Lora M. Levett, *Investigating Predictors of True and False Guilty Pleas*, 42(5) L. & HUM. BEHAV. 427 (2018).

3. Lucian E. Dervan, *Bargained Justice: Plea Bargaining's Innocence Problem and the* Brady *Safety-Valve*, 2012 UTAH L. REV. 51, 97.

4. Human Rights Watch, *An Offer You Can't Refuse: How US Federal Prosecutors Force Drug Defendants to Plead Guilty* (Dec. 5, 2013), https://www.hrw.org/report/2013/12/05/offer-you-cant-refuse/how-us-federal-prosecutors-force-drug-defendants-plead.

5. *Id.* at 3.

Given the inherent lack of transparency in the plea process, *An Offer You Can't Refuse* pioneered a methodology that, as will be discussed later, provided a template for future projects designed to expose the trial penalty. The report relied upon interviews, case law, legal articles and other literature, and sentencing statistics compiled by the U.S. Sentencing Commission. In so doing, the report was able to document the human dimension of the trial penalty, demonstrating how specific provisions carrying harsh statutory minimums are manipulated to coerce pleas and severely punish those who reject them. Overall, based on data for 2012, sentences were three times longer for those charged with drug offenses who were convicted after trial (16 years) than for those who were convicted by guilty plea (five years and four months).[6]

The HRW report also extensively addressed how U.S. jurisprudence has ratified the use of coercive and retaliatory plea practices and upheld the constitutionality of excessively severe and disproportionately long prison sentences as falling outside the constitutional proscription on cruel and inhuman sentences.[7] And interestingly, particularly in light of the next major report in support of reform, *An Offer You Can't Refuse* also contrasted the U.S. approach to that of other jurisdictions, where threats of enhanced punishment are prohibited by various international standards or national law and where constructive judicial engagement in the plea process is permitted.[8]

Ultimately, the HRW report concluded with a series of recommendations aimed at the executive and legislative branches designed to eliminate the laws that make the trial penalty possible, such as various statutes that provide mandatory minimums that can vastly increase penalties imposed upon drug offenders, and to establish policies that would establish new benchmarks for fair sentencing and prohibit coercive tactics.[9]

The Disappearing Trial

Fair Trials is a global criminal justice watchdog organization with offices in Brussels, London, and Washington, D.C., that campaigns for fairness, equality, and justice in criminal legal systems. It brings a unique international comparative focus to the study of criminal justice. In 2017, after two years of extensive research, Fair Trials published *The Disappearing Trial: Towards a Rights-Based Approach to Trial Waiver Systems*, a research effort that was conducted jointly by Fair Trials staff and a team of pro bono attorneys from the law firm Freshfields, Bruckhaus, Deringer, LLP.[10] This was an audacious effort to document the astonishing rise of trial waiver systems throughout the world. The research conducted in the two years leading up to publication indicated that in 1990 only 19 of 90 countries studied had some form of trial waiver. By 2015, that number had risen exponentially to 66 of 90 countries.[11] Worse, once waivers are introduced, the frequency with which they are employed grows exponentially. For example, in the Republic of Georgia, waivers (known as plea bargaining) accounted for only 12.7 percent of cases in 2005, but by 2012 the percentage grew to 87.8. In Russia,

6. *Id.* at 2.
7. *Id.* at 114–20.
8. *See, e.g.*, *id.* at 88 n.277, 116, 119–20.
9. *Id.* at 13–14, 121.
10. Fair Trials, *The Disappearing Trial: Towards a Rights-Based Approach to Trial Waiver Systems* (2017), https://www.fairtrials.org/articles/publications/the-disappearing-trial/ (last updated Jan. 28, 2022).
11. *Id.* at 4.

trial waivers increased from 37 percent in 2008 to 64 percent in 2014. And in South Africa, where waivers, which are known as "plea and sentence agreements," are not that prevalent, nevertheless there was an increase in 2014–2015 of 33 percent from the prior year.[12] Significantly, however, *The Disappearing Trial* also observed that it is not uniformly the case that trial waivers necessarily consume the system. For example, Italy introduced trial waiver procedures in 1989, and the number of cases resolved through this vehicle has remained constant at 4 percent. And in the state of New South Wales in Australia, the number has remained constant at about 60 percent.[13]

Perhaps the most disturbing finding in *The Disappearing Trial*, particularly from the standpoint of this publication and the work of the ABA in addressing the problem of coercive pleas, is the outsize role that the United States plays in propagating waiver systems around the world. Researchers found that sources throughout the world spoke of the influence of the U.S. example, and the report offered this sobering observation:

> The US model is often seen as the ideological inspiration for adoption of trial waiver systems worldwide. The US has also worked actively to support other countries in developing trial waiver systems to pursue a range of rule of law and human rights objectives. This has been done through the provision of development funding and technical support for rule of law projects, often taking the form of US experts (e.g., prosecutors primarily through the Office of Overseas Prosecutorial Development and Training (OPDAT)) travelling to train foreign judges and lawyers in US models of adversarial practice, including trial waiver systems.[14]

In noting the influential role of the U.S. approach to plea bargaining, the report also notes how, in contrast to most of the world, the United States countenances questionable plea practices in cases involving juveniles and those with psychosocial or intellectual disabilities and in capital cases. It also provides documentary support for the racially disparate impact of plea bargaining in the United States.

Overall, *The Disappearing Trial* contributed immensely to the reform movement by analyzing various approaches to trial waivers, some far less abusive than in the United States, and contextualizes waivers within an international and regional human rights perspective that identifies safeguards that are essential to protect fundamental rights within a waiver construct. These include the following, most of which are lacking in the United States: (1) enhanced protection of procedural rights; (2) regulation of benefits offered in exchange for trial waivers, for example by limiting sentencing discounts; (3) limitations on the types of cases or defendants for which trial waivers may be used; (4) greater judicial oversight over procedural and evidentiary requirements; (5) the development of international and regional frameworks to govern the use of trial waiver systems; (6) a commitment to an audit of human rights protections in trial waiver systems; (7) vastly improved data collection to measure the scope and impact of waiver systems on arrest, pretrial detention, prosecution, conviction, and incarceration rates and correlation of that

---

12. *Id.* at 32.
13. *Id.*
14. *Id.* at 9 (citations omitted).

data to the impact on vulnerable groups; and (8) international knowledge exchange on good and bad practices and the risks and safeguards related to waiver systems.[15]

The Trial Penalty: The Sixth Amendment Right to Trial on the Verge of Extinction and How to Save It[16]

One year after the release of Fair Trials' *The Disappearing Trial*, in 2018, the National Association of Criminal Defense Lawyers (NACDL) published *The Trial Penalty: The Sixth Amendment Right to Trial on the Verge of Extinction and How to Save It*. The report, which was the culmination of four years of research and analysis, was the combined effort of NACDL's professional staff, a task force of volunteers comprised of distinguished criminal defense practitioners from across the United States, and a team of volunteer attorneys from the firm of Skadden Arps Slate Meagher & Flom LLP. Although *The Trial Penalty* roughly followed the approach HRW employed in *An Offer You Can't Refuse*, the NACDL report focused on all federal cases and provided an in-depth analysis of how federal criminal defendants are coerced to plead guilty by extreme sentencing disparities that essentially eliminate the option to take a case to trial.[17]

The NACDL report, which was based on meticulous analysis of federal sentencing data, found that fewer than 3 percent of federal cases proceed to trial and that, for those who do invoke their right to a trial, the sentence imposed after conviction is exponentially enhanced.[18] Essentially, a coercive regime has eliminated trials.

> Guilty pleas have replaced trials for a very simple reason: individuals who choose to exercise their Sixth Amendment right to a trial face exponentially higher sentences if they invoke their right to a trial and lose. Faced with this choice, individuals almost uniformly surrender the right to trial rather than insist on proof beyond a reasonable doubt.[19]

In a whole range of offense categories, the post-trial sentence was on average more than three times longer than the sentences imposed for the same crime following a guilty plea. For example, the average sentence for drug trafficking after trial was 14.5 years as against 5.2 years after a plea. For firearms offenses, the average sentence post-trial was 17.6 years as opposed to 5.8 years after a plea. And some of the most draconian disparities were observed with respect to economic crimes such as embezzlement, fraud, larceny, and tax offenses where sentences post-trial were found to be four, five, or even six times longer than those imposed after a guilty plea.[20] This phenomenon was ascribed to prosecutorial manipulation of sentencing guideline provisions that relate to

---

15. *Id.* at 5, 72–73.

16. Nat'l Ass'n of Crim. Def. Laws., *The Trial Penalty: The Sixth Amendment Right to Trial on the Verge of Extinction and How to Save It* (July 10, 2018), https://www.nacdl.org/Document/TrialPenaltySixthAmendmentRighttoTrialNearExtinct.

17. *Id.* at 6.

18. Specifically, in 2016, 97.3 percent of defendants in the federal system entered guilty pleas. And in 2017, the number held steady at 97.2 percent. *Id.* at 14.

19. *Id.* at 5.

20. *Id.* at 20–21.

loss amount and offense characteristics that imbue prosecutors with unbridled opportunities to enhance penalties.[21]

Perhaps the most enduring contribution of the NACDL report was the articulation of ten principles that address the multifaceted harms inflicted by the trial penalty and broadly outline the reforms necessary to alleviate those harms. Beyond that, the report provides ten specific recommendations to alleviate coercive plea practices in the federal criminal system.[22] It is beyond the scope of this chapter to describe each of these principles and recommendations. But one recommendation does bear mention because it gets to the heart of the problem and has found unusual resonance with lawmakers. *The Trial Penalty* proposes an amendment to the U.S. Sentencing Guidelines that would authorize a court to address sentencing disparity among similarly situated defendants who pleaded guilty and a defendant who was convicted after trial and assess whether the differential between similarly situated defendants would undermine the Sixth Amendment right to trial. In the 117th Congress, Républican Victoria Spartz introduced H.R. 8092, the Right to Counsel Act, which would essentially codify the NACDL recommendation, giving judges the authority to consider the sentences of similarly situated defendants and plea offers that were extended and determine whether the required sentence would constitute a penalty for exercising the right to trial and, in appropriate cases, sentence below the mandatory minimum. Significantly, the proposed legislation received important bipartisan support. Although the legislation did not advance, it is noteworthy that it was cosponsored by eight other Republicans and three Democrats, including now–Minority Leader Hakeem Jeffries.[23]

A Coalition Begins to Form

A great concern when publishing even the best-researched and most insightful report is that it will "just sit on a shelf." That, however, was not the fate of the NACDL trial penalty report. To the contrary, from its inception the report resonated with reformers across the ideological spectrum unlike anything this author has seen in decades of involvement in criminal justice reform. NACDL leadership decided to hold a launch event to coincide with the report's publication with the initial idea of inviting a couple of other groups to provide endorsements for the report. Interest was so great, however, that invitations had to be limited. On July 10, 2018, at a luncheon at the National Press Club, NACDL formally released the report. As a testament to the level of concern with the trial penalty and coercive plea practices, the following major organizations participated in person or through endorsing statements: the American Civil Liberties Union (ACLU), Cato Institute, Families Against Mandatory Minimums (now known as FAMM), Fair Trials, Human Rights Watch, Charles Koch Institute, Innocence Project, Texas Public Policy Foundation, and Right on Crime. Additionally, several leading criminal defense practitioners and academics participated in the event, as did former U.S. District Judge John Gleeson, who authored the foreword to the NACDL report,

21. *Id.* at 32–36.
22. *Id.* at 11–13.
23. Right to Trial Act, H.R. 8092, 117th Cong. (2022), https://www.congress.gov/bill/117th-congress/house-bill/8092/cosponsors?r=75&s=1.

thus underscoring the resonance of the issue among bench and bar. By 2018, a sense of urgency and community was growing around the need to address coercive bargaining and to reform a system that had for too long permitted the trial penalty to flourish.

To give a sense of how this issue unites the most divergent viewpoints in American society and to underscore the building coalition beginning to take shape around this issue, consider the following comments by some of the key participants in the event.[24] Jordan Richardson, Senior Policy Analyst at the Charles Koch Institute, observed, "The diminished power of the jury and the rise of plea bargaining is a danger to liberty." Jeffery Robinson, Deputy Legal Director and Director of the Trone Center for Justice and Equality at the ACLU, noted that the report "tells a not-so-hidden secret about the criminal legal system. Specifically, that innocent people plead guilty because they are faced with a 'trial penalty.'" Kevin Ring, President of FAMM, noted, "The slow disappearance of our constitutional right to trial gets far too little attention. This report should serve as a wake-up call for lawmakers and lay people alike." And Marc Levin, Vice President of Criminal Justice Policy at the Texas Public Policy Foundation and Right on Crime, explained, "From a conservative perspective, for those of us who believe in limited government and individual liberty this is a really important issue. The trial process and juries represent a crucial check on the otherwise unlimited power of government . . . The trial penalty also violates the principle of proportionality and consistency in sentences . . . ."

The breadth of support garnered by the release of this seminal report was by no means aberrational.

The Federal Sentencing Reporter Trial Penalty Double Issue

Not long after the release of the NACDL report, the author of the report along with then–NACDL Vice President Martin Sabelli, who led the NACDL task force that helped craft the principles and recommendations, were invited by the Federal Sentencing Reporter (FSR) to guest edit an issue of the FSR. The FSR is a journal published by the University of California Press with a focus on sentencing law, practice, and theory. Again, interest by potential authors was so keen that the result was the publication of a special double issue of the FSR, *The Tyranny of the Trial Penalty: The Consensus That Coercive Plea Practices Must End.*[25]

The issue featured 16 articles by 24 authors who tackled virtually every aspect of the trial penalty and described in stark terms the impact of coercive plea bargaining. As with the launch event, the authors reflected a broad spectrum of thought from academia, the practicing bar, major national reform groups from the left and right, and even the quintessential victim of the trial penalty—exoneree Chris Ochoa who, as discussed later, pleaded guilty to a rape and murder he did not commit. This publication was the next step in the building of a diverse and effective coalition to bring attention to the trial penalty.

---

24. *See* Norman Reimer, *NACDL's Efforts to Expose and Limit the Trial Penalty Garners Broad Support with the Launch of a National Reform Effort* 9, The Champion (July 2018), https://www.nacdl.org/Article/July2018-InsideNACDLNACDLsEfforttoExpos and https://www.nacdl.org/Document/TrialPenaltySixthAmendmentRighttoTrialNearExtinct (including the full text of remarks by participants at the National Press Club event).

25. 31 Fed. Sentencing Rep., Issues 4–5 (Apr./June 2019).

Collectively, the articles show the various ways in which the trial penalty and coercive plea practices wreak havoc on the U.S. justice system by eviscerating basic rights, overriding all other considerations, vastly exacerbating racial and ethnic disparities, and largely excluding the general citizenry from its constitutionally ordained role as a bulwark against governmental overreach. The FSR issue is both a tour de force of the scope of the problem and a prescriptive text presenting a wide range of solutions. There can be little doubt that the emerging consensus reflected in this extraordinary treatment of the issue presaged the eventual work of the ABA Plea Bargain Task Force.

The Creation of the ABA Plea Bargain Task Force

As discussed more fully in Chapter 1, it was at this point that the ABA Plea Bargain Task Force was created. Recognition by the nation's leading bar association that plea bargaining and its consequences have become so problematic as to warrant a focused study was an extraordinarily important development. By its very nature, the ABA brings together all key actors in the justice system, including prosecutors, defenders, judges, and academics. Since meaningful systemic reform is rarely feasible in the absence of a consensus that there is a problem and broad agreement on the remedies, the creation of the task force provided an essential platform to foment reform. If disinterested academics, impartial judges, and prosecutors can agree with reputable NGOs and the defense community that plea bargaining practices have become abusive and undermine the legitimacy of criminal justice, then reform is inevitable.

The New York State Trial Penalty: The Constitutional Right to Trial under Attack

HRW, Fair Trials, and the NACDL authored their reports from a national and international perspective. Similarly, the ABA Plea Bargain Task Force, which was now busy at work, was exploring the issue with an expansive national lens, though cognizant of the many versions of plea bargaining that existed across jurisdictions throughout the country. It was at this point that other groups began to explore plea bargaining at a more local level. The NACDL's *The Trial Penalty* report noted that "it is well-established that the trial penalty is just as prevalent in state and local criminal prosecutions [as in the federal system]" and pledged to partner with its affiliates and others to tackle the problem throughout the nation's criminal legal system.[26] The first jurisdiction in which that pledge was realized was New York state.

The New York State Trial Penalty: The Constitutional Right to Trial under Attack was released on March 26, 2021.[27] It was a project led by the New York State Association of Criminal Defense Lawyers (NYSACDL) in partnership with NACDL and supported by a team of pro bono lawyers from the Skadden law firm. The report provided a statistical analysis of the prevalence of the trial penalty in New York, personal stories demonstrating how the issue impacts all New Yorkers by effectively removing a critical check on the state's justice system, and recommendations for how policymakers and

26. Nat'l Ass'n of Crim. Def. Laws., *supra* note 16, at 8.

27. N.Y. State Ass'n of Crim. Def. Laws., *The New York State Trial Penalty: The Constitutional Right to Trial under Attack* (2021), https://nysacdl.org/page/NYTrialPenalty21.

prosecutors can reverse the trend and protect New Yorkers' constitutional rights. The report found that 96 percent of felony cases in New York are resolved by guilty plea as well as 99 percent of misdemeanor cases.

Additionally, based on extensive attorney surveys, the report confirmed that to obtain the benefit of a plea offer, accused individuals also routinely waived numerous valuable rights. For example, respondents reported the following waiver rates: 23.66 percent waived time for meaningful investigation; 25.24 percent waived discovery; 35.33 percent waived pretrial suppression motions; and a staggering 68.14 percent waived the right to appeal.[28] Further, with the benefit of data aggregated by two defender offices, researchers were able to establish that in 66 percent of all cases (including misdemeanors where the maximum penalty in New York state is one year in jail), the individual received a more severe sentence after trial, and that number soars to 89 percent where the offered time was at least four years.[29] The New York trial penalty also falls more harshly based upon age and race, with data showing that those less than 25 years old and Black were more likely to receive a trial penalty than those who were older or White.[30]

An especially important finding in the NYSACDL report relates to the role of judges. Unlike in the federal system, New York judges are permitted to be actively involved in plea negotiations. It was found that judges routinely follow the recommendations of prosecutors. But an even more problematic finding is that judges routinely pressure defendants to plead guilty. Indeed, survey results showed that 72 percent of respondents responded affirmatively to the question of whether judges actively encouraging the accused to plead guilty through the use of an enhanced penalty after trial was a factor that contributed to the trial penalty. Just over half—51 percent—reported that this was the most significant factor driving the trial penalty.[31] And 64 percent responded that judicial manipulation of bail/pretrial release determinations to induce guilty pleas contributed to the trial penalty.[32]

As observed by New York attorney Susan J. Walsh, who served as NYSACDL's Trial Penalty Project Chair, "The report makes absolutely clear the trial penalty has metastasized in the system well beyond individual punishment. It is a threat to our constitutional rights and simultaneously allows—even encourages—the abuse of power by prosecutors and judges and too often buries police misconduct which never sees the disinfecting light of a courtroom."[33] The report includes a set of ten principles and 15 specific reform recommendations to address the trial penalty in New York. It confirms the need for state-specific research and remedies. Similar state-level projects are now under way in California and Georgia, with more to follow.

---

28. *Id.* at 19.
29. *Id.* at 59–60.
30. *Id.* at 62.
31. *Id.* at 40.
32. *Id.* at 43.
33. N.Y. State Ass'n of Crim. Def. Laws., *NYSACDL and NACDL Publish Groundbreaking Report on Trial Penalty in New York* (Mar. 26, 2021), https://nysacdl.org/news/news.asp?id=558160&hhSearchTerms=%22new+and+york+and+state+and+trial+and+penalty%22.

The Coalition to End the Trial Penalty

While policy statements and reports from influential national organizations such as the ABA, in conjunction with state-by-state research, are key to creating a defined path forward, there is also a need for a coordinated national reform movement. To that end, Martin Sabelli, who served as NACDL president from 2021 to 2022, devoted NACDL's annual presidential summit to laying the groundwork for such a movement. On December 8 and 9, 2021, in Washington, D.C., NACDL convened *The Constitutional Right to Trial: Organizing a National Movement to End the Trial Penalty*. The program brought together representatives from the groups that supported the launch of the NACDL report in 2018, as well as representatives from dozens of additional groups including community activists, academics, employees of numerous NGOs, prosecutors, judges, practitioners, political operatives, journalists, and media consultants.[34]

The program was designed to establish a platform for the creation of a national coalition to end the trial penalty and address the excessively coercive aspects of plea bargaining. To facilitate this work, the summit featured numerous panels, including one that reflected on other successful national reform campaigns, such as the efforts to limit capital punishment, curtail the abuse of fees and fines, and promote marriage equality. Another panel focused on effective media strategies and the indispensable role of research projects to document the extent and nature of the problem. Additionally, the program included panels that highlighted the racial disparity that emanates from the trial penalty as well as the vital role that judges must play in curtailing the culture of coercion. The final panel in the program, which was moderated by Rebecca Shaeffer, Interim Global Legal Director for Fair Trials and member of the ABA Plea Bargain Task Force, presented an international perspective. Panelists not only described how other nations have limited the most abusive aspects of plea bargaining but also featured a representative of the U.S. Department of State, who explained and defended U.S. efforts to support the implementation of plea bargaining systems, especially in jurisdictions where processing delays result in long periods of incarceration without adjudication of the case. As of the date that this chapter is written, NACDL is on the cusp of publishing a comprehensive report summarizing the various presentations at the summit.[35]

The program had the desired impact. A national coalition, #EndtheTrialPenalty,[36] was launched in the spring of 2023. This extraordinary effort, which will include policy and legislative initiatives and a coordinated communications strategy, already includes a remarkable array of groups whose participation underscores an emerging consensus that coercive plea practices must be curtailed.[37]

---

34. Nat'l Ass'n of Crim. Def. Laws., *The Constitutional Right to Trial: Organizing a National Movement to End the Trial Penalty Agenda* (Aug. 31, 2022), www.nacdl.org/document/111621_TrialPenaltySummitAgenda.

35. Nat'l Ass'n of Crim. Def. Laws., *The Constitutional Right to Trial: Organizing a National Movement to End the Trial Penalty* (Aug. 9, 2023), www.nacdl.org/Document/NationalMovementtoEndtheTrialPenaltyReport.

36. End the Trial Penalty, www.endthetrialpenalty.org (last visited Feb. 13, 2024).

37. As of the date this chapter was drafted, the following groups have joined the coalition: ACLU, Association of Prosecuting Attorneys, The Bail Project, Brennan Center for Justice, Center for Justice Innovation, Northwestern Pritzker School of Law Center for Wrongful Conviction, Drug Policy Alliance, Fair and Just Prosecution, Fair Trials, FAMM, Federal Public and Community Defenders, Innocence Project, Inter-

The Plea Bargaining Institute

Given the obstacles to reform that arise from the jurisprudential landscape, which has essentially provided legal protection for coercive plea practices, and the ingrained culture, which has exalted expedience over justice to sustain a massive overuse of criminal law, there is one additional critical ingredient to nurture a sustainable reform movement in addition to the policy and coalition work described earlier: original research and data to fuel a multifaceted reform strategy. That need is now met as well.

On December 13, 2022, Fair Trials and Professor Lucian Dervan, professor of law and director of Criminal Justice Studies at Belmont University College of Law and convener and cochair of the ABA Plea Bargain Task Force, launched the Plea Bargaining Institute (PBI). The PBI provides a global intellectual home for academics, policymakers, advocacy organizations, and practitioners working in the plea bargaining space to share knowledge and collaborate.[38] With an ambitious goal of seeking to devise multiple strategies to limit coercive plea practices, the PBI will aggregate, digest, disseminate, and solicit original academic research and analysis to provide the intellectual capital to transform practice in the United States and internationally. As noted in the beginning of this chapter, academics have produced a growing body of research related to plea bargaining in the last decade, just as national advocacy organizations began to focus and organize in this space. With the creation of both the Coalition to End the Trial Penalty and the PBI in 2023, the stage is set for significant and meaningful reform guided by the 14 Principles from the ABA Plea Bargain Task Force Report and the recommendations and insights found in the previously described reports from others in the reform community.

The ABA Report, Its Adoption by the ABA House of Delegates, and the Future of Reform

The publication of the ABA Plea Bargain Task Force Report and the adoption of its 14 Principles at the ABA's 2023 Annual Meeting could not have come at a more propitious time for trial penalty reform. That report now has the invaluable imprimatur of the organized bar for a reform movement that has been gaining momentum for more than a decade. Its principles are now official ABA policy. This establishes a consensus reform agenda that reflects the views of prosecutors, judges, defenders, academics, and think tanks. Viewed in the context of the emergence of a broad national coalition to address the trial penalty and the establishment of an institute whose mission is to transform plea practices, the principles enunciated in the ABA report give reason to hope that they will engender broad systemic reform.

---

national Legal Foundation, Howard S. and Deborah Jonas Foundation, Legal Defense Fund, NACDL, Right on Crime, Sentencing Project, Stand Together, and Tzedek Association, as well as the following individuals affiliated with several entities that as a matter of organizational policy do not join coalitions: Lucian Dervan, Marc Levin, Clark Neily, Norman L. Reimer, Robert Rose III, and Somil Trivedi.

38. *See* Fair Trials, *Plea Bargaining Institute Launched to Reform Plea Bargaining Practices in the U.S. and Internationally*, Fair Trials News (Dec. 13, 2022), https://www.fairtrials.org/articles/news/plea-bargaining-institute-launched/.

Coercive plea practices were born of systemic accommodations that were necessary to facilitate overcriminalization and founded on willful indifference to the reality that when the cost of a basic right is years of freedom, or life itself, most rational human beings will not pay the price. The exaltation of efficiency over justice must end. The extraction of waivers of fundamental rights through the threat of legitimized coercion disgraces the American legal system. The trial penalty and the larger problem of coercive plea bargaining did not arise overnight. They were decades in the making. And it may take decades to restore a semblance of balance. But the foundation to end the tyranny of the trial penalty is now in place.

CHAPTER 5

Plea Bargaining in the United States

Current and Future Contributions of Social Science

Vanessa A. Edkins

Reform of the criminal justice system is more likely to be successful if it has a solid foundation in empirical research, and plea bargaining is no exception to this rule. Throughout the task force's work, we considered what social science has learned about the modern plea bargaining system. Some of those findings and research are discussed in the report itself. But, given the report's length, it could not delve deeply into this field and all it has to offer those interested in plea bargaining and efforts to reform the current system. This chapter will explore the social science of plea bargaining in greater detail to bring more light to the issues touched upon in the report. In addition to outlining current contributions, the chapter will end with a discussion of important new directions for research in the field.

Plea Bargaining Research

In the field of psychology and law, much of the last 30 years of research has been directed toward the jury; in criminology and criminal justice, it has been sentencing (mostly at the federal level). For both areas, plea bargains were often seen as inaccessible to the typical researcher. The lack of transparency in the process meant that collecting comprehensive court data on pleas was nearly impossible, and the inaccessibility of the players (especially prosecutors and defendants) made experimental studies prohibitive. Still, it was clear that an honest discussion about any sort of criminal justice system reform could not be had without a discussion of pleas.

With increased access to electronic records,[1] judicial system players,[2] and prosecutors who believe in transparency in the system,[3] social scientists have been able to shed some light on the plea bargaining process. In addition, laboratory approaches have been able to recreate the psychological processes involved in the decisions.[4] The sections that follow will summarize some of the current research on the main players in the process (the prosecutor, the defense attorney, and the defendant) and discuss where the research needs to be headed to fully advise those interested in criminal justice system reform.

The Prosecutor

One of the core components of the current "system of pleas"[5] that is the U.S. criminal justice system is the incredible power (with virtually no oversight) given to prosecutors in the process. Prosecutors not only have the power to decide which charges to pursue but, once the defendant is charged, are also the party that typically gives the first offer in a plea negotiation.[6] The prosecutor's unfettered discretion has raised concerns with legal scholars for decades[7] and is compounded by a lack of transparency in the plea process. Prosecutors could cite the efficiency and cost-saving benefits of being able to have plea discussions informally, without a judge, a court reporter, or even a defendant (who may be held in pretrial detention and not readily available). They may also argue that the plea process allows for the exercise of leniency and for the protection of a defendant concerned about providing information that will aid in prosecuting a codefendant.[8] But of course, the potential for coercion and disparate treatment weighs heavy. Social science contributions to this area suggest that those concerns are warranted.

1. *See* Carlos Berdejó, *Criminalizing Race: Racial Disparities in Plea-Bargaining*, 59 B.C.L. Rev. 1187, 1187–249 (2018); Meghan Sacks & Alissa R. Ackerman, *Pretrial Detention and Guilty Pleas: If They Cannot Afford Bail They Must Be Guilty*, 25 J. Crim. Just. 265, 265–78 (2012); Marisa Omori & Nick Petersen, *Institutionalizing Inequality in the Courts: Decomposing Racial and Ethnic Disparities in Detention, Conviction, and Sentencing*, 58 Criminol. 678, 678–713 (2020).

2. *See* Allison D. Redlich, Shawn D. Bushway & Robert J. Norris, *Plea Decision-Making by Attorneys and Judges*, 12 J. Experimental Criminol. 537, 537–61 (2016).

3. Besiki L. Kutateladze, Victoria Z. Lawson & Nancy R. Andiloro, *Does Evidence Really Matter? An Exploratory Analysis of the Role of Evidence in Plea Bargaining in Felony Drug Cases*, 39 L. & Hum. Behav. 431, 431–42 (2015).

4. *See* Lucian Dervan & Vanessa Edkins, *The Innocent Defendant's Dilemma: An Innovative Empirical Study of Plea Bargaining's Innocence Problem*, 103 J. Crim. L. & Criminol. 1 (2013); Miko M. Wilford et al., *Guilt Status Influences Plea Outcomes beyond the Shadow-of-the-Trial in an Interactive Simulation of Legal Procedures*, 45 L. & Hum. Behav. 271, 271–86 (2021).

5. Missouri v. Frye, 566 U.S. 134, 144 (2012).

6. *See* Robert Wright, Jenny Roberts & Betina Wilkinson, *The Shadow Bargainers*, 42 Cardozo L. Rev. 1295, 1295–371 (2020). Of course, many jurisdictions limit the prosecutor's charging power by requiring grand juries for more serious offenses, but even that process is skewed in the prosecution's favor.

7. *See* Stephanos Bibas, *Plea Bargaining outside the Shadow of Trial*, 117 Harv. L. Rev. 2463, 2463–547 (2004). *See also* Jed S. Rakoff, *Why Prosecutors Rule the Criminal Justice System—and What Can Be Done about It*, 111 Nw. U. L. Rev. 1429, 1429–39 (2017).

8. For a full discussion of the benefits and pitfalls of keeping plea bargains in the shadows, see Jenia I. Turner, *Transparency in Plea Bargaining*, 96 Notre Dame L. Rev. 973, 973–1024 (2021).

One major apprehension with prosecutor discretion is the possibility that the charges brought are not solely the result of what the prosecutor feels they may be able to prove in court, based on the evidence, but are instead being used as leverage to induce a guilty plea. Perhaps the prosecutor is tacking on additional charges (i.e., overcharging), communicating to the defense the possibility of dropping some of the charges in exchange for a guilty plea (charge bargaining). Or maybe the prosecutor is charging the highest count possible while allowing for the possibility of reducing the severity or recommending a sentence at the lower end of what the statute dictates—again, in exchange for a guilty plea (sentence bargaining). Shermer and Johnson utilized a large sample of federal sentencing data and were able to clearly establish a pattern of both charge and sentence bargaining.[9] Not only that, but the use of these tactics was not uniform from case to case; certain groups were less likely to benefit from the sentence and charge reductions (e.g., men compared to women).

A separate study created an online platform to mimic accessing or reading a case file, using over 1,500 defense attorneys, prosecutors, and judges as participants.[10] The legal system players were able to click on various parts of the file prior to making a plea recommendation, and the number of evidentiary factors/case variables accessed and the time spent on each were measured. Prosecutors may state—and may even believe—that strength of evidence is the main impetus behind the favorableness of the plea bargain (i.e., the weaker the evidence, the better the deal), but the actual effect of evidence is quite small. For all the actors, plea discounts differed by about 4 to 6 percent when comparing the presence and the absence of various types of evidence (e.g., confession, eyewitness, and DNA).

This leads to the second concern with the current level of prosecutorial discretion: what else—outside of evidentiary factors—is actually influencing the charge and sentencing bargaining? Kutateladze and colleagues investigated this possibility using a sample of over 1,100 felony drug cases disposed of by the New York County district attorney's office in 2010–2011.[11] Through an agreement with the DA's office, the researchers had access to full case files and prosecutor notes and were able to conduct interviews with prosecutors to get the most accurate picture of case disposition. The data here did show a clear relationship between strength of evidence and punitiveness of plea offers—for example, when drugs, drug paraphernalia, cash, or other incriminating items were found on the defendant, the most common offer was a plea to the charge with no charge reduction. In those cases, sentence reductions were also small, and final sentence recommendations still usually had a custodial component. But the researchers did find that additional extralegal factors were also at play. Specifically, prior record increased punitiveness (possibly because it affected perceived blameworthiness of the defendant), as did the presence of pretrial detention.

For detained defendants, the likelihood of receiving a custodial sentence in the plea offer increased by six times compared to those not detained.[12] Some of this difference may be accounted for by the fact that violent or repeat offenders are more likely to be

9. Lauren O'Neill Shermer & Brian D. Johnson, *Criminal Prosecutions: Examining Prosecutorial Discretion and Charge Reductions in U.S. Federal District Courts*, 27 Just. Q. 394, 394–430 (2010).

10. Redlich, Bushway & Norris, *supra* note 2.

11. Kutateladze, Lawson & Andiloro, *supra* note 3.

12. *Id.*

detained compared to nonviolent or first-time offenders. Still, prosecutors may benefit from the constraints placed on a detained accused person; the sheer pressure from the desire to be released may motivate acceptance of a plea deal.

Social science research provides support for the idea that not only are defendants detained pretrial significantly more likely to end up pleading guilty, but they are also willing to plead to worse offers, and prosecutors are using this knowledge to their own advantage and offering less favorable plea deals to those detained.[13] Leslie and Pope looked at almost one million arraignments for felonies and misdemeanors in New York City between 2009 and 2013 and found a clear link between pretrial detention and increased plea rates. Not only that, but the researchers were able to parse the effect and show that the difference in conviction rates at trial between those detained and not detained, compared to the difference in conviction rates by plea for those detained and not detained, suggests that the reason pretrial detention increases likelihood of pleading is because it is inducing individuals who would have taken their case to trial (if they were free) to instead plead guilty.

The pretrial detention effect contributes to the racial inequality in our justice system, with studies showing anywhere from a 4–8 percent[14] to a 14 percent[15] increase in likelihood of pretrial detention for Black offenders compared to White offenders. And since pretrial detention is directly correlated with likelihood of conviction *and* sentence length,[16] inequalities propagate. Not only that, but research has demonstrated a clear correlation between being Black and having your plea offer include a custodial sentence.[17] And when the crime is a violent one, minorities are less likely than their White counterparts to even receive the benefit of a plea offer.[18]

Empirical research has clearly established that the unconstrained power of prosecutors has the potential for disparate treatment and outcomes, but plea bargains are not one-sided affairs, and the other side of the aisle is not immune from biases.

The Defense Attorney

In recent terms, the Supreme Court has acknowledged that a client's right to effective representation is not simply reserved for trials but also includes representation during the plea process.[19] Such representation is important during plea negotiations because of the many perils and pitfalls that may be encountered. Navigating these elements of plea bargaining is challenging even for counsel, let alone an individual left to fend for themselves. While the presence of counsel offers the possibility of more effective

---

13. *See* Emily Leslie & Nolan G. Pope, *The Unintended Impact of Pretrial Detention on Case Outcomes: Evidence from New York City Arraignments*, 60 J.L. Econ. 529, 529–57 (2017).

14. Omori & Petersen, *supra* note 1.

15. Leslie & Pope, *supra* note 13.

16. See Ram Subramanian et al., *In the Shadows: A Review of the Research on Plea Bargaining*, Vera Inst. Just. (Sept. 2020), for an overview of the research looking at detention and conviction rates.

17. Berdejó, *supra* note 1; Leslie & Pope, *supra* note 13.

18. *See* Ira Sommers, Jonathan Goldstein & Deborah Baskin, *The Intersection of Victims' and Offenders' Sex and Race/Ethnicity on Prosecutorial Decisions for Violent Crimes*, 35 Just. Syst. J. 178, 178–204 (2014).

19. *See* Lafler v. Cooper, 566 U.S. 156 (2012); Missouri v. Frye, 566 U.S. 134 (2012); Padilla v. Kentucky, 559 U.S. 356 (2010).

representation and the accompanying benefits for the defendant, research also indicates that there are potential detriments associated with the presence of counsel. For example, simply not being able to afford a private attorney drastically increases the chances of the defendant's case ending in a guilty plea; it is in a private attorney's best interest to keep the case going, and it is in an overworked public defender's best interest to end the case as quickly as possible.[20] As this example illustrates, the role of defense counsel in plea bargaining is multifaceted and complex. Fortunately, while the prosecutor decision-making process is very much a closed-off system, social science research has fared much better at accessing the defense side—both the defense attorney and the defendant—and we have amassed an important body of work summarizing the influences on these players' decisions.

The defense attorney, of course, is not the individual making the actual decision to accept or reject the plea offer, but as the defendant's advocate, they are the "interpreter" for that offer; defense attorneys will be the ones stating that the offer is good or bad and encouraging the defendant to accept or discouraging the defendant from accepting. Two research questions naturally arise from this fact: What influences that interpretation/recommendation? Does the defendant take the advice? Similar to the discussion of prosecutors, the hope is that evidentiary factors are the main contributor to defense attorney recommendations to accept or reject a plea—and in fact research does support that as a very important influence[21] but certainly not the only influence.

The previous section discussed the correlation between being Black and receiving a plea deal that includes jail time.[22] It would be a mistake to assume this disparity was stemming only from unchecked prosecutorial discretion.[23] In a study utilizing defense attorneys from multiple states as participants, the attorneys made recommendations for mock defendants considering plea deals. When the defendant was depicted as Black, the attorneys were more likely to recommend that the defendant take a plea and to recommend a plea that included a custodial sentence.[24] When attorneys were asked how likely it was that the client was guilty of the offense, and how likely it was that the client would be convicted by a jury, there were no differences by race—this appears to be less about strategy or logic and more about a simple, unconscious association of "Black" with "behind bars." Given the fact that inequalities in the justice system have led to African Americans making up 37 percent of the incarcerated population but only 13 percent of the general population,[25] we can see how this association occurs—and how it is perpetuated.

20. *See* Burton M. Atkins & Emily W. Boyle, *Prisoner Satisfaction with Defense Counsel*, 12 CRIM. L. BULL. 427, 427–50 (1976).

21. *See* Kelsey S. Henderson, *Examining the Effect of Case and Trial Factors on Defense Attorneys' Plea Decision-Making*, 27 PSYCH., CRIME & L. 357, 357–83 (2021).

22. Berdejó, *supra* note 1.

23. For an overview of how multiple players contribute to racial disparities in the "post-arrest, pretrial" period, see Joseph J. Avery & Joel Cooper, *Racial Bias in Post-Arrest and Pretrial Decision Making: The Problem and a Solution*, 29 CORNELL J.L. & PUB. POL'Y 257, 257–94 (2019).

24. *See* Vanessa A. Edkins, *Defense Attorney Plea Recommendations and Client Race: Does Zealous Representation Apply Equally to All?*, 35 L. & HUM. BEHAV. 413, 413–25 (2011).

25. *See* E. Ann Carson, *Prisoners in 2014*, BUREAU JUST. STAT. No. 248955 NJC 33, 33 (Sept. 2015), http://www.bjs.gov/index.cfm?ty=pbdetail&iid=5387.

Most surprising may be what is *not* being considered (or at least not to the extent that we may expect) in the defense attorney recommendations: innocence. Some legal scholars have suggested that actual innocence might have a protective factor, leading individuals to protest their guilt more strongly and reject offers of a plea,[26] but, as you will read in the following section on defendant decision-making, that is simply not the case; innocence is not the protective factor that many hoped it would be.[27] If innocent defendants are willing to plead guilty, can the defense attorney act as the gatekeeper? It appears that even the innocent defendants are trusting their attorney's recommendation. In fact, a laboratory study showed that advice from an advocate to plead guilty was more likely to be heeded by those who were innocent of the alleged misdeed than those who were guilty.[28] A study utilizing interviews with juvenile offenders confirmed the innocent defendants are listening. The researchers showed that pressure tactics exhibited by attorneys are more likely to lead to increased acceptance of guilty pleas for those who are self-proclaimed as factually innocent of the crime compared to those who state that they are actually guilty.[29] In other words, those who are most likely to be heeding the advice from the expert are also those who possibly have the most to lose and are the least deserving of the conviction.

Perhaps this is a concern only if attorneys are actually encouraging innocents to lie to the court and accept the consequences for a crime they did not commit. Such is the "system of pleas," though. Indeed, a defense attorney recommending that an innocent individual plead guilty is a very real possibility. Interviews with attorneys from nine U.S. states (New York, Tennessee, Wisconsin, Wyoming, Vermont, Idaho, Iowa, Arizona, and Rhode Island) showed that roughly 78 percent of those asked indicated that there were definitely cases in the current system where an innocent individual should plead guilty.[30] This included times when the outcome at trial was particularly severe, when it would make for a faster or easier resolution, when a cost-benefit analysis showed the plea as the more favorable outcome (considering chances of conviction and the plea sentence vs. trial sentence), and when the plea offer would help avoid significant future repercussions. Even in cases where the defense attorney felt there was less than a 50 percent chance of conviction, a significant proportion stated they would recommend to an innocent client to plead guilty.

The research, then, suggests biases and extralegal influences on both sides. And in the middle is the defendant, expected to choose a path based on unknowable outcomes and probabilities.

---

26. *See* Avishalom Tor, Oren Gazal-Ayal & Stephen M. Garcia, *Fairness and the Willingness to Accept Plea Bargain Offers*, 7 J. EMPIR. LEGAL STUD. 97, 97–116 (2010).

27. *See* Michael Beenstock, Josh Guetzkow & Shir Kamenetsky-Yadan, *Plea Bargaining and the Miscarriage of Justice*, 37 J. QUANT. CRIMINOL. 35, 35–72 (2019). The authors demonstrate that factually innocent defendants are quite likely accepting pleas.

28. *See* Kelsey S. Henderson & Lora M. Levett, *Investigating Predictors of True and False Guilty Pleas*, 42 L. & HUM. BEHAV. 427, 427–41 (2018).

29. The juveniles self-reported as factually innocent or guilty of the charges that they had pleaded guilty to. *See* Lindsay C. Malloy, Elizabeth P. Shulman & Elizabeth Cauffman, *Interrogations, Confessions, and Guilty Pleas among Serious Adolescent Offenders*, 38 L. & HUM. BEHAV. 181, 181–93 (2014).

30. *See* Rebecca K. Helm et al., *Limitations on the Ability to Negotiate Justice: Attorney Perspectives on Guilt, Innocence, and Legal Advice in the Current Plea System*, 24 PSYCH., CRIME & L. 915, 915–34 (2018).

The Defendant

In a perfect system, entry into a plea bargain will benefit the defendant as much as it does the prosecution—a reduced sentence, reduction in or dismissal of charges, a speedy outcome, and so on. In practice, this benefit assumes that every defendant is guilty of the crime charged. Unfortunately, innocent people do plead guilty,[31] and possibly at a significant rate, as we demonstrated in laboratory research employing a "cheating paradigm."[32] The idea behind the cheating paradigm was born of laboratory research on false confessions[33] and involves having two students (one who is posing as a naïve participant but is actually working with the researchers; that is, a *confederate*) participate in a study, solving individual logic problems. After the students are explicitly told it is against the rules to work together, the researcher leaves the room and, in certain conditions of the study, the confederate proceeds to follow a script asking for assistance. The researcher, who is blind to the study condition, returns and accuses the students of collaborating, since their answers are too similar. Questioned alone, accused of cheating, the student is offered a "deal" to go home that day and lose credits but avoid the academic dishonesty panel (a fictitious body that is depicted as resembling a court trial). Across conditions, more than half (56 percent) of innocent students who were never even approached to cheat signed a statement saying that they had cheated and were accepting a punishment. Repeating this research in the United States, South Korea, and Japan simultaneously found similar rates of pleading guilty by the innocent students and even found them indicating a willingness to testify in front of a review board, implicating their partner in the cheating incident—an incident that *never even occurred.*[34]

The National Registry of Exonerations has catalogued the important details for hundreds of individuals who have been falsely convicted in the U.S. criminal justice system. Of the first 1,700 exonerations documented on the registry, 15 percent had entered a guilty plea. The actual rate of innocents pleading guilty is unknowable, and while the registry focuses mainly on felonies (and frequently those that have DNA evidence), the consensus seems to be that the risk of innocents pleading guilty is likely to be most prominent at the misdemeanor level, where the process is rushed and the pressure to get out of detention is high.[35]

It is hard for defendants to resist the temptation to accept a plea offer—the combination of charge or sentence bargaining from the prosecutor and potential pressure from the defense attorney can make the plea deal seem like the only rational choice, regardless of guilt. As mentioned previously, the status of the defendant also weighs heavy. Laboratory and field data shows a direct link between pretrial detention and the

---

31. *See* Nat'l Registry of Exonerations, *Innocents Who Plead Guilty* (Nov. 24, 2015), https://www.law.umich.edu/special/exoneration/Pages/about.aspx.

32. Additional research suggests that specific populations are most at risk. *See* Dervan & Edkins, *supra* note 4.

33. *See* Melissa B. Russano, Christian A. Meissner, Fadia M. Narchet & Saul M. Kassin, *Investigating True and False Confessions within a Novel Experimental Paradigm*, 16 Psych. Sci. 481, 481–86 (2005).

34. *See* Andrew M. Pardieck, Vanessa A. Edkins & Lucian E. Dervan, *Bargained Justice: The Rise of False Testimony for False Pleas*, 44 Fordham Int'l L.J. 469, 469–528 (2020).

35. *See* John H. Blume & Rebecca K. Helm, *The Unexonerated: Factually Innocent Defendants Who Plead Guilty*, 100 SSRN Elec. J. 157, 157–91 (2012).

likelihood that someone will plead guilty,[36] impacting minorities the hardest because we know that even for lower-level offenses, Black defendants are more likely to face larger bail determinations and longer pretrial detention times.[37]

Still, one of the largest factors is the deal itself. The *plea discount* (or trial penalty) is very real and may be difficult to resist. In a vignette study of both juveniles and adults, for those who said they would plead guilty for a particular scenario, the fear of a conviction at trial and the belief that the offer was a good deal were most often listed as the important factors in their decision.[38]

And the offer, frequently, *is* a good deal. Zottoli and colleagues interviewed adult and juvenile offenders who had pleaded guilty in New York and found that for adult offenders, the sentence offered with the plea deal was on average an 80 percent reduction from the sentence defendants were told they could expect at trial.[39] For juveniles, the discount was closer to 95 percent. An analysis of serious felony cases in Pennsylvania found the sentences for those who were convicted at trial were about 57 percent longer than for equivalent defendants who had chosen to accept a plea.[40] While the amount may differ from jurisdiction to jurisdiction or by level of offense, there is no denying that pleading guilty is a direct route to a more lenient sentence.[41]

The effects of pretrial status and the impact of the plea discount on expected sentence mean that defendants may find it difficult to consider other important factors—like collateral consequences.[42] The collateral consequences attached to a conviction can affect everything from federal student loans to housing aid to licensure for many occupations. Yet, even when those factors are on the table, it is difficult for a defendant to fully integrate them into the decision—they are overshadowed by the plea deal and the possible release from detention.

Future Directions

Even with limited access to the plea bargaining process, social science has managed to amass a great deal of research. Our findings can contribute to policy initiatives and changes in practices at every level of the system. Promising new directions and methods will help fill in remaining holes.

---

36. *See* Vanessa A. Edkins & Lucian E. Dervan, *Freedom Now or a Future Later: Pitting the Lasting Implications of Collateral Consequences against Pretrial Detention in Decisions to Plead Guilty*, 24 Psych., Pub. Pol'y & L. 204, 204–15 (2018); *see also*

37. *See* Nick Petersen & Marisa Omori, *Is the Process the Only Punishment?: Racial–Ethnic Disparities in Lower-Level Courts*, 42 L. & Pol'y 56, 56–77 (2020).

38. *See* Allison D. Redlich & Reveka V. Shteynberg, *To Plead or Not to Plead: A Comparison of Juvenile and Adult True and False Plea Decisions*, 40 L. & Hum. Behav. 611, 611–25 (2016).

39. *See* Tina M. Zottoli et al., *Plea Discounts, Time Pressures, and False-Guilty Pleas in Youth and Adults Who Pleaded Guilty to Felonies in New York City*, 22(3) Psych., Pub. Pol'y & L. 250, 250–59 (2016).

40. *See* Jeffery T. Ulmer & Mindy S. Bradley, *Variation in Trial Penalties among Serious Violent Offenses*, 44 Criminol. 631, 631–69 (2006).

41. For a thorough discussion of the various studies addressing plea discounts, see Subramanian et al., *supra* note 16.

42. Edkins & Dervan, *supra* note 36.

For example, in our laboratory studies, there is a new focus on the role of simulation—using computer technology to create an environment similar to first-person-player video games. Researchers are designing platforms to allow individuals to play the role of various legal system actors and progress through a case from crime to plea negotiations and beyond.[43] The platform has been adapted as semi–open source, allowing labs around the world to use the simulation to test various research questions.

Another very recent addition to the field is the adoption of computational modeling to help capture the process behind a defendant's decision to plead.[44] Fields such as economics and biology have used computational modeling for decades, but it has been slower to catch on in most areas of social science. The dynamic nature of plea bargains and the vast number of variables that could contribute to any one outcome make the area perfect for modeling. Rather than attempting to control for outside influences in the lab or trying to make different jurisdictions align in the field, computational modeling can rapidly simulate outcomes, combining the various complexities and measuring their influence. For example, we could very quickly assess—given the particular parameters of a case—what sort of plea offer would be optimal for enticing those actually guilty to plead while not tempting those who may be innocent.

We should also consider more innovative approaches to the actual practice of plea bargaining. There has been a great deal of focus on progressive prosecutors[45] being elected around the country and the creation of Conviction Integrity Units.[46] Wanting to right wrongs of the past is a valiant cause, but those same offices should be as willing to implement initiatives to prevent future injustices. For example, a trial lottery[47] approach would take a small amount of cases that have pleaded out and send them to a jury trial anyway, with the plea sentence set as the upper limit for the sanction and the possibility of an acquittal at the other end. The idea is to audit jurisdictions to see if the plea deals are actually being applied in a manner that saves resources or if they are simply contributing to the problem of mass incarceration.

Judge Jed Rakoff has suggested another pioneering approach: require that part of prosecutors' time is spent serving as defense counsel for indigent defendants.[48] Perhaps seeing the other side of the case will help prosecutors rein in overcharging or sentence bargaining and better use (or at least not abuse) the discretion they have been afforded. Data would show if plea offers from these jurisdictions significantly differ from similarly situated jurisdictions without this requirement.

All of these research approaches will help inform the plea process. In particular, the focus on furthering social science research in plea bargaining speaks directly to Principle 13, which states that all officers of the court should be collecting data at every step

---

43. Wilford et al., *supra* note 4.

44. *See* Tina M. Zottoli, Rebecca K. Helm, Vanessa A. Edkins & Michael T. Bixter, *Developing a Model of Guilty Plea Decision-Making: Fuzzy-Trace Theory, Gist, and Categorical Boundaries*, 47 L. & Hum. Behav. 403, 403–21 (2023).

45. Angela J. Davis, *The Progressive Prosecutor: An Imperative for Criminal Justice Reform*, 87 Fordham L. Rev. 8, 8–12 (2018).

46. For a discussion of these units, see Barry Scheck, *Conviction Integrity Units Revisited*, 14 Ohio St. J. Crim. L. 705 (2016).

47. *See* Kiel Brennan-Marquez, Darryl K. Brown & Stephen E. Henderson, *The Trial Lottery*, 56 Wake Forest L. Rev. 1 (2021).

48. Rakoff, *supra* note 7.

of the plea process. This data will not only provide the necessary oversight and monitoring of the plea process that is so sorely lacking but also inform the scientists seeking to better our justice system.

Summary

Plea bargaining research has been progressing at a rapid pace. We have a great deal of knowledge about various aspects of the system, with a lot of possible future directions. In addition, the access to public records and large data sets seems to be growing by the day. But one issue that will continue to arise is what is actually recorded. If the plea negotiations themselves stay in the shadows, the majority of the process will also be lost to researchers. For the data to speak loudest, we need things like records of offers, summaries of evidence, records of the back-and-forth between attorneys, and any other formal or informal input to be captured. The old computer science adage of "garbage in, garbage out" comes to mind—our conclusions about the process are only as good as the information we use to reach those conclusions. The hope is that increased scrutiny of the process will help spur a similar increase in understanding plea bargaining's inner workings. Moving plea bargaining out of the shadows will do more for advancing the research than any other reform we could suggest.

CHAPTER 6

Practitioners' Nightmare/ Reformers' Dream

The Tyranny of the Trial Penalty

Norman L. Reimer

Introduction

As the Task Force Report and 14 Principles make clear, the plea bargaining system should be just, fair, and transparent. As a practitioner, however, one sees the many ways in which the plea bargaining system fails to create such an environment. While the report details many examples of the system's failures, this chapter dives more deeply into the experiences of practitioners and explores the current system they work within each and every day. And it highlights one of the most glaring injustices that emerges from the current plea bargaining system: the lack of proportionality.

Without proportionality in sentencing, there is no justice in the administration of the criminal law. To the extent that punishment is warranted, it should be appropriate to the individual, the offense, and the circumstances of the case, including the punishment imposed upon other participants in the offense. Further, the punishment should be no more severe than necessary to meet legitimate sentencing objectives, such as deterrence, rehabilitation, retribution, and public protection. But the stark truth is that today these fundamental precepts are in tatters in the U.S. criminal legal system. Consider six cases, all of which are noteworthy not because they are exceptional, but because they are shockingly routine. These are the stories that prompt the need for reform and the 14 Principles described in the Task Force Report.

Demetric Savoy was arrested at Penn Station in New York and charged with narcotics trafficking. Although no drugs were found on Demetric, Antoine Williams, with whom Demetric was planning to travel, implicated Demetric after Williams's other traveling companion, Ida Avarista, was found to be in possession of roughly two ounces (69 grams) of crack cocaine. Demetric had one prior conviction from five years earlier for possession of a weapon when he was 17 years old. Williams had four previous convictions for drugs, battery, and weapons offenses, admitted to selling cocaine since he was a minor, and faced the prospect of mandatory penalties that would result in decades in prison. He quickly decided to cooperate with the government and testified that Demetric was working with him on the day of their arrest at Penn Station. Williams received a sentence of time served, which was approximately 21 months. Demetric, asserting his innocence, went to trial, rejecting a pretrial offer to plead guilty to a count that would have required him to serve approximately seven years in prison and possibly more under the then-mandatory U.S. Sentencing Guidelines. At the trial, he was acquitted of possession but convicted of conspiracy to possess with intent to distribute. Following his conviction, Demetric faced a ten-year statutory mandatory minimum, and additionally the prosecution asked the court to enhance the sentence based on Williams's testimony that Demetric had been involved in other drug transactions besides the one for which he was arrested and convicted. Demetric Savoy was sentenced to 15 years and eight months. Despite the manifest disparity between the two individuals, there was no legal impediment to subjecting an individual with the demonstrably lesser criminal history to a sentence nine times greater.[1]

Daniela Gozes-Wagner, a single mother of two children, worked as a midlevel manager for a company that improperly received Medicare and Medicaid funds. Her role in the case was less central than two codefendants, one of whom became a cooperating witness and was permitted to plead guilty to a count with a ten-year maximum; the other was permitted to plead to a five-year maximum. Daniela was also initially facing a five-year maximum, but when she opted to proceed to trial, the government added a count that subjected her to a maximum of 30 years. After conviction on both counts at trial, she was sentenced to 20 years. The sentencing judge several times referenced the fact that Daniela had gone to trial and ultimately said that was the "bottom line" for why she faced a far more severe penalty than the others in the case.[2]

Chris Ochoa was convicted of rape and murder in Texas when he was 22 years old. Faced with the threat of capital punishment, under pressure from his ailing mother, who feared that he would be put to death, and with the strong recommendation of his attorneys, Chris pleaded guilty to the offense, even though he was innocent. He served 12 years in prison before he was conclusively exonerated through DNA evidence.[3]

---

1. United States v. Savoy, 98—CR 284 (S.D.N.Y. 1998); United States v. Williams, 98—CR 0055 (S.D.N.Y. 1998). Several years after he was originally sentenced, the district court reduced Demetric Savoy's sentence to 12½ years, reflecting amendments to the U.S. Sentencing Guidelines that modestly reduced the guideline calculation for crack cocaine offenses. United States v. Savoy, 567 F.3d 71 (2d Cir. 2009).

2. On appeal, Daniela Gozes-Wagner challenged her sentence on several grounds, including that the trial penalty imposed upon her was unconstitutional. An amicus brief in support of that argument was submitted by numerous groups, including the ACLU, Cato Institute, NACDL, and Texas Public Policy Foundation. Brief of National Ass'n of Criminal Defense Lawyers et al. as Amici Curiae in Support of Defendant-Appellant and Reversal, United States v. Gozes-Wagner, 977 F.3d 325 (5th Cir. 2020), https://www.nacdl.org/brief/United-States-v-Gozes-Wagner. The Fifth Circuit rejected the claim. United States v. Gozes-Wagner, 977 F.3d 325 (5th Cir. 2020). In December 2020, Daniela Gozes-Wagner's sentence was commuted by the president of the United States.

3. Chris Ochoa & Carlita Salazar, *How the Threat of the Trial Penalty Coerces the Innocent to Plead Guilty: A First-Hand Account of an Exoneree*, 31 FED. SENTENCING REP. 299, 299–302 (Apr./June 2019).

Angelina H. was 22 years old when she was charged with the armed robbery of a gas station attendant. Angelina maintained her innocence. The sole evidence against her was the eyewitness identification by the robbery victim. She was offered one to three years in prison, and during the plea discussions the judge advised counsel that if Angelina was convicted after trial, the judge would impose a sentence of five to 15 years, which would have required Angelina to serve at least five years in state prison before becoming eligible for parole. Counsel was legally and ethically obligated to communicate that threat to Angelina. Despite her insistence that she did not commit the crime, Angelina was terrified of possibly spending at least five years and possibly more of her young life in prison and opted to plead guilty and accept the sentence of one to three years. Prior to sentencing, in the section of the presentence report in which there is usually a victim impact statement, it was noted that the victim was not interviewed because he left the jurisdiction immediately after the incident and could not be located. Under the prevailing law, the prosecutor was under no obligation to disclose to the defense or the court that the sole witness to the crime was unavailable, and the failure to make such a disclosure was not a ground to withdraw the guilty plea.[4]

Robert Rose was a young man when late one night he got into an altercation on the porch of his home with an older man who was in an abusive relationship with his mother. During the fight, Robert shot and killed the man. He had no criminal record and voluntarily surrendered to the police the next day. Despite being charged with homicide, he was permitted to remain free on bail for the three years his case was pending. At trial, he asserted that he acted in self-defense. The jury rejected his defense and convicted him of homicide. He was sentenced to serve 25 years to life in prison. Although the mandatory minimum was only 15 years, the judge opted to impose the maximum possible sentence. After Robert had served nearly 20 years in prison, lawyers working on a clemency petition on Robert's behalf discovered that before trial the district attorney offered Robert an opportunity to plead guilty and serve a minimum of three years. For asserting his right to go to trial, Robert was sentenced to serve at least eight times longer in prison.[5]

Gilbert Lopez was the chief accounting officer of a company that was engaged in fraud. It was undisputed that James Davis, the chief financial officer, played a pivotal role by falsifying public reports and bribing government regulators and the company's external auditor. As conceded by the government, Gilbert was unaware that Davis paid bribes to cover up the scheme. But in his role as chief accounting officer, Gilbert was aware of the false reports before they were made public. Accordingly, he was indicted along with Davis and the owner of the company. Davis immediately pleaded guilty and agreed to testify against Gilbert, who was unable to implicate anyone other than Davis. Because he had nothing to offer, the government made no offer to Gilbert. He

---

4. The author of this article represented Angelina H., whose true name is not disclosed for privacy reasons.

5. N.Y. State Ass'n of Crim. Def. Laws., *The New York State Trial Penalty: The Constitutional Right to Trial Under Attack* 47 (2021), https://nysacdl.org/page/NYTrialPenalty21; Nat'l Ass'n of Crim. Def. Laws., *The Trial Penalty: The Sixth Amendment Right to Trial on the Verge of Extinction and How to Save It* (July 10, 2018), https://www.nacdl.org/Document/TrialPenaltySixthAmendmentRighttoTrialNearExtinct; *see* Nat'l Ass'n of Crim. Def. Laws., *The Vanishing Trial Panel Discussion* 28:55–33:35, YouTube (June 30, 2020), https://www.youtube.com/watch?v=oGxbDZ3-WrI (Robert Rose discussion).

proceeded to trial and was sentenced to 20 years in prison when he was 70 years old—a veritable life sentence. James Davis, who was demonstrably more culpable than Gilbert, was sentenced to five years in prison. On appeal, Gilbert raised the gross disparity, but the Fifth Circuit blithely dismissed the claim, noting that plea bargaining "often does lead to more lenient sentences for more culpable defendants who choose to cooperate," and as to Gilbert's plight, the court observed, "This is simply the way that cases against multiple co-defendants are often prosecuted."[6]

The blatant injustice reflected in these cases, whose origins span the past four decades, is a phenomenon often referred to as the trial penalty or trial tax. The trial penalty—the likelihood and the ubiquitous threat that an exponentially greater punishment will be imposed upon those who assert fundamental rights—is at the core of the most pervasive injustices in the American criminal legal system. The trial penalty is the hammer that is wielded at every phase of a criminal prosecution to extract waivers. It is the inevitable result of the emergence of plea bargaining and the accretion of prosecutorial power with the concomitant diminution of judicial discretion. It is the principal engine that supports an assembly-line approach to criminal justice, which in turn is a key driver of overcriminalization and racial and ethnic disparities. And the trial penalty was the principal motivation for the author of this chapter to gratefully accept the offer to serve on the ABA Plea Bargain Task Force, which has produced the Plea Bargain Task Force Report.

Defining the Trial Penalty and How It Is Deployed

Just what is the trial penalty and how does it operate in practice? In the most basic sense, the trial penalty is the imposition of a more severe sentence if one is convicted after trial than if one accepts a pretrial sentencing offer. It is a cost that is imposed as the price of asserting the constitutional right to a trial. But it is usually not a financial cost. Rather, it is a cost that imposes additional years in captivity. In three of the cases cited previously, the trial penalty is obvious. An offer was made at or before the trial, and if the individual rejected the offer, they faced an exponentially increased penalty after trial, not because of new evidence of criminality but merely for asserting the basic right to have the evidence against them evaluated by a jury. Notions of proportionality are completely disregarded.

Look closely at the case of Robert Rose. Rose, who had a spotless history and a highly plausible defense, was offered a minimum sentence of three years with a maximum of nine years. When considering all the rationales for imposing punishment, including deterrence, rehabilitation, retribution, and public protection, the prosecutor concluded that such a sentence was appropriate. Yet because Robert Rose elected to avail himself of the fundamental right to have a jury of his peers determine whether he acted in self-defense or with some mental state short of an intent to kill, after conviction for homicide he faced a mandatory minimum sentence of 15 years to life. Not satisfied with a minimum sentence that was five times greater than what the prosecutor felt was appropriate, the judge opted to impose a sentence of 25 years to life—a sentence whose minimum was more than eight times greater than the prosecutor's offer and with

6. *The Trial Penalty*, *supra* note 5, at 46; United States v. Lopez, 788 F.3d 403, 425 n.12 (5th Cir. 2015).

a potential maximum that would have kept Robert Rose imprisoned for the rest of his life. This is the quintessential example of the trial penalty. Although the U.S. Constitution and the constitution and laws of every state guarantee the accused the right to a trial by jury, establish a presumption of innocence, and require the government to prove guilt beyond a reasonable doubt, the assertion of those basic rights comes at enormous cost: the risk of losing years of a person's life.

But the actual imposition of far greater sentences after a trial is just part of the tyranny of a system that penalizes the assertion of rights. The mere existence of the looming threat of the trial penalty prompts rational individuals who are actually or arguably innocent to plead guilty.[7] This is evident in the cases of Chris Ochoa and Angelina H. Chris Ochoa, who was irrefutably innocent, chose to plead guilty and face life in prison rather than risk death. Indeed, it is estimated that roughly 15 percent of all exonerations involve individuals who pleaded guilty to a crime they did not commit, and for exonerations involving drug crimes, the percentage rises to a staggering two-thirds.[8] And, of course, cases of actual exoneration are only the tip of the iceberg. Over the years, countless thousands of individuals for whom exonerating evidence cannot be uncovered have done the same thing. After all, if they have family members who depend upon them, and there is a chance that asserting their rights will result in a far longer separation, is it not entirely rational to choose to limit the risk? That is precisely the calculation that motivated Angelina H. She may very well have been innocent. And had she asserted her right to a trial, the absence of the sole witness would have resulted in the charges being dismissed. But, facing a system that is designed to impose unreasonable pressure, she chose to spend one year in prison rather than risk at least five years and possibly as many as 15.

From a systemic perspective, however, there is an aspect to the threat of an increased penalty that is more harmful than the imposition of significantly more severe sentences upon those few who assert their right to a trial. Throughout the United States it is routine practice to employ coercive plea practices at every stage of a criminal proceeding. Often, beginning at the first appearance, sometimes even in venues where counsel has not yet been provided to an accused person, the individual is encouraged to waive basic rights and plead guilty to some criminal offense. They are told that if they do not do so, they will have to return to court—possibly many times over a long period of time—without regard to the consequences for their jobs or family responsibilities. Or worse, if they do not immediately plead guilty, they may be subject to the imposition of monetary bail that they cannot post. This, too, is a manifestation of a trial penalty. If an accused individual wants to avail themselves of fundamental rights, including the right

---

7. Lucian E. Dervan, *Bargained Justice: Plea Bargaining's Innocence Problem and the* Brady *Safety-Valve*, 2012 Utah L. Rev. 51, 95 ("At some point, the sentencing differential becomes so large that it destroys the defendant's ability to act freely and decide in a rational manner whether to accept or reject the government's offer.").

8. Nat'l Registry of Exonerations, *Innocents Who Plead Guilty* 1 (Nov. 24, 2015), https://www.law.umich.edu/special/exoneration/Documents/NRE.Guilty.Plea.Article1.pdf; Branden A. Bell, *Not for Human Consumption*, 31 Fed. Sentencing Rep. 226 (Apr./June 2019). *See also* Glinda S. Cooper, Vanessa Meterko & Prahelika Gadtaula, *Innocents Who Plead Guilty: An Analysis of Patterns in DNA Exoneration Cases*, 31 Fed. Sentencing Rep. 234–38 (Apr./June 2019); Lucian Dervan, *Bargained Justice: The History and Psychology of Plea Bargaining and the Trial Penalty*, 31 Fed. Sentencing Rep. 239–47 (Apr./June 2019).

to counsel and the attendant rights to obtain discovery and conduct an appropriate investigation, it comes at the cost of facing an increased penalty. The increased penalty may be that a harsher penalty will be offered later in the case, or it may simply be that they have to languish in jail for weeks, months, or years until counsel can be provided and take the essential steps to effective representation and the proper litigation of the case.

Indeed, another common prosecutorial tactic is the practice of increasing the length of the offer as the case progresses. Thus, for example, an accused will often be told that a particular offer will remain available only if there is a waiver of a right to challenge unlawfully obtained evidence, a questionable identification procedure, a purported inculpatory statement, or other law enforcement misconduct. This not only forces the accused to choose among fundamental constitutional rights, but it also creates a system in which law enforcement conduct is routinely insulated from judicial review. Indeed, often, even after a suppression hearing is conducted, prosecutors will condition a plea offer on an agreement to waive the right to challenge the court's ruling on appeal. In fact, in most jurisdictions in the country, a plea offer will routinely include a requirement that the accused waive the right to an appeal as a condition of the plea offer.

And, of course, there is the well-documented practice of increasing charges on the eve of trial for those who do not capitulate and enter a guilty plea. The case of Daniela Gozes-Wagner perfectly illustrates this phenomenon. Never mind the fact that she was demonstrably less culpable than other participants in the criminal scheme. The enhancement of the charges against her, which resulted in her receiving a sentence two to four times greater than more blameworthy codefendants, is perfectly acceptable under the trial penalty regime.

Viewed globally, the American criminal legal system, which the Supreme Court observed has largely become a plea bargaining system,[9] has placed such a premium on the disposition of cases that coerced waivers are simply standard operating procedure.

Causes of the Trial Penalty: The Levers of Coercion

There are so many factors that have contributed to the rise of the trial penalty and the general prevalence of coercive plea practices that it is a challenge to catalogue all of them. Indeed, they emanate from myriad sources, with virtually every component of the criminal legal system, including all branches of government, contributing to the problem. The following is a summary of significant contributing factors.

Mandatory Minimum Sentences

Without question, statutorily mandated minimum sentences are a major component of the trial penalty architecture. For decades, politicians of all stripes sought to outdo one another in playing the "tough on crime" card by enacting a panoply of mandatory minimum sentences, which created the illusion of addressing criminal behavior at no financial cost. Of course, while there may be no immediate cost to enact laws that establish a minimum term of imprisonment for specific crimes, eventually the bill comes due when a government must pay for the prisons, staff, vendors, and products necessary to support an outsize incarceration infrastructure. Beyond that, there are the enormous, intangible

9. *See* Lafler v. Cooper, 566 U.S. 156, 170 (2012); Missouri v. Frye, 566 U.S. 134 (2012).

societal costs imposed on families and communities when parents, spouses, and children are long deprived of the emotional and financial support of a loved one. Mandatory minimum sentences are the means by which the executive and legislative branches strip the judicial branch of sentencing discretion, inevitably placing the greatest power in the hands of prosecutors, who enjoy unbridled discretion over the charging function.

Mandatory minimum sentences also give the participants a moral escape valve from accepting responsibility for manifest injustice. So, as in the case of Robert Rose, a prosecutor who offers a sentence of three years on a plea to manslaughter can stand back after the conviction on the murder count, which triggers a mandatory minimum of 15 years, and disavow any responsibility for the unconscionable disparity. Judges, of course, can resort to adopting the same mantra with the accurate but rather casual comment "My hands are tied."

Sentencing Guidelines

To the extent that guideline sentencing regimes are compulsory, they are no different than mandatory minimum sentences. For example, in the era before the Supreme Court held that judges have authority to vary from the U.S. Sentencing Guidelines, federal judges had no discretion to fashion a sentence that reflected the true culpability of the accused. Even when guidelines are not compulsory, though, there is a tendency for judges to hew to the guidelines rather than write on a blank slate in fashioning a just sentence.[10] Because guidelines authorize courts to consider not just the actual crime of conviction but other relevant conduct, prosecutors routinely engage in "fact bargaining," whereby they may threaten to bring forth or withhold facts that may impact the sentence as a tool to extract a guilty plea. And for those who exercise their rights, the threat is all too real. This is precisely what was done in the case of Demetric Savoy. As a penalty for going to trial, the government obtained enhancements that vastly increased the sentence, which the court felt obligated to impose. The judge expressed sympathy for Demetric's plight but brusquely dismissed the entreaties of counsel by stating that his oath required him to impose the additional time.[11]

Prosecutorial Manipulation of Charges and Guidelines

The unbridled authority of prosecutors to determine what charges to bring and to select the facts that can influence guideline calculation provides extraordinarily coercive leverage. The well-documented example of prosecutors threatening to enhance charges on the eve of trial if an accused person refuses to plead guilty is just one example. Often prosecutors will also threaten to bring charges against family members or other loved ones, and they routinely bring more severe charges than may be warranted to invoke higher mandatory minimums or elevated guideline calculations.

---

10. *The Trial Penalty*, *supra* note 5, at 54–58.

11. The official court transcript reflects the following statement by the judge: "You are unfortunately preaching to the choir, Mr. Reimer. I just don't think the oath I took to work here lets me do anything other than that." Brief for Defendant-Appellant at 19, United States v. Savoy, 567 F.3d 71 (2d Cir. 2009) (on file with attorney Norman L. Reimer).

Unilateral Prosecutorial Control over the Power to Avoid the Application of Mandatory Minimum Sentences

Another weapon in the prosecutorial arsenal, which is especially prevalent in the federal system, is the unilateral power to exempt cooperating defendants from mandatory minimum sentences and to charge bargain to limit the amount of prison time the cooperator will face. The multifaceted injustice that flows from this power was plainly evident in the cases of Gilbert Lopez, Demetric Savoy, and Daniela Gozes-Wagner. That a cooperator who is far more culpable than the person against whom they cooperate gets a substantially lighter sentence is only one aspect of the injustice. What is even worse is that the less culpable person often has nothing to offer the government to obtain the benefit of a cooperation agreement. Essentially, the system perversely incentivizes the most blameworthy offenders to rush to be the first to cooperate so that they can avoid the most severe penalties and the less blameworthy bear the consequences.[12] Or, as the court so cavalierly put it in the case of Gilbert Lopez, that's "simply the way that cases against multiple co-defendants are often prosecuted."[13]

The Culture of Efficiency over Justice

The inherent compulsion to resolve cases expeditiously, especially in high-volume felony and misdemeanor courts, creates a culture in which coercive waiver is the norm. From the very beginning of the case, it is routine to use the imposition of bail as a bludgeon to induce accused persons to waive basic rights. Sadly, this is not just done by prosecutors who have enormous caseloads; it is also part of judicial culture. There are some jurisdictions where judicial performance is assessed based on "disposition rates," where resolution of cases is seen as the ultimate objective. And this is not just done at the beginning of the case; it is manifest throughout the pendency of the case, where often the plea offer will go up at each phase at which an accused asserts basic rights.

It must be noted that in many jurisdictions, defense entities also succumb to this culture of efficiency. Inadequate resourcing of the defense function necessarily forces defender entities to prioritize certain cases at the expense of others. Fixed-rate contracts, which obligate an individual defender or a defender organization to handle a fixed number or percentage of cases, necessarily incentivize defenders to dispose of cases as expeditiously as possible. Hence, the defense can very well be complicit in the coercive milieu in which waivers are essential to prevent a collapse of overburdened systems.

The simple fact is that the culture of efficiency over justice is an inevitable consequence of a society addicted to overcriminalization. Over the past several decades, the United States has increasingly turned to the use of criminal penalties to address all manner of disfavored personal, social, and economic behavior. Rather than invest the resources to address underlying pathologies such as mental health issues, addiction, pervasive poverty, and other challenges, politicians of all stripes reflexively resorted to the seemingly quick fix of expanding penal sanctions. This is what has given rise to mass incarceration, which in turn undermines family and community stability, thereby perpetuating a cycle of criminality. The only way that the system could adjust to accommodate

12. *The Trial Penalty*, *supra* note 5, at 42–47 and citations therein.
13. United States v. Lopez, 788 F.3d 403, 425 n.12 (5th Cir. 2015).

the influx of criminal cases was to adopt an assembly-line approach that exalts case processing as the ultimate attribute of the justice system. The conviction conveyor belt depends upon coercive plea practices and a cultural acquiescence to the routine waiver of basic rights.

Judicial Disengagement or Judicial Complicity

Judges play a vital role in perpetuating the culture of waiver. Ironically, in some cases it is because of their direct involvement in a coercive plea process, and in others it is their utter lack of involvement that facilitates the process.

In some systems, such as generally speaking the federal criminal system, judges are wholly disengaged from the plea process.[14] Discussions about possible disposition of the case occur solely between the prosecution and defense. What judges see in the vast majority of cases that result in a guilty plea is the defendant admitting to a particular crime on the record accompanied by a required statement that the guilty plea is being entered freely and voluntarily and under no threat whatsoever. Often, this statement is a sham. The fact that the accused may have been told that they will face a vastly more severe sentence if they proceed to trial is not considered a relevant factor. Competent defense counsel must advise the client that should they reference the coercive threat of an enhanced sentence if convicted after trial or after refusing to waive other valuable rights, the guilty plea will not be accepted by the court. Similarly, should the client reference any other leverage that may have been employed by the prosecutor, such as threats to add additional charges or charge other persons who may be near and dear, as a factor inducing them to plead guilty, the plea will not be accepted. And in those jurisdictions where judges are not involved in the plea bargaining process, they have no compunction about how the disparities unfold. Thus, in the case of Gozes-Wagner a vast sentencing disparity was the "bottom line" consequence of the accused taking the case to trial. In Gilbert Lopez's case, the disparity is blithely accepted as simply the way that cases are prosecuted in multiple defendant cases. Simply put, there is a pervasive understanding shared by the judiciary that a significantly increased sentence is the price of asserting fundamental rights.

Conversely, in many state systems, judges are fully engaged and complicit in the imposition of a trial penalty. In jurisdictions where judges participate in plea negotiations, they are just as inclined as prosecutors to threaten to enhance or actually enhance penalties if the individual is convicted after trial. Thus, in the examples cited previously, the judge sentenced Robert Rose to 25 years to life, despite the prosecutor's preconviction offer of three to nine years, and notwithstanding that 15 to life was the mandatory minimum. And in the case of Angelina H., the judge affirmatively put his thumb on the scale by threatening a far more severe sentence if she were convicted.

---

14. Federal Rule of Criminal Procedure 11(c) provides in pertinent part:

(c) Plea Agreement Procedure.

(1) *In General.* An attorney for the government and the defendant's attorney, or the defendant when proceeding pro se, may discuss and reach a plea agreement. The court must not participate in these discussions.

Jurisprudential Disengagement

Although historically the U.S. Supreme Court viewed plea bargaining as essentially unconstitutional, that view was jettisoned as criminalization burgeoned.[15] In 1970, the Court held that it is not unconstitutional for prosecutors to induce guilty pleas with the threat of seeking a higher sentence after trial.[16] Within a few years, the Court even went so far as to uphold a life sentence that a prosecutor obtained by making good on a threat to reindict a defendant charged with passing a single forged check in the amount of $88.30 under a Habitual Criminal Act for refusing to plead guilty and accept a sentence of two to ten years in prison.[17] The Court essentially removed any legal limitation on the use of prosecutorial leverage when it stated that "[i]ndeed, acceptance of the basic legitimacy of plea bargaining necessarily implies rejection of any notion that a guilty plea is involuntary in a constitutional sense simply because it is the end result of the bargaining process. By hypothesis, the plea may have been induced by promises of a recommendation of a lenient sentence or a reduction of charges, and thus by fear of the possibility of a greater penalty upon conviction after a trial."[18]

Within a few decades, the Court recognized that plea bargaining had become so ingrained in the system that it issued a series of opinions in which it held that the constitutional right to effective assistance of counsel imposes specific duties upon defense counsel to ensure that clients are adequately advised with respect to the consequences of accepting or rejecting a plea offer.[19] In rejecting the notion that a fair trial cures any deficiency in representation during the plea process, the Court acknowledged the veritable end of trials: "That position ignores the reality that criminal justice today is for the most part a system of pleas, not a system of trials. Ninety-seven percent of federal convictions and ninety-four percent of state convictions are the result of guilty pleas."[20]

Unless and until the Court recognizes that plea bargaining has become so inherently coercive that it is more akin to extortion than bargaining—so much so that rational people routinely plead guilty to avoid a trial penalty—there is no legal limit on how much pressure may be brought to bear to extract a waiver of rights.

Plea Bargaining Is a Constitution-Free Zone That Unfolds with Virtually No Transparency

Although the accused in the United States enjoy the right to a public trial, currently neither constitutions nor statutes require that plea offers or threats to seek sentencing enhancements be placed on the record and available for public review. This is hardly surprising given the jurisprudence described in the preceding section. Indeed, in jurisdictions where judges either are prohibited from participating or choose not to participate

15. *See* Dervan, *supra* note 7; see also Chapter 3 regarding the history of plea bargaining's rise.

16. Brady v. United States, 397 U.S. 742, 751 (1970). *See also* Parker v. North Carolina, 397 U.S. 790, 795 (1970).

17. Bordenkircher v. Hayes, 434 U.S. 357 (1978).

18. *Id.* at 363.

19. Padilla v. Kentucky, 559 U.S. 356 (2010); Missouri v. Frye, 566 U.S. 134 (2012); Lafler v. Cooper, 566 U.S. 156, 170.

20. *Lafler*, 566 U.S. at 169–70.

in plea discussions, such discussions are kept from them as well. And those discussions are certainly never disclosed to juries, who in most jurisdictions are told that their only function is to decide guilt or innocence and that they have no role to play in sentencing. In fact, in many cases juries are unwittingly complicit in the trial penalty regime, such as where prosecutors add charges for the sole purpose of seeking convictions on counts that will increase the penalty beyond the pretrial offer. In jurisdictions with harsh mandatory minimum sentences, jurors are often shocked to learn the severity of the sentence that must be imposed after they have returned a verdict of guilt. And in cases where after verdict jurors have been advised of the differential between a plea offer that was rejected and the required sentence after conviction, they are often dismayed and sometimes quite angered to learn the true consequences of their verdict.

Without meaningful constitutional guardrails, with little or no transparency, and with prosecutorial domination of a process with limited opportunity for judicial discretion, it is no wonder that plea bargaining has become inherently coercive. Indeed, it is really a misnomer to call it "bargaining." Rather, it should be termed "plea begging." Nothing about the process reflects the kind of arm's-length negotiation that one sees in other areas of the law. The prosecutor holds all the levers of coercion that produce the trial penalty, and the defense lawyer's only tool is the power to seek mercy from the prosecuting authority.

The True Costs of the Trial Penalty and Coercive Plea Practices

The most obvious impact of the trial penalty is the imposition of a sentence that far exceeds that which is necessary to meet the legitimate objectives of sentencing. Cases in which an individual rejects an offer and suffers an exponentially greater penalty simply for asserting fundamental constitutional rights are a human catastrophe and a stain on the justice system.

But in practice, since all available data indicates that at least 97 percent of all cases are resolved through guilty pleas, the bulk of which occur in the context of an inherently coercive process, the systemic costs are more pervasive and corrosive than the injustice that is visited upon those who gamble on asserting their rights and lose.[21] The induced waiver of all manner of rights not only prevents individuals who may be innocent from avoiding the life-altering consequences of a criminal conviction, but it also insulates all manner of law enforcement conduct from public exposure and judicial oversight.

When an accused person is induced to plead guilty early in a case to avoid being held in custody or to minimize the burden of repeated court appearances, they do so without the benefit of full discovery and a comprehensive investigation, which contributes to wrongful conviction. When the accused gives up the right to challenge unlawfully obtained evidence, questionable police practices go undetected and uncorrected.

---

21. It is important to note that of the small percentage of cases that do proceed to trial, a significant portion of those cases involve facts that are so awful that prosecutors make no plea offer, and therefore the accused really has no alternative but to have a trial.

These practices perpetuate systemic deficiencies that undermine public confidence and foster racial and ethnic disparities.[22]

Further, the unrestrained ability of prosecutors to extract guilty pleas incentivizes government overreach by bringing cases based on dubious evidence and unreliable witnesses, secure in the knowledge that most often the evidence will never be subjected to a public trial at which the evidence and witnesses will be subject to the crucible of cross-examination and independent assessment. Indeed, many prosecutors candidly acknowledge that the weaker the case, the more they will employ the plea process to avoid a trial.

A factor closely related to the prospect of government overreach is the exclusion of the citizenry from the criminal process. The Framers intended cases to be decided by juries, but the current system essentially ousts the public from engagement in any oversight over the criminal legal system, thereby eliminating a core check on government excess. Similarly, through the routine practice of extracting waivers of appeal as a condition of a guilty plea, the judicial oversight role is severely constricted. Thus, even if some aspects of a case are litigated at the trial level, the eventual extraction of a guilty plea will shield trial court rulings from appellate review.

Finally, and perhaps most troubling, the trial penalty and coercive plea practices have been conclusively shown to induce innocent people to plead guilty. As noted earlier, Chris Ochoa and Angelina H. are by no means aberrational cases.[23] While Chris Ochoa was eventually exonerated, rare are the cases in which there is a clear evidentiary basis to eventually exonerate an innocent accused. It is impossible to speculate how many individuals falsely plead guilty to avoid the tyranny of the trial penalty.

The Defense Practitioners' Perspective

From the standpoint of an accused person, the trial penalty and the looming threat of an ever-increasing penalty for the assertion of basic rights must always be the paramount concern. Thus, in reflecting upon how these practices impact the defense lawyer, the reader should not lose sight of the fact that the ultimate burden falls upon the person who is facing the peril of a prosecution and whose entire future, and often the future of their family, is on the line.

With that as context, consider the plight of the defense lawyer who represents a client who asserts their innocence. The lawyer is absolutely obligated not only to convey a plea offer to a client but also to explain the potential sentence if the plea offer is rejected. The relationship between any lawyer and client is sacred and confidential. The client places their trust in the attorney's skill, experience, and judgment to guide them through a legal thicket. In the criminal context, however, where the stakes are neither property rights nor money but rather a person's freedom—or life—this relationship is unlike any other. In this context, the client necessarily looks to the lawyer to make the most consequential decisions they may ever face in their life. And the conscientious lawyer must provide advice in a situation in which a misestimation of the likely outcome

---

22. Rick Jones & Cornelius Cornelssen, *Coerced Consent: Plea Bargaining, the Trial Penalty, and American Racism*, 31 FED. SENTENCING REP. 265, 265 (Apr./June 2019).

23. *See* Dervan, *supra* note 7; Nat'l Registry of Exonerations, *supra* note 8.

of the process can cost a client many additional years in prison. And depending upon the circumstances, the lawyer may have to provide that advice at a point at which the full scope and nature of the evidence against the client cannot be accurately assessed.

Barry Pollack, a noted defense practitioner and a former president of the National Association of Criminal Defense Lawyers, explained the conundrum this way:

> The United States Constitution sets the gold standard for criminal justice. No one should be convicted unless the evidence is fully tested in a public trial. Yet we have layered on every reason not to use that gold standard. The trial penalty presents a basic math problem. I have to tell my client: I have looked at the evidence the government has presented to me thus far. You have a great defense. I think if you go to trial, there's a 75 percent chance we will win. If you plead guilty, you will get no more than one year in jail. But if you exercise your constitutional right to go to trial and we lose, you will get ten years. Do you want to take a 25 percent risk that you will go to prison for ten years? And we know that 97 percent of the time the answer is "no." And so the evidence is never tested.[24]

To be sure, where the evidence against a client is clearly strong and the likelihood of conviction is great, the lawyer's duty to try to persuade the client to accept a lesser offer is clear. But where the client asserts innocence and the evidence is weak, unknown, or at best ambiguous, what is the duty of the lawyer when confronted with the prospect of a significant trial penalty? How can a lawyer in good conscience advise a client to assert their defense when the risk is an exponentially greater term of imprisonment? There is clearly something rotten in a system in which the assertion of fundamental rights is so heavily taxed that in practice the rights are nothing more than an illusion. Clearly, it is past time to reform coercive plea practices and end, or at least significantly limit, the trial penalty in the U.S. criminal legal system.

The 14 Principles recommended in the Task Force Report, which have now been adopted as formal ABA policy,[25] start us on that path. These principles acknowledge the important role that litigation plays in promoting the legitimacy and accountability of the criminal process. More importantly, the principles now place the ABA firmly on record as recognizing the coercive aspects of current plea bargaining practices, which includes coercive incentives that overbear the will of the accused and induce the innocent to plead guilty. At the same time, they embody a wide array of prescriptive measures to promote transparency, oversight, and accountability and process reforms designed to rein in prosecutorial overreach and ensure that the defense has the necessary resources, materials, and opportunity to assess a plea offer. In sum, the 14 Principles provide a groundbreaking road map to a future in which the kinds of injustices highlighted in this chapter can be avoided.

---

24. Barry Pollack, Remarks Delivered at NACDL Trial Penalty Report Launch Event (July 10, 2018), 13:00–16:15, https://www.nacdl.org/Document/TrialPenaltySixthAmendmentRighttoTrialNearExtinct.

25. The ABA House of Delegates adopted the 14 Principles in the Task Force Report as formal policy at its Annual Meeting on August 7, 2023.

CHAPTER 7

A View from the Innocence Bar

Adnan Sultan

I began my career as a public defender practicing in a busy urban jurisdiction where plea bargaining played an almost central role in my representation of my clients. My time on the ABA Plea Bargain Task Force required me to take a critical look at the role of plea bargaining as it currently exists in the criminal legal system.

As a public defender, one of the first things I did with a case was approach the prosecutor and initiate plea discussions, making the best case for why the prosecution should reduce my client's charges and offer a more lenient punishment. In the jurisdiction in which I practiced, judges often participated in the plea bargaining process, questioning me about why my client would not accept the prosecution's plea offer or haranguing the prosecution about why they would not make a plea offer, or why their plea offer was not better.

Within this system, many of my clients took pleas—often at my urging. My client consultation was a risk assessment: it was safer to take a plea to a lesser charge and less severe punishment than go to trial, where if we lost, punishments would get far harsher. In less serious cases, my consultation focused on the impact the case had on my client's life. Often, the client could move on with their life if they took the plea that day. Otherwise, they could spend the next year fighting the case, having to miss work every day they came to court. I advised my clients to take pleas only because I believed it was in their best interest, but my advice had little to do with whether my client actually committed the crime.

Now as an attorney at the Innocence Project working on post-conviction cases where we try to prove our clients' innocence, I see the downstream problems pleas can pose to innocent people accused of crimes. Our system values process and finality over getting the correct result. As a result, our post-conviction system imposes limitations on a convicted person's ability to appeal their convictions. Some states flatly prohibit people who pleaded guilty from conducting post-conviction DNA testing on evidence. There are states that prevent people who pleaded guilty from seeking to vacate their convictions, despite the existence of evidence that proves their innocence or undermines the State's case against them.

The deliberations of the task force required me to think about pleas from a system-wide perspective rather than on an individual client basis. I concluded that our system of plea bargaining perpetuates the problems with the criminal legal system, including innocent people accused of crimes pleading guilty to crimes they did not commit.

In this chapter, I examine, based on my experience, how forces within the criminal legal system push innocent clients to plead guilty to crimes they did not commit on the front end and how the system of pleas impacts innocent clients on the back end who wish to prove their innocence.

Too Many Cases in the System

Plea bargaining perpetuates the overcriminalization and mass incarceration that currently plagues the criminal legal system. One of the biggest issues confronting the United States is the sheer number of people who are ensnared in the criminal legal system. In the second half of the 20th century, there was an explosion of conduct that legislatures deemed illegal and attached criminal penalties to.[1] This overcriminalization of conduct has directly led to the current problem of "mass incarceration" where poor Black and Brown people are disproportionately incarcerated for crimes.[2]

As a result of this overcriminalization, prosecutor and public defender caseloads have ballooned. Public defenders provide representation to 85 percent of those accused of crimes.[3] During my time at the Bronx Defenders—a well-resourced office full of dedicated lawyers—my caseload was often in the triple digits. Thankfully, my caseload did not consist entirely of felony cases, but there are jurisdictions where public defenders carry triple-digit caseloads consisting entirely of felonies.[4] Many of these public defender offices do not have paralegals, law clerks, or full-time investigators, so lawyers are expected to do everything.[5] The combination of these high caseloads and lack of resources has a detrimental impact on the quality of representation that even a dedicated public defender can have on a case. The simple math suggests, and my own experience confirms, that with such high caseloads, attorneys do not have enough time to spend on each case. Research commissioned by the ABA found that in certain states, public defenders had two to three times the maximum number of cases consistent with standards of adequate representation.[6] The study found that in Louisiana, public defenders had five times the maximum number of cases.[7]

---

1. James R. Copland & Rafael A. Mangual, *Overcriminalizing America: An Overview and Model Legislation for States*, MANHATTAN INST. (Aug. 18, 2018), https://manhattan.institute/article/overcriminalizing-america-an-overview-and-model-legislation-for-states.

2. Jeff Fagan et al., *Reciprocal Effects of Crime and Incarceration in New York City Neighborhoods*, 30 FORDHAM URB. L.J. 1551, 1568 (2003).

3. Emily Galvin-Almanza, *To Prevent Wrongful Convictions, Invest in Public Defense Solutions*, THE HILL (Dec. 18, 2021), https://thehill.com/changing-america/opinion/586305-to-prevent-wrongful-convictions-invest-in-public-defense-solutions.

4. Richard A. Oppel Jr. & Jugal K. Patel, *One Lawyer, 194 Felony Cases, and No Time*, N.Y. TIMES (Jan. 31, 2019), https://www.nytimes.com/interactive/2019/01/31/us/public-defender-case-loads.html.

5. *Id.*

6. *Id.*

7. *Id.*

When lawyers do not have sufficient time to work on their cases, they miss things—both legal issues and factual investigation. Attorneys do not have time to consider all the legal issues present in the case and file the necessary motions. They do not have time to review State-provided discovery, assuming the jurisdiction requires the State to provide discovery prior to trial, or to conduct their own investigation beyond the universe of facts developed by the police. All too often this means that overworked public defenders fail to visit the crime scene, interview witnesses who spoke with police, locate and interview witnesses who did not speak with the police, or find surveillance videos. Overworked public defenders also lack time to consult with experts to challenge forensic evidence the State seeks to introduce against their clients or to challenge the admissibility of such evidence.

Clients are often the best source of information about the case, so an overwhelmed public defender is at a significant disadvantage when their client is incarcerated before trial. Visiting clients in jail is more time-consuming than meeting clients at the office. Clients can also be helpful in locating important witnesses for their attorneys. Without the time or resources to conduct an investigation or thoroughly assess legal issues in the case, defense attorneys and clients cannot adequately assess the strength of the State's case against them and whether there is evidence or legal issues that could significantly undermine the State's case.

The overcriminalization and the resulting high volume of cases that enter the criminal legal system also impact prosecutors, who are the gatekeepers of the system. They decide whether to formally charge a person who has been arrested with a crime. In making this charging decision, prosecutors must determine not only whether there is sufficient evidence to prove the case beyond a reasonable doubt, but also whether the evidence is credible. In many jurisdictions, "individual prosecutors handle more than one thousand felony cases per year."[8] This means that there are hundreds of open felony cases and multiple felony cases set for trial on any given day.[9]

With such heavy caseloads, prosecutors do not scrutinize their cases early in the process. They cannot "thoroughly investigate cases, subpoena witnesses, meet with experts," or complete other essential tasks.[10] They completely rely on the information and representations made by law enforcement. In my experience, prosecutors often do not work up their case until the brink of trial—if the case goes to trial. They do not question witnesses or police officers and evaluate their credibility until they prepare them to testify. This is particularly problematic because, as mentioned earlier, they are the gatekeepers of the system. Although prosecutor offices may be hamstrung by not having enough prosecutors to keep up with the number of cases that come through the system, they have a distinct advantage over public defenders and defense attorneys: they have access to law enforcement to investigate their cases.

The high number of cases also impacts courts themselves. In many jurisdictions, there are not enough judges to handle the volume of cases that come through the system. At the Bronx Defenders, on any given day there were hundreds of cases on the court's calendar. Many of these cases were scheduled for trial, but there were only three judges

8. Adam M. Gershowitz & Laura R. Killinger, *The State (Never) Rests: How Excessive Prosecutorial Caseloads Harm Criminal Defendants*, 105 Nw. U. L. Rev. 261, 262–63 (2011).

9. *Id.* at 263.

10. *Id.* at 265.

designated to conduct misdemeanor trials. If there was not a judge available to hear a case scheduled for trial, the case would get adjourned to another day. Often a misdemeanor case can get continuously adjourned for years before a trial judge becomes available to hear it. In this system, judges are incentivized to clear cases; it reflects poorly upon them if they keep adjourning cases for prolonged periods of time.[11]

Coercive Plea Bargaining Is the Only Way for This System to Continue

The only way this high-volume system can survive is if there is a less rigorous, less resource-intensive way to dispose of cases, short of trial and litigation. Plea bargaining provides a solution to this problem. As Albert Alschuler long ago pointed out, "By lowering the price of imposing criminal punishment, plea bargaining gave America more of it."[12] "Prosecutors took up plea bargaining in part to escape the enormous burdens of their office."[13] Prosecutors aim "to reduce or limit their workload where possible," and this requires "limiting the cost of the process per case."[14] To accomplish this, prosecutors seek to "convert potential trials into guilty pleas," which "are not simply cheaper than trials" but "enormously cheaper. And prosecutors' bargaining strategies tend to ensure that this remains so."[15]

This incentive to convert trials into guilty pleas is also shared by the courts because, as described earlier, they want to clear cases and do not have the resources to try every trial-eligible or -ready case.[16] The joint incentive of prosecutors and judges for pleas rather than trials means that enormous pressure is put on defendants to plead guilty, and these two powerful actors have at their disposal the power to ensure that defendants do just that.

System of Coercion

Pretrial Detention

Both the court and prosecution have several tools at their disposal to enact leverage over a person accused of a crime to coerce them into taking a plea. One common way is through pretrial detention. Prosecutors can request and judges can impose bail and incarcerate a person accused of a crime pretrial while the case is pending. The purpose

11. William Glaberson, *In Misdemeanor Cases, Long Waits for Elusive Trials*, N.Y. TIMES (Apr. 30, 2013), https://archive.nytimes.com/www.nytimes.com/2013/05/01/nyregion/justice-denied-for-misdemeanor-cases-trials-are-elusive.html.

12. Albert W. Alschuler, *Lafler and Frye: Two Small Band-Aids for a Festering Wound*, 51 DUQ. L. REV. 673, 705 (2013).

13. George Fisher, *Plea Bargaining's Triumph*, 109 YALE L.J. 857, 893 (2000).

14. William J. Stuntz, *The Pathological Politics of Criminal Law*, 100 MICH. L. REV. 505, 535–36 (2001).

15. *Id.*

16. *See* Medlin v. State, 280 S.E.2d 648, 650 (S.C. 1981) (Littlejohn & Gregory, JJ., concurring and dissenting) ("It is true that the judge, at least in theory, reserves to himself the right to honor or reject any plea bargain; however, as a practical matter, he accepts the sentence and disposition recommended by the office of the prosecutor in a great majority of the cases in order to expedite their disposition.").

of bail is to ensure a person's return to court, but often, prosecutors will request and a judge will impose a bail amount that a person cannot pay, and as a result, that person remains in jail. It goes without saying that being held in jail can have disastrous effects on a person's life (not only the trauma of being incarcerated but also loss of employment, housing, or custody of children). A person will do almost anything to get out of that predicament, and courts and prosecutors know this. Both my research and my personal experience as a public defender show that there is a big discrepancy in outcomes when a client is held pretrial compared with when they are out.

Given the length of time it takes a case, even and especially a misdemeanor case, to go to trial, if the prosecutor makes a plea offer that gets a client out of jail before the case would go to trial, that plea offer is almost certain to be accepted. This means that poor clients who do not have the means to pay bail are hurt and that the fate of the case and the client is sealed at arraignment or whenever release conditions are decided. I have been in situations at arraignment where, in a misdemeanor case, a prosecutor offered my client a nonincarceratory plea offer, which indicated that the prosecutor did not think my client should be incarcerated for the crime. However, when my client turned down the plea offer, the same prosecutor asked the court to impose bail. As a result of this threat, my client reluctantly pleaded guilty and took the nonincarceratory offer.

Overcharging and the Trial Penalty

Prosecutors routinely make charging decisions. Attached to each criminal charge is a range of punishments that must be imposed for that crime. The more serious the crime, the higher the punishment range. In making the charging decision, the prosecutor sets the parameters for how the case will get resolved. For many of these crimes, however, the penalty that the prosecutor can impose for a charged offense is more severe than they or society would consider just or fair for the conduct and/or defendant. As Professor Andrew Crespo has explained:

> [W]hile defendants always want to minimize their potential sentences, prosecutors rarely want to maximize them, hoping instead to obtain only their preferred sentence, in the most efficient way possible. This asymmetry allows prosecutors to trade away "extra" years of incarceration that the defendant desperately wants to avoid but that the prosecutor doesn't particularly value . . . this free leverage is typically overwhelming because most criminal codes authorize sentences much higher than what a typical prosecutor—or a typical person for that matter—would actually want to see imposed in a given case. Thus, by threatening a seriously inflated set of charges and then offering to replace it with the charges that she truly desires, the prosecutor is able to control the defendant's incentive to plead guilty, and with it the outcome of any subsequent "negotiation."[17]

This means that the prosecutor can charge a client with a particularly serious offense that they may legally be able to prove but do not necessarily believe is the correct charge, simply because it gives them more leverage in plea negotiations. This

---

17. Andrew M. Crespo, *The Hidden Law of Plea Bargaining*, 118 Colum. L. Rev. 1303, 1311–12 (2018).

overcharging has an adverse impact on cases going to trial because if there is a significant difference between the plea offer and maximum sentence of the charged crimes, a client will likely accept the plea offer to avoid the longer potential sentence. Judges can and often do push people accused of crimes to accept these pleas by threatening them with the maximum sentence should they lose at trial.

Exploding Plea Offers

Another tactic prosecutors use is the exploding plea offer. Because prosecutors control the plea process, they can set deadlines by which a client must accept the plea offer. If the client does not accept the offer by the deadlines, the offer disappear. That's what makes it "exploding." These deadlines can coincide with points in the litigation process when prosecutors must perform work or provide defense counsel with information about the case. In my experience, I have had prosecutors hold a plea offer open until I filed a suppression motion or requested or litigated discovery issues or other legal issues. The reason these offers disappeared after I filed a suppression motion, requested discovery, or litigated legal issues is because my actions required prosecutors to respond to my motions and disclose information about their case—it required them to do work. This put me in the impossible position of advising a client to take a plea without having complete information about the State's case against my client or knowing whether all of the State's evidence against my client would be admitted at trial.

Road Map for How Innocent Defendants Plead Guilty

In this underresourced and high-volume system, where institutional actors do not have adequate resources to handle their workload, it is understandable how an innocent client would plead guilty. An overworked prosecutor who is looking to clear cases is presented with an arrest by the police. The prosecutor, looking to gain leverage on the defendant, charges the defendant with a more serious charge than the case deserves and requests bail to incarcerate the client pretrial. The prosecutor does not have the time to properly review the case and makes what seems like a generous plea offer if the client accepts the plea by a certain time.

An overworked public defender meets this client at arraignments; their client says that they are innocent. Despite the public defender's best efforts, the judge imposes bail. The public defender has not been provided discovery in the case and has not had time to conduct their own investigation or file motions challenging the admissibility of the evidence against the defendant. Despite this, the prosecutor's offer will get the client out of prison much sooner than if they took the case to trial, but the client must accept the offer before any motions are filed or before the prosecutor has to turn over discovery. If the prosecutor has to put more work into the case, they will change the plea offer. The public defender, concerned about getting the client out of jail, advises the client to take the offer. The public defender is forced to give this advice even though they do not know about all the evidence the State has against their client or the reliability of that evidence.

At a status hearing for the case, the judge typically asks the prosecution about the plea offer. When the prosecutor tells the judge that the offer will get the client out of prison but will go away once the State has to turn over discovery and file motions, the judge will likely inform the client that they will impose the maximum sentence if the client is found guilty at trial.

Hearing all of this, the innocent client, who did not commit this crime—and there may be evidence to prove they did not commit the crime—will almost certainly take the plea because under the circumstances it simply makes the most sense. In this system, not only has the innocent client agreed to a false guilty plea, but also the causes of this wrongful conviction will likely never be exposed because no one will scrutinize either the legal or the factual issues in the case.

Plea Bargaining Allows Systemic Issues That Cause Wrongful Convictions to Continue

The inability of public defenders to vigorously contest most cases gives rise to many problems, including the proliferation of the use of problematic forensic evidence. According to the Innocence Project, the misapplication of forensic science is a contributing factor in 45 percent of its DNA exonerations.[18] As the 2016 President's Council of Advisors on Science and Technology (PCAST) report demonstrated, there are serious questions about the reliability of forensic evidence that has been routinely introduced at trial.[19] Even sophisticated DNA evidence can be challenged, and in some cases it has been deemed inadmissible.[20] But challenging such evidence is resource intensive. Public defenders must consult with experts to understand the forensic evidence, request certain types of discovery from the State, file substantive motions, and conduct lengthy evidentiary hearings that involve presenting expert testimony and challenging the State's expert testimony.[21] These challenges do not happen, however, when public defenders do not have the time or resources or when prosecutors make exploding plea offers contingent on not filing motions.

Bad actors like corrupt police officers and prosecutors continue to thrive in a system where cases are not scrutinized. The only way a bad police officer is exposed is if their conduct and history are scrutinized through discovery, examining their past conduct, and testimony at hearings or trials. Police officers have been exposed telling falsehoods on the stand, which has in some circumstances forced prosecutors not to call them again at a hearing or trial.[22] NYPD narcotics detective Joseph Franco, for example, has been

18. Innocence Project, *Misapplication of Forensic Science*, https://innocenceproject.org/misapplication-of-forensic-science/ (last visited Feb. 15, 2024).

19. Forensic Science in Criminal Courts: Ensuring Scientific Validity of Feature-Comparison Methods, President's Council of Advisors on Sci. & Tech. (Sept. 2016), https://obamawhitehouse.archives.gov/sites/default/files/microsites/ostp/PCAST/pcast_forensic_science_report_final.pdf.

20. Jesse McKinley, *Judge Rejects DNA Test in Trial over Garrett Phillips's Murder*, N.Y. Times (Aug. 26, 2016), https://www.nytimes.com/2016/08/27/nyregion/judge-rejects-dna-test-in-trial-over-garrett-phillipss-murder.html.

21. People v. Collins, 49 Misc. 3d 595 (N.Y. Sup. Ct. 2015) (describing months-long evidentiary hearing where defendant presented numerous experts in challenging the admissibility of DNA evidence developed from a probabilistic genotyping software program).

22. Tim Prudente & Jessica Anderson, *State's Attorney Mosby Releases Names of Baltimore Police Officers She Won't Call to Testify, but Most Are No Longer with the Department*, Balt. Sun (Oct. 29, 2021), https://www.baltimoresun.com/news/crime/bs-md-ci-cr-marilyn-mosby-do-not-call-list-20211029-rplz7z7nlnbfnhnfslhtrmmphu-story.html.

alleged to have lied in hundreds of cases that resulted in indictments based on supposed observations he made. Many of those cases resulted in guilty pleas, which has now required district attorney offices throughout the city to dismiss hundreds of cases he worked on.[23]

Prosecutors who hide exculpatory *Brady* evidence or engage in other types of misconduct will also not get exposed unless cases are scrutinized and litigated. No one will know if a prosecutor hid evidence unless there is a robust investigation and discovery process and litigation. A system that does not give public defenders the resources to review discovery or litigate discovery issues prior to advising a client to take a plea will not uncover such misconduct.

Guilty Plea Issues after Vacatur of Conviction

The forces that push clients to plead guilty pretrial also lead clients who have had their convictions vacated to take guilty pleas. After a court vacates a conviction based on new evidence—either DNA or non-DNA evidence—the case goes back to a pretrial posture where the prosecution has the option to retry or dismiss the case.

In the history of the Innocence Project, only one case has ever been retried after the court vacated the conviction, and that client was acquitted. In most cases, the State will dismiss the charges against the client, but there are instances where clients, who are demonstrably innocent, still plead guilty after their convictions have been vacated.

These guilty pleas are particularly troubling because many of the factors described earlier that lead innocent clients to plead guilty are absent. A case that has been vacated because of newly discovered evidence has presumably been thoroughly investigated by either trial counsel or post-conviction counsel because they learned of evidence proving innocence. Many of the legal issues have been litigated during post-conviction proceedings, and because the case has already been tried, the client knows the strength of the State's case against them and knows about the existence of this new evidence and how it will undermine the State's case. Through trial and post-conviction proceedings, the client has been provided with all the discovery that exists in the case. Given the notoriety of these cases, they tend to be insulated from pressures by the judiciary. Yet despite all of this, innocent clients still accept plea offers.

For example, Raymond Tempest was convicted in 1992 of second-degree murder and sentenced to 85 years in prison.[24] In 2015, a Rhode Island trial judge reversed Tempest's conviction, and the Rhode Island appellate court upheld the reversal because the police and prosecution failed to turn over evidence that pointed to Tempest's innocence.[25] This evidence included witnesses who came forward and significantly contradicted a key piece of the State's case and an important state witness who had significantly changed her story during the course of a conversation with the prosecution shortly before trial.[26]

23. Tamar Lapin, *Bronx DA Dropping 133 Cases Linked to Indicted NYPD Detective Joseph Franco*, N.Y. Post (Jan. 20, 2022), https://nypost.com/2022/01/20/bronx-da-darcel-clark-dropping-133-cases-linked-to-nypd-detective-joseph-franco/.

24. Innocence Project, *Guilty Plea Series: The Case of Raymond Tempest* (Oct. 17, 2017), https://innocenceproject.org/guilty-plea-series-the-case-of-raymond-tempest/.

25. *Id.*

26. *Id.*

Post-conviction counsel also learned that police had fed information to four witnesses who testified against Tempest.[27] Despite this evidence of innocence, which undermined the State's case, the State would not drop the charges against Tempest and threatened to retry him for this crime.[28] Tempest was released on bail pretrial on this murder charge, and the State offered Tempest an opportunity to accept an Alford plea, which allowed him to maintain his innocence and get time served.[29] After spending 24 years in prison for a crime he did not commit and fearful that he could lose at trial, Tempest accepted the offer to end the case.[30]

The Tempest case shows that even when a client knows they are innocent and can prove it, they still will accept some form of guilt if it leads to immediate freedom and they are receiving a steep discount from the State in exchange for the plea. This suggests the importance of two factors: pretrial detention and steep discounts in plea offers. A client who remains incarcerated after their conviction is vacated, who has spent years, perhaps decades, incarcerated, will take a plea offer that allows them to get released immediately, even if it means admitting to a crime they did not commit and there exists evidence that proves their innocence. Similarly, even clients who have evidence that proves their innocence engage in a risk assessment when deciding how to handle their case. If there is a significant difference between the plea offer and the punishment they may face after trial, they will accept the plea.

Legal Obstacles for Pleading Clients to Prove Their Innocence

In this system where trials rarely happen, and innocent clients are pressured to plead guilty, innocent people convicted of crimes shockingly face legal obstacles in the post-conviction context to prove their innocence. Several states prevent people who pleaded guilty from conducting post-conviction DNA testing on evidence because either the statute explicitly prevents them from testing evidence or courts in the state have interpreted the DNA testing statute to mean they do not meet one of the statutory requirements.[31]

This is troubling in a system where a vast majority of cases are resolved through plea bargains. Additionally, the data proves that innocent defendants plead guilty, and post-conviction DNA testing confirms that terrible fact. I recently represented an individual in West Virginia, which thankfully allows people who have pleaded guilty to conduct post-conviction DNA testing. My client had been convicted of a homicide, but the West Virginia Supreme Court reversed his conviction because of an evidentiary issue. My client then took an Alford plea for fear he would lose again at trial. We conducted post-conviction DNA testing on multiple pieces of crime scene evidence that not only excluded my client but also matched a convicted sex offender whose profile was in

27. *Id.*

28. *Id.*

29. *Id.*

30. *Id.*

31. Colin Miller, *Why States Must Consider Innocence Claims after Guilty Pleas*, 10 U.C. Irvine L. Rev. 671, 675–86 (2020).

the FBI convicted offender database. Based on these DNA results, the State vacated my client's conviction.

There are states that also do not allow clients who pleaded guilty to raise actual innocence claims in post-conviction proceedings based on non-DNA evidence. In *People v. Tiger*, the Court of Appeals in New York held that the State's post-conviction relief statute did not allow pleading defendants to raise actual innocence claims based on non-DNA evidence. The court reasoned that the recognition of such an error would have enormous ramifications for the criminal justice system, including undermining the finality of the proceedings.[32]

What this means is that a person who availed themselves of an exploding plea offer where their underresourced public defender could not fully investigate the case cannot get relief on actual innocence grounds when there may be alibi witnesses or a surveillance video that shows they could not have committed the crime and that their trial lawyer never obtained. This seems remarkably unfair in a system not equipped for people to develop evidence of their innocence at trial.

The court's reasoning in *Tiger* and cases like it ignores the reality of how the criminal legal system functions and the coercive environment in which pleas are extracted. Valuing finality over getting the correct results seems to ignore the fact that 18 percent of known exonerees pleaded guilty to crimes they did not commit.[33]

Recommendations to Prevent Innocent Clients from Pleading Guilty

The task force has made a number of important recommendations on how to reform plea bargaining within the criminal legal system. Following are two recommendations that I think address the issue of innocent people accused of crimes pleading guilty in our system. The thrust of these recommendations is to incentivize litigation and trials because I believe the best way to protect innocent clients is by scrutinizing their cases. It is my belief that this does not happen unless cases are litigated and tried. While I understand hundreds of innocent clients have been wrongfully convicted after trials, the hope of these recommendations is to set up a system where defendants are represented by well-resourced attorneys at trial and that this would address the issues that lead to wrongful convictions.

Provide Adequate Resources to Public Defenders

As described earlier, public defenders represent most people accused of crimes and have crushing caseloads that prevent them from spending adequate time on their cases. There should be caps on the number of cases an individual defender handles at one time. This will ensure that defenders can spend the requisite time on each case, which will allow them to file the necessary motions, review and litigate discovery issues, and conduct

32. 32 N.Y.3d 91, 101 (2018). In 2023, the New York legislature passed the Challenging Wrongful Convictions Act, which would allow pleading defendants to raise actual innocence claims based on non-DNA evidence. As of publication of this book, Governor Hochul had not signed the act.

33. Innocence Project, *Why Do Innocent People Plead Guilty to Crimes They Didn't Commit?*, https://guiltypleaproblem.org/#about (last visited Feb. 15, 2024).

investigations. Public defender offices should be equipped with full-time investigators who can interview witnesses and track down other evidence that may exculpate their clients.

Public defender offices should also have specialized departments that assist attorneys in litigating the admissibility of forensic evidence. As described earlier, the misapplication of forensic sciences has played a significant role in wrongful convictions. In order to challenge the admissibility of these forensic sciences, defenders must learn about the forensic science, consult with experts, draft motions, and conduct contested hearings. This can be difficult for a public defender with a full caseload. A specialized unit, consisting of lawyers without a caseload, would be equipped to make these necessary challenges.

Limit Plea Differentials

Defendants and their attorneys engage in a risk assessment when deciding whether to accept a plea offer. At the heart of this assessment is comparing the potential punishment if the client is convicted following a trial against the plea offer. When there is a significant difference between the two possible sentences, defense attorneys, such as me, will counsel clients to accept the plea, regardless of the strength of the case. Sometimes, it is precisely because the defense has a strong case that there may be a steep differential.

Although generous plea offers benefit individual clients, they also have the adverse impact of making trials riskier propositions with more downside.[34] As a result, most cases do not go to trial, and the numbers bear this out. Prosecutors make generous plea offers on weaker cases rather than dismissing such cases because they know clients will accept such offers and not risk trial.[35]

If there is a limit on this differential, then clients will view going to trial as a less risky option, which should lead more cases to go to trial. If prosecutors knew that every case they charged or indicted would go to trial, they would presumably scrutinize cases earlier in the process, and only cases with credible evidence that they knew they could prove at trial would move forward and weaker cases would be dismissed. These resulting dismissals would mean innocent clients who would have strong cases at trial would not be faced with the dilemma of whether to accept a plea.

If more cases go to trial, then better-resourced public defender offices will have the opportunity to litigate those cases, including filing motions challenging the admissibility of evidence and discovery issues. Presumably, through such litigation, issues with the State's case will get exposed. Innocent clients will not be put in a situation of accepting a plea simply because it is far safer than going to trial.

---

34. Josh Bowers, *Punishing the Innocent*, 156 U. Pa. L. Rev. 117, 119 (2008).
35. Oren Gazal-Ayal, *Partial Ban on Plea Bargains*, 27 Cardozo L. Rev. 2295, 2298–99 (2006).

CHAPTER 8

The Problem of Fictional Pleas

Thea Johnson

Introduction: What Is a Fictional Plea?

The Task Force Report operates in a liminal space between the criminal justice system that currently exists and an ideal that it envisions for the future. Operating in this liminal space means that we acknowledge that our recommendations for an ideal criminal justice system might confront the reality of the current system. As we noted in the report, "The Task Force prepared this Report with an eye toward the criminal justice system we would like to see, rather than account for all the potential ripples that might flow from our recommendations in the world that exists now."[1] Of course, we understand that many of our proposals will indeed have ripples. Therefore, we constantly asked ourselves how to address the problems we have now while pushing the system and system actors toward the system we hope to see in the future. But addressing current problems while envisioning a new future can sometimes create conflict.

Nowhere was this clearer than in our efforts to address fictional pleas. A fictional plea is one in which the defendant pleads guilty to a crime they have not committed with the knowledge of the defense attorney, prosecutor, and judge.[2] (In the report, we alternate between calling such pleas "baseless pleas"[3] and "fictional pleas." For the purposes of this chapter, I will adhere to the term "fictional plea.") In a fictional plea, the plea of conviction often has only a passing resemblance, or sometimes no resemblance at all, to the facts as the parties understand them. For instance, in one jurisdiction, a

1. ABA Crim. Just. Section, 2023 Plea Bargain Task Force Report 12, https://www.americanbar.org/content/dam/aba/publications/criminaljustice/plea-bargain-tf-report.pdf. (Subsequent citations to the report in this chapter refer to the original page numbers of the report as they appear in the PDF available online, not the page numbers as they appear in this book.)

2. Thea Johnson, *Fictional Pleas*, 94 Ind. L.J. 855, 860 (2019).

3. Mari Byrne, *Baseless Pleas: A Mockery of Justice*, 78 Fordham L. Rev. 2961 (2010).

defendant charged with downloading child pornography resolved the charge by pleading guilty to assault, even though there were no facts that would support an assault charge.[4] This apparently allowed him to bypass the sex offender registration that would be mandatory on a child pornography charge. In another part of the country, a defendant accused of robbery pleaded guilty to a charge of "creating no less than one thousand illegal music recordings without consent." The defense attorney later acknowledged in an interview that this was just "creative" plea bargaining so the parties could reach the desired result at sentencing.[5] In other places, defendants may plead guilty to crimes with an attempted reckless mens rea—a legal impossibility in most jurisdictions.[6] This means that the defendant is pleading guilty to a crime they could never be convicted of at trial because there would be no statute on which to charge the jury. These legally baseless pleas generally allow a defendant to escape a particular mandatory minimum sentence that is associated with the original charge.

As these examples demonstrate, the fictional plea exists to meet a need. It can help defendants avoid often-unfair collateral consequences, such as immigration effects or mandatory sentences associated with the charge that would actually match the facts. The fictional plea also allows the prosecutor to come to a resolution that they believe is fair and that the defendant is likely to agree to. For instance, a defendant may want to avoid the immigration consequences associated with a drug charge. The prosecutor may agree that immigration consequences on the particular facts in the case are unfair but nonetheless be disinclined to drop the case. The compromise often reached in such cases is a fictional plea that allows the parties to come to a fair resolution without the imposition of unwanted collateral consequences. Certainly, the terms "unfair" and "fair" are both notoriously ambiguous and undefined. This ambiguity facilitates the creation of the fictional plea. What is interesting about a fictional plea is that parties from both sides of the aisle often reach these resolutions on the shared belief that they are reaching a fairer—or, perhaps, less unfair—result than that which would otherwise occur.

What's the Problem with the Fictional Plea?

As just described, the fictional plea is often used to avoid a particular unfair outcome, which solves a problem in an individual case. In this sense, the fictional plea can be a valuable tool in particular cases where the parties agree that charges based on the facts might lead to unwanted consequences. But there are broader problems associated with fictional pleas that have implications for the entire criminal justice system. Fictional

4. Thea Johnson, *Lying at Plea Bargaining*, 38 GA. ST. U. L. REV. 673, 691 (2022).

5. *Id.* at 691–92.

6. *See, e.g.*, People v. Martinez, 611 N.E.2d 277, 278 (N.Y. 1993); State v. Wickman, No. CA 76-40, 1977 Ohio App. LEXIS 10210, at *7 (Ohio Ct. App. Sept. 28, 1977); Spencer v. State, 942 P.2d 646, 647, 649 (Kan. Ct. App. 1997); People v. Myrieckes, 734 N.E.2d 188, 194 (Ill. App. Ct. 2000); McPherson v. State, 163 P.3d 1257, 1261, 1264 (Kan. Ct. App. 2007); State v. Pollman, 441 P.3d 511, 517 (Kan. Ct. App. 2019); People v. Guishard, 789 N.Y.S.2d 332, 333 (App. Div. 2005); People v. Genes, 227 N.W.2d 241, 242–43 (Mich. Ct. App. 1975). Although they are beyond the scope of this chapter, there are many other common types of plea bargaining that I would label as forms of "lying" akin to fictions. For instance, many Alford pleas operate as a sort of fiction, as does the process of the plea colloquy itself, which often requires defendants to lie about the nature of the bargain. For more on these other forms of lying, see Johnson, *supra* note 4, at 687–709.

pleas may also pose problems even at the case level for defendants and victims. Following is just a sampling of some of these problems.

For one, fictional pleas distort our ability to rely on crime statistics as a reliable measure of behavior. This is one of the most important concerns in a system that relies on plea bargains that do not reflect the truth of what the defendant actually did.[7] Recently, the Supreme Court of Michigan considered changing the procedural rules for guilty pleas to make it more difficult for a defendant to accept a fictional plea.[8] The rule would have required defendants to enter into the record a factual basis for the particular crime they were pleading guilty to—that is, the parties would have to provide some factual support for the charge of conviction. This rule stood in contrast to the standing (and current) Michigan procedural rule that allows a defendant to enter a factual basis that supports either the charge of conviction or the arrest charges.[9]

Local attorneys and judges universally opposed the change. One letter to the court from a defense attorney noted that in a driving while intoxicated (DWI) case, he was able to negotiate a plea for the defendant to two separate charges: careless driving and failure to report an accident. As the attorney admitted, the latter charge was not supported by the facts.[10] If the Court or a researcher wanted to study the rate of Michiganders failing to report an accident, one would imagine that the first place they would look is the number of convictions for the crime. This is because we assume that a conviction for failure to report an accident stands for the proposition that someone failed to report an accident. A local government might make many policy decisions based on these statistics. If it seemed that the citizens of Michigan were regularly failing to report accidents, the government might decide to launch a campaign to educate people about the need to report accidents. But if failing to report an accident is instead a way of resolving a DWI case that the parties have decided should not be resolved with the penalties associated with the initial charge, then the conviction no longer indicates that a person committed the crime. Resolving a case this way may also mean that the state is undercounting the number of DWI cases.

Furthermore, if we accept that truth-seeking is a fundamental goal of the criminal legal system (although many reasonable people would dispute this characterization of the system), then there is a problem with attaching a conviction to conduct that does not, in fact, resemble the charge of conviction. The purported purpose of the trial is to determine whether the defendant is guilty or innocent of the charges against them—both legally and factually. Although plea bargains resolve cases more efficiently than trials, they should also be truth-seeking mechanisms. Because plea bargains generally do not have a developed factual record, the conviction at disposition takes on even greater significance.

---

7. Part of this section of the chapter is drawn from my letter to the Michigan Supreme Court at the time it was contemplating this rule. *See* Letter from Thea Johnson & Russell Covey to Larry S. Royster, Sup. Ct. Clerk, Mich. Sup. Ct. (June 17, 2021), https://www.courts.michigan.gov/4a5647/contentassets/0bfa5a1e17f441c59ed928da0b1f0047/approved/2018-29_2021-06-17_commentfromtheajohnson-russellcovey.pdf.

8. Order Seeking Comment on Proposed Amendments of Rule 6.302 and Rule 6.610 of the Michigan Court Rules, ADM File No. 2018-29 (Mar. 25, 2021).

9. Mich. Ct. R. 6.302, R. 6.610.

10. Email from Stephen Adams, Att'y at Law, to Mich. Sup. Ct., at 39–40 (Mar. 31, 2021), https://www.michbar.org/file/generalinfo/pdfs/6-11-21_PPC_agenda.pdf.

There are many barriers to seeking truth in the criminal system. Sometimes truth is legitimately difficult to determine and may never be known. But many times, the parties know the truth and, for the sake of efficiency, come to a resolution that does not represent the truth. Although fictional pleas help keep the system from grinding to a halt, we should be deeply concerned if the courts have given up the goal of truth-seeking in exchange for an efficient way to process their caseloads.

Even on the individual level, a fictional plea may create problems for those who may seemingly benefit from such a plea. A fictional plea might be a fiction at the time the defendant accepts it, but once the plea is accepted, it will forever be associated with the defendant as a true characterization of their conduct. In prior work, I discussed a defendant who turned one felony sex assault charge into three separate misdemeanor sex assault convictions by using a fictional plea. As I noted: "Although the three acts are categorized as misdemeanors and therefore less 'serious' crimes, to the outside world they indicate a pattern of abusive behavior where one may not actually exist. It is not hard to imagine a future prosecutor in a potential future criminal case pointing to the defendant's criminal record and harping on the defendant's *repeat* crimes."[11] The reality—that two of the three sex assault convictions are fictions—falls away as soon as the defendant enters the plea. While the fictional plea may have had many benefits at the moment the defendant accepted it, there is the potential for various unintended consequences down the road.

Crime victims may also be harmed by the use of fictional pleas. The victims of Jeffrey Epstein are a prime example. Epstein was an extraordinarily wealthy financier who was accused by dozens of girls of sexual assault. Despite the number and severity of the charges, Epstein was able to plead guilty to soliciting a prostitute, a clear fiction.[12] This plea was largely kept hidden from his victims, who would have objected to it.[13] The victims were not prostitutes but instead girls who had been lured to Epstein's home by his associates, where they were then assaulted. The message of the fictional plea in those cases was that the victims' real harm could be transformed into a petty crime. The criminal system hid Epstein's true crimes behind the façade of a fictional plea.

How to Reform the Fictional Plea

The fictional plea is a necessary solution for the current problem of the huge range of mandatory consequences, both sentencing and collateral, that result from a criminal conviction. For this reason, many members of the task force, myself included, hesitated to suggest banning it. It is impossible to have a fair system if it requires that defendants regularly engage in lying and fictions to get to what the parties believe are just results. So, how do we envision a system that meets existing needs while creating something new? We recognize that no problem or practice is an island. Indeed, as the report notes,

---

11. Johnson, *supra* note 2, at 898.

12. David Enrich, *How Jeffrey Epstein Got Away with It*, N.Y. Times (July 13, 2021) (reviewing Julie K. Brown, Perversion of Justice: The Jeffrey Epstein Story (2021)), https://www.nytimes.com/2021/07/13/books/review/perversion-of-justice-julie-k-brown.html.

13. Laurel Wamsley, *Labor Secretary Alex Acosta Defends His Handling of Jeffrey Epstein Plea Deal*, NPR (July 10, 2019), https://www.npr.org/2019/07/10/740425294/labor-sec-alex-acosta-defends-his-handling-of-jeffrey-epstein-plea-deal.

> many of the problems addressed in [the] Report do not stem from the practice of plea bargaining itself, but rather are manifestations of problems in other parts of the criminal justice system, such as overly harsh sentencing rules or one-size-fits-all collateral consequences that impose unjust or intolerable conditions on individual defendants. Problems and imbalances in these other areas inevitably manifest in plea bargaining practice.[14]

The report also notes that baseless or fictional pleas are "a symptom of broader problems with the criminal justice system."[15]

Fictional pleas remind us that plea bargaining is about much more than just the negotiation of the case between the parties. Plea bargaining is about sentencing, the substantive criminal law, the policies of individual prosecutors, the practice of judges, and the many other consequences that flow from convictions. This is why the report took a holistic look at the system to see where these levers and pressure points exist and can be reformed.

So, what should be done about fictional pleas? Unsurprisingly, there are no clear answers. In some ways, fictional pleas are just a microcosm of the problems with plea bargaining more generally. Fictional pleas are made possible because plea bargaining is so flexible and opaque. One might say that the solution to fictional pleas is to make the system more transparent and less flexible, but there are drawbacks to limiting flexibility that might make many reformers balk. The task force "does not suggest that courts limit the ability of the parties to negotiate 'creatively,' even while [it] acknowledges its deep discomfort with factually and legally baseless pleas."[16] The task force offered no clear solutions to the issue of fictional pleas because there simply are not any. Next, however, I lay out some ways we might think about reform in this area, drawing from the report's suggestions more broadly. I also offer my own opinion on which of these reforms are more viable than others.

Do Nothing

One option, of course, is to do nothing. Doing "something" about fictional pleas assumes that they are a problem. Many, perhaps even most, stakeholders in the criminal system dispute that these pleas pose a problem. In fairness to the majority view, I offer here one solution to the problem, which is no solution at all. Fictional pleas meet a need and, as such, should not be particularly addressed. Because fictional pleas are a symptom, and not a cause, of a broader dysfunction within the system, we shouldn't touch them.

However, this theory holds up only if you think that treating the symptoms of an illness makes no sense unless you can eradicate the illness itself. In a system in which the illness has many causes, though, it may be nearly impossible to eradicate the disease. For this reason, although I see the appeal and wisdom of the "do nothing" approach, I reject it. While searching for a broader cure, we may be well served to treat the various symptoms of the problem.

---

14. 2023 Plea Bargain Task Force Report, *supra* note 1, at 13.
15. *Id.* at 23.
16. *Id.*

Ban Fictional Pleas

On the other end of the spectrum, if you worry that fictional pleas are corrosive to the criminal system, you could ban them. One could certainly imagine legislation or criminal rules that prohibit certain types of bargaining or certain plea deals. Indeed, many jurisdictions already place limits on the types of bargaining that can happen in a case.[17]

But a total ban on fictional pleas is unlikely to be effective. History tells us that banning plea bargaining more generally has not been particularly successful. Legislators have experimented with plea bans for various reasons. As I noted in previous work, "[S]omewhat ironically, plea bans are sometimes put in place to fight both perceived leniency towards defendants and to combat overly punitive measures towards defendants."[18] But no matter the reason behind the bans, lawyers tend to figure out ways around them. Most bans have usually given way "to business-as-usual plea bargaining."[19]

More importantly, even if one imagines that these bans could be effective, they would be very painful for defendants, often at a high cost that none of the parties—defense attorney, prosecutor, or judge—think is fair. A total ban on these bargains would essentially be trying to combat a problem created by mandatory outcomes with yet another mandatory outcome. It is likely that a ban on fictional pleas would distort the system even further. The ban would only address the symptoms of plea bargaining practice without taking into account the broader illness. For this reason, a ban on fictional pleas strikes me as unwise.

Require a More Meaningful Factual Record

As the report notes, "[P]lea colloquies almost always are tightly scripted and largely ceremonial events, often consisting entirely of leading, yes-no questions asked by the judge."[20] As a result, they tend not to represent a meaningful inquiry into whether the defendant is pleading guilty knowingly and voluntarily or even if the state has a strong basis for believing that the defendant truly committed the crime. Although some jurisdictions require a full factual record, others require only a brief recitation of the facts or none at all. Fictional pleas flourish in a system without a meaningful testing of the facts.

One option to either curb fictional pleas or, as I explain later, track them more effectively is to enhance the procedures at the plea colloquy by requiring that the parties develop a meaningful factual record before the defendant enters a plea. A more meaningful factual basis would have many salutary effects on the plea system. At the moment, pleas take the place of a trial with none of the truth-seeking mechanisms or procedural protections of a trial. The guilty plea process should be significantly more robust so that we may have more faith in the colloquy as a stand-in for the ever-disappearing trial.[21] That requires making the colloquy a more meaningful process, including by making sure that there is a robust factual basis for the plea.

---

17. Andrew Manuel Crespo, *The Hidden Law of Plea Bargaining*, 118 Colum. L. Rev. 1303, 1363–66 (2018) (discussing the ways that some states limit charge bargaining by procedurally limiting when the prosecutor may make an offer to a lesser charge).

18. Thea Johnson, *The Efficiency Mindset and Mass Incarceration*, 74 Okla. L. Rev. 115, 136 (2022).

19. *Id.* at 137.

20. 2023 Plea Bargain Task Force Report, *supra* note 1, at 22.

21. *Id.*

A clear critique of this proposal is that it poses the same problems as a plea ban in that it will prevent defendants from taking advantage of the fictional plea when it is necessary to avoid an unfair outcome. If defendants must plead guilty only to the charges that are supported by the facts of the case, they will be prohibited from taking advantage of fictional pleas and their benefits. This, indeed, was the argument made by many of the lawyers and judges who opposed the rule change in Michigan.[22] Such a change would have required defendants to provide a factual basis for the charges they are pleading to. This contrasts with the current rule, which only requires defendants to create a factual record that supports either the arrest or the conviction charges. This means that a defendant might create a factual record that does not support the conviction charge.

Michigan's competing procedural rule—the proposed rule versus the actual rule—provides an interesting way to explore the potential effects of the factual basis requirements. For instance, if one wanted to curb fictional pleas, then it would make sense to adopt a rule that requires a factual basis that matches the conviction charge. Although many fictional pleas are clandestine, there is still good reason to believe that requiring an accurate factual basis for a plea bargain would lessen the number of fictional pleas. Defense attorneys and prosecutors may be disinclined to have defendants openly lie on the record to achieve the plea bargain. In this sense, the requirement of a more meaningful factual record would make fictional pleas less common without banning them. Of course, this would have many of the same negative effects as a ban.

But if a jurisdiction simply wanted to understand when and how fictional pleas are being used, then it could adopt a rule similar to the one that Michigan currently has in place but with added transparency about the nature of the bargain. For instance, a defendant could plead guilty to a charge but make clear that the facts would not support the conviction. Part of the problem with the current system is that while the parties *at the time of the plea* might understand that the defendant is entering a fictional plea, that fiction later functions as truth about the defendant's conduct. Nowhere on the defendant's rap sheet will it note that the facts did not support the conviction. In this way, "the fiction is transformed into truth."[23]

But one could imagine a system in which the parties could explain the reasons that they opted for fiction rather than the truth in resolving the case. In this way, the defendant can secure the benefit of a plea without the process requiring that the parties engage in what is essentially a lie in open court. As other scholars have noted, guilty pleas are not formal confessions and, for the most part, do not rely on the defendant taking an oath.[24] We could see guilty pleas as allowing for the same sort of flexibility one sees in the civil system, where advocates frequently reach resolutions that no one claims represent the "truth." A jurisdiction could adopt a more meaningful guilty plea colloquy that allows the defendant to be truthful about the reasons why they are pleading guilty to a particular charge. Many members of the task force would discourage judges from asking defendants if they are pleading guilty to the charges because they are guilty precisely because we know that defendants plead guilty for various reasons, sometimes

22. Johnson, *supra* note 18, at 121–25.
23. Johnson, *supra* note 2, at 898.
24. Brandon L. Garrett, *Why Guilty Pleas Are Not Confessions*, 57 WM. & MARY L. REV. 1415 (2016).

unrelated to guilt on the charge.[25] To take this concept a step further, instead of judges avoiding the question, they may ask the question and then accept the honest answer.[26]

Such a system would have the benefit of helping us track fictional pleas. We would not have the problem outlined earlier where a jurisdiction relies on conviction statistics to understand how many people have committed a certain offense that year. Instead, we could track when a conviction reflects the conduct that a defendant admits to on the record. In addition, this type of honesty at the guilty plea phase might also have a feedback loop effect on legislatures. To stick with the DWI example, knowledge that defendants are regularly avoiding DWIs because of mandatory consequences associated with the DWI charges may encourage legislatures to rethink such mandatory consequences to encourage truth in the system.

Eliminate Mandatory Outcomes

Fictional pleas are caused primarily by the parties attempting to avoid mandatory outcomes, like mandatory minimums, deportation, and sex offender registration. Although the source of these mandatory consequences varies, they all must be imposed upon conviction on certain charges. As a result, the lawyers in a case will often get creative to avoid these consequences.

Part of the problem is that mandatory outcomes attach to *a lot* of crimes. Nearly all drug convictions require deportation for noncitizens.[27] Nearly all sex crimes require sex offender registration.[28] In many states, felony convictions automatically deny a person the rights to vote and participate in jury service and the ability to obtain or keep licensing for many types of jobs, to name just a few of the thousands of potential collateral consequences that mandatorily attach to felony convictions.[29] Further, mandatory minimum sentences are common in every single jurisdiction in the United States.

Part of the reason that legislators have been so cavalier about imposing mandatory consequences is because they know that prosecutors have the discretion to charge and bargain in ways that allow them to work around unfair results. What is so interesting about fictional pleas is that they make clear that there are certain cases in which a prosecutor's only charging or bargaining options are to resort to fiction. And that resort to

25. 2023 Plea Bargain Task Force Report, *supra* note 1, at 22.

26. A system where defendants can give more honest answers about the reasons they are pleading guilty poses the question of how to deal with innocent people who plead guilty. The task force has acknowledged that innocent people plead guilty in the system we have. 2023 Plea Bargain Task Force Report, *supra* note 1, at 20. The question is whether a transparent system should embrace this reality by allowing defendants to plead guilty while proclaiming innocence. The Alford plea already allows defendants to do this, but in many jurisdictions Alford pleas are limited or even prohibited. For the purposes of this chapter, I focus here on how transparency might work in cases where the defendant is guilty of *something* and wants to plead to a fictional plea. But I acknowledge the difficult question of how such transparency applies to people who are not guilty of anything.

27. Johnson, *supra* note 2, at 883 ("Virtually all drug crimes—both misdemeanor and felony—are removable offenses under immigration law.").

28. *Id.* at 888 ("In the case of sex offenses . . . sex offender registration [] is attached to almost any [sex offense] conviction and affects all defendants who plead guilty, regardless of their background.").

29. A search of the Collateral Consequences Inventory demonstrates the thousands of collateral consequences at the national and state level. *See Collateral Consequences Inventory*, Nat'l Inventory Collateral Consequences Conviction, https://niccc.nationalreentryresourcecenter.org/consequences (last visited Feb. 16, 2024).

fiction is nearly always the product of the parties trying to maneuver around a mandatory consequence associated with the crime that matches the actual alleged conduct of the defendant.

Throughout the report, the task force recommends eliminating or curbing mandatory minimum sentences and mandatory collateral consequences.[30] To start, there are many reasons that this move would have widespread salutary effects. First, eliminating mandatory minimums would be a major step toward ending the trial penalty. Defendants would be able to pursue their constitutional right to trial with less fear of massive mandatory sentences. Removing mandatory sentencing would also empower judges to make individualized sentencing decisions based on the facts of each case. Eliminating mandatory collateral consequences associated with professional licensing would mean greater access to jobs and stability for those who are convicted of crimes. Getting rid of mandatory deportation would keep families together. There are many good reasons to challenge these consequences.

But, for the purposes of this chapter, I argue that at least one substantial reason for removing mandatory outcomes is that it would very likely decrease the need for fictional pleas. Defendants could plead guilty to the thing *they were actually guilty of*,[31] instead of participating in the charade required for fictional pleas. Reformers who care about creating a more truthful and legitimate criminal system ought to be committed to the end of mandatory consequences of all kinds. They fly in the face of a system that is meant to determine criminal liability with a careful weighing of the facts and law.

Conclusion

This chapter presents modest reforms that may address some of the concerns surrounding fictional pleas. But the reality is that the only real solution to fictional pleas—one that addresses the truth-seeking problems with these pleas while also getting at the underlying roots of why they exist—would be a total overhaul of the criminal system. Only reforms that address the interlocking nature of the substantive criminal law, procedural law, sentencing law, and other collateral consequences can have a long-term impact on fictional pleas. As I've noted in prior work, "[A] failure to think big and focus only on [discrete] reform is unlikely to have a meaningful impact because [fictional pleas are] a product of these knitted inputs."[32] The report is an attempt to get lawyers, judges, policymakers, and other stakeholders to think big about these issues. If all the suggestions in the report were adopted, it is quite likely that fictional pleas would not be needed. The report acknowledges the reality of the current system but is ultimately moving us toward a system that is more transparent, accountable to the public, fair, and legitimate.

---

30. 2023 Plea Bargain Task Force Report, *supra* note 1, at 15 (noting that some members of the Task Force would call for an outright elimination of all mandatory outcomes. All members of the Task Force agree that "where mandatory minimums remain in statutory form, they should not be used to induce pleas of guilt through the plea bargaining process.").

31. This, of course, assumes that they are actually guilty of something, which is not always the case. *See supra* note 26.

32. Johnson, *supra* note 4, at 729.

CHAPTER 9

Plea Formalization

Russell D. Covey

Plea bargaining has been described as "informal" and a practice more subject to experience than rule and more often characterized by local variation than uniformity imposed at the state or federal level.[1] The informality of plea bargaining stands in stark contrast to the formality of the charging process, which is governed by grand jury procedures and/or substantive judicial review and subject to state and federal constitutional standards. The contrast between the virtually unregulated plea bargaining process and highly regulated trial procedures is even greater. This disparity in procedural rigor between plea bargaining and most other features of criminal law is striking, all the more so given that the vast majority of criminal cases are resolved through negotiated guilty pleas. The obsessive fixation on the regulation of trial procedures seems like a peculiar fetish in the broader context of mass criminal justice, which is practically dependent on the day-in day-out functioning of the almost completely unregulated plea system. For decades, plea bargaining scholars have called for greater regulation of the practice. It is past time that we take these calls seriously. Plea bargaining is a procedural renegade that can, and must, be brought to heel. To that end, this chapter will propose a set of reforms intended to bring more rigor and formality to the plea bargaining process.

Over the course of two-plus years, the ABA Plea Bargain Task Force heard testimony and reviewed reports from criminal justice reform–minded organizations and research from the top plea bargaining scholars in the nation. Task force members, who represent a wide range of perspectives and roles, including prosecutors, defense attorneys, state and federal judges, innocence advocates, representatives of various organizations from across the ideological spectrum working on criminal justice reform, and academics, debated all aspects of contemporary plea bargaining practice. After months

1. As Andrew Manuel Crespo puts it: "Thus, the conventional account: Plea bargaining operates 'outside the law's shadow,' governed instead only by brute prosecutorial power that is exercised in ways 'not usually written down anywhere,' let alone 'governed by formal legal standards.'" Andrew Manuel Crespo, *The Hidden Law of Plea Bargaining*, 118 COLUM. L. REV. 1303, 1305 (2018). As Crespo argues in his work, though, plea bargaining is governed largely through "subconstitutional law" and norms. *Id.* Stephen Schulhofer proposed a one-level guideline reduction for guilty pleas, which varies in effect on sentence but appears to range from about 20 to 35 percent. *See* Stephen Schulhofer, *Due Process of Sentencing*, 128 U. PA. L. REV. 733, 791 n.225 (1980).

of discussion and often-heated dialogue, this diverse group was able to reach broad agreement on the essential attributes of a fair plea bargaining system. While there were inevitable disagreements about the details, there was a consensus that plea bargaining as it is currently practiced is undermining fundamental American values that are central to the core constitutional project. The plea bargaining system we have, in short, is not a system of justice, it is a system of convenience.

In my view, what is needed is a fundamental rethinking of plea bargaining as an institution. We need to formally regulate plea bargaining so that, while preserving alternative dispute resolution of criminal accusations, we remove the excesses of discretion that are built into the system and that lead to the worst forms of abuse and injustice. This includes, perhaps controversially, the need to remove "bargaining"—or at least bargaining in the way it typically is conducted—from our guilty plea practices.

Many critics of plea bargaining have called for its complete abolition. If such calls are meant to signal that all cases should be resolved at trial, then the call for abolition is neither a practical solution given the way in which our criminal legal system has evolved, nor is it in my view a superior solution even if it were possible. Resolution of criminal charges through the taking of guilty pleas offers several advantages that would be lost were abolition somehow made possible. First, guilty pleas deliver comparatively speedy resolution of criminal cases. For a multitude of reasons, criminal trials are complex, time-consuming, and resource intensive. While far from perfect, they provide what constitutes Anglo-American law's best approximation of a fair opportunity to establish some sort of objective factual and moral "ground truth," arrived at in that messy sausage-factory way. Trials are not always pretty to observe, but they do allow relatively wide participation from people with varying vantage points, including prosecutors and defense attorneys, judges, victims, witnesses, scientific experts, and jurors drawn from the community in which the alleged criminal offenses occurred. Criminal trials are undoubtedly the premier events in our criminal legal system pantheon, but the features that make them so invaluable—live witnesses, cross-examination, neutral fact finders, subject matter experts, and adversarial process—are the very features that limit their broad availability. We have never lived in a world where such resources were routinely used to resolve the garden-variety criminal allegations that characterize the administration of a modern mass society, and we likely never will.

Voluntary guilty pleas, at least in theory, offer a much more efficient way to resolve criminal disputes while preserving the rights of the accused to individualized and fair outcomes. As such, they are viewed as a vital tool by prosecutors, the criminal defense bar, and judges alike. Guilty pleas, though, are not and should never be simply a mechanism to economize on the costs of criminal procedure. Guilty pleas also perform the important function of minimizing uncertainty. For prosecutors, such pleas help ensure that offenders receive the prompt punishment so central to effective deterrence and community safety. For defendants, a guilty plea offers some control over ultimate outcomes, helping well-counseled defendants manage risk and identify least-worst alternatives.

These functions make guilty pleas indispensable to the world we currently inhabit. If we didn't already have a system that permitted people to plead guilty, we would almost certainly have to invent it. At the same time, our current system of plea bargaining carries with it excesses that are obvious and seriously detrimental to the basic fairness of our criminal legal system. The widespread obsession with efficiency has resulted in the normalization of oppressive and coercive practices that treat the infliction of massive and life-destroying punishments on criminal defendants as little more than bureaucratic routine. These ruinous punishments are often imposed in the absence of basic safety measures designed to prevent legal accidents from inflicting harm on innocent persons. Such an absence of safety measures would be considered gross negligence in other regulatory fields and reflects a basic failure of respect for the humanity of the people on the receiving end of the criminal legal system. The critical project facing reformers of our guilty plea practices, therefore, is to figure out how to rein in the excesses and abuses without undermining the core benefits of the system as it has evolved. Formalizing plea procedures could well provide the mechanism to make this possible.

Formalization as I envision it would encompass several critical components. I will provide a brief summary of the elements of formalization here and then later in the chapter explore each idea more fully. First, bargaining would be removed from back hallways and courthouse lobbies and returned to where the resolution of significant legal accusations belongs: the courtroom. What this means, in practical terms, is that plea offers would take on the characteristics of legal instruments that serve similar functions in the trial process. Most importantly, plea offers should always be in writing, and they should always be filed in court. Second, the consequences of accepting, or declining, a plea offer should be transparent. Defendants need to understand, at minimum, what the maximum sentence is if they accept or decline the offer. (It would be better yet if defendants understood the actual sentence that would be imposed if they agreed to enter a guilty plea, and if they retained the ability to withdraw their plea if the sentence imposed by the court varied materially from what they were led to expect.)

Formalization of the plea process also necessarily means regulating the conditions under which decisions to plead guilty are made. There is no justification for forcing defendants to make high-pressure decisions to accept or reject exploding plea offers or preventing them from obtaining thoughtful, well-considered counsel from their lawyers and their loved ones before making decisions on which years or decades of their freedom may hinge. The amount of time that defendants have to consider whether or not to plead guilty must be standardized.

Of critical importance, the range of penalties must be limited by law. As legal scholar Darryl Brown has noted, prosecutors have increasingly "recognized that the power to dictate enhanced post-trial sentences through charging decisions" has given them "enormous leverage in convincing defendants to plead guilty."[2] Prosecutors simply cannot be allowed to continue to exercise unfettered discretion over the size of the trial penalty and thereby ensure that they can compel just about any defendant to plead guilty in just about every case.

The contents and terms of guilty pleas should also be standardized, particularly with respect to the rights that defendants are asked to waive. The range of rights currently thought to be "fair game" for bargaining runs the gamut. Plea formalization would put an end to this variance by standardizing terms of plea agreements. Some waivers are appropriate and, indeed, inherent in the entry of a guilty plea (e.g., when one pleads guilty, one necessarily waives the right to trial, the right to cross-examine witnesses,

---

2. Darryl K. Brown, *How to Make Criminal Trials Disappear without Pretrial Discovery*, 55 AM. CRIM. L. REV. 155, 194 (2018).

etc.); some are arguably sufficiently advantageous to the goals of the State that they should be treated as standard even if not absolutely necessitated by the plea process (e.g., the right to appeal pretrial rulings); and some may be the proper subject of bargaining. But there is simply no justification for the anarchic scrum that constitutes contemporary waiver practice.

Finally, certain types of commonly used pleas should be banned, particularly those most likely to coerce innocent defendants to plead guilty. The two most common of those are guilty pleas to avoid death sentences and guilty pleas that reward pleaders with immediate release from jail. Death sentences and administrative tools such as pretrial detention should not be available to induce defendants to waive their trial rights.[3]

That is a quick overview. The next part of the chapter will dive deeper into some of the complexities that formalization would entail.

The Nitty-Gritty of Formalization

Formalization of the plea process might seem relatively simple in the abstract, but once one turns to the concrete implications of formalization, difficult issues quickly emerge. In this section, I take a closer look at some of these complexities.[4]

Writing Requirement

The critical first step in any effort to formalize the plea process is to transform it from a predominantly oral tradition into a written practice. Anglo-American law has from time immemorial placed a writing requirement at the center of its formal charging procedures. As English jurist Sir James Fitzjames Stephen explained:

> The indictment is the foundation of the record in all criminal cases, and is indeed the only document connected with the trial which in all cases is in writing. It is in the form of a statement upon oath by the grand jury that the prisoner committed the offence with which he is charged. This assertion in former times went a long way (as I have already shown), to his conviction . . . I cannot say when it was first enacted that indictments should be in writing. It is said . . . that a statute to that effect was passed under Edward I., but however this may be, I think it is clear that the form of indictments, and the extreme strictness

3. Other types of highly dubious pleas include "linked" pleas, in which one defendant agrees to plead guilty in exchange for an agreement not to prosecute another person—often a family member or loved one—and group pleas, in which the offer made to one defendant is contingent on other defendants also agreeing to plead guilty. Consideration of such pleas is beyond the scope of this chapter. *But see* ALI Model Code of Pre-Arraignment Proc. § 350.3 commentary at 616–17 (1975) (noting unanimous rejection by ALI Council of recommendation to forbid plea bargains containing third-party benefits) (cited in United States v. Marquez, 909 F.2d 738, 742 (2d Cir. 1990)) (discussing numerous cases involving third-party beneficiaries; defendant pleaded guilty to avoid prosecution of wife).

4. Among the most challenging concerns are the costs and benefits of limiting the discretion of various legal actors. The principal players in the criminal legal system—legislators, judges, criminal defense attorneys, and prosecutors most of all—are deeply invested in the power and accompanying benefits that their discretionary authority provides. Getting sufficient buy-in poses even greater hurdles in the plea context than is typical of most proposed reforms to the criminal legal system.

> with which rules respecting them have been observed, were derived principally from the laws relating to appeals. . . .
>
> [I]n all common cases the pleadings in a criminal trial have always consisted, and still consist, of an indictment engrossed on parchment, and a plea given by the accused person orally in open court, of guilty or not guilty.[5]

In contrast to charging by indictment (or information or complaint), the haphazard practice of plea bargaining—which is often carried out orally and, in more recent times, also by phone, text message, and email—lacks this traditional rigor. And yet, a plea agreement is as much a solemn instrument of accusation as an indictment. Indeed, the plea offer—a statement of charges and terms made by a state official authorized to resolve criminal accusations on behalf of the government—is at least as significant as, if not more significant than, the indictment, information, or complaint itself. There is no logical reason that a plea offer should receive any less formal treatment than a traditional indictment. Moreover, as will be discussed later, the substantive aims of plea reform, including diminishing its fundamentally coercive form, would be greatly advanced by memorializing plea offers in ways that create binding obligations on the State.

What might a writing requirement look like in practice? Currently, plea negotiations are typically carried out in an informal, on-the-fly fashion. Not always, mind you. In some cases, especially federal white-collar investigations in which potential targets are well represented or in which the stakes are high and a significant expenditure of investigatory resources has been made, plea negotiations may proceed in a more measured fashion. But these types of negotiations are the rare exception. In typical cases, the bargaining process is quick, casual, and expeditious.

Imagine instead a world in which plea offers were not negotiated in hallways but were filed in court. Such filing would provide notice to the defendant and the court of the terms on which the State is prepared to resolve the charges. It would also trigger a clock that would both protect and limit the time a defendant has to consider an offer—perhaps 14 days. This would ensure that the defendant had an opportunity to consult with family and counsel. It would provide counsel an opportunity to review discovery, interview witnesses, and research the law. A uniform 14-day clock would contrast sharply with the variable bargaining practices followed in different jurisdictions around the country, which sometimes include routine use of so-called exploding plea offers that require defendants to accept within hours or minutes a deal on which years or decades of imprisonment might turn.

Although a written filing requirement would not prevent defense counsel from making a counteroffer, any counteroffer that the prosecutor agreed to would still need to be filed in court by the prosecutor. Filing would signify the State's willingness to settle

---

5. Sir James Fitzjames Stephen, A History of the Criminal Law of England (1883). Sir Stephen continues:

> The requisites of an indictment at common law differed hardly at all from the earliest times till our own, indeed the only statutes which much affected them up to the year 1827 were what was called the Statute of Additions (1 Hen. 5, c. 5), which provided that the names of the defendants should be followed by a statement of "their estate or degree or mystery, and of the towns, hamlets, or place, and counties, in which they were," and the 4 Geo. 2, c. 26, which enacted that all indictments should be in English. Subject to these alterations an indictment under George IV. was what an indictment under Edward III., and probably under Edward I., had been.

the case on the terms of the offer. Importantly, however, the presentation of a counteroffer would not be binding on the defendant. To preserve the core purposes of formalization, it is necessary to place the onus on the State to identify the terms on which it is amenable to resolving the case—while still preserving the defendant's ability to accept or reject those terms without risk. The aims of formalization would be defeated if reforms simply shifted the onus of proposing actionable offers from the prosecution to the defense.

Preplea Sentencing Hearings

In addition to requiring that plea offers be memorialized in writing and filed in court, plea bargaining reformers must take steps to dissipate the fog of uncertainty that surrounds current plea sentencing practices. A variety of ideas have been floated by plea bargaining scholars over the years, but the gist of those ideas has remained constant. To make informed and rational plea decisions, defendants need to know the consequences of taking a plea, and they need to know the consequences of declining to do so. As it now stands, in most cases defendants are forced to make plea decisions without either piece of information. They may be aware of the maximum penalty possible as a result of a plea or a trial, but in most instances, because of extremely punitive statutory sentencing provisions, actual sentences will fall well below the statutory maximums. In some cases, authorized sentences may cover a vast range—from probation to 30 years or more. In other cases, sentencing guidelines might constrain the ability of the court to sentence anywhere along the authorized range but nonetheless still create sentencing uncertainty. This uncertainty stems from the impact of various sentencing factors and the ability of sentencing courts to depart from guideline sentences for a wide variety of reasons. Criminal defendants simply cannot make voluntary and intelligent plea decisions—as the Constitution requires—without a concrete understanding of the consequences of those decisions.

This problem, however, can be solved with remarkably little cost simply by shifting the timing of sentencing hearings from post- to preconviction. While at first blush this might sound extravagant—a sentencing hearing even for defendants who are ultimately acquitted at trial!—the reality is that pretrial sentencing hearings would impose very little additional burden. After all, upwards of 95 percent of all criminal convictions are secured by guilty plea. In all such cases, sentencing hearings are required. Of the remaining 5 or so percent of cases that do proceed to trial, conviction rates tend to hover around 80 percent. Moving the sentencing hearing to the pretrial process thus would, in reality, require an extra sentencing hearing in approximately 1 percent of total cases. The benefits of making sentencing information available to defendants before they must make crucial procedural decisions, meanwhile, would flow to 100 percent of defendants. Moreover, challenges to sentencing decisions could be delayed until post-conviction appeals, further diminishing the costs of conducting earlier sentencing proceedings.

One adjustment to the typical sentencing process would be required. As the plea bargaining scholar Albert Alschuler noted when he discussed a similar proposal many decades ago, the probation officer responsible for preparation of the sentencing memorandum should not interview a defendant prior to conviction, which otherwise might put in jeopardy the defendant's Fifth Amendment right to be free of compelled self-incrimination.[6] While the costs of shifting sentencing hearings to an earlier point in the process are minor, this change would provide significant advantages. The main benefit of conducting pretrial sentencing hearings is that by fixing the consequences of both a guilty plea and a trial conviction ahead of time, a mechanism would be created to effectively control the trial penalty. While there are other mechanisms available to limit the trial penalty, such as capping post-trial sentences at or modestly above any plea sentence offer, enforcing such caps is difficult and leaves substantial room for punitive sentencing practices. By establishing the parameters of both plea sentences and trial sentences up front, pretrial sentencing hearings would allow jurisdictions to set firm boundaries on the differential that is permitted between plea and trial sentences.

Pretrial sentencing hearings would have the added advantage of educating judges about the cases on their dockets. This information might empower judges to play a more active role in the resolution of charges, rather than sidelining them as current practices do until after proceedings have essentially concluded.

Subjecting the Trial Penalty to Legal Regulation

Professor John Langbein once famously compared modern plea practices, and in particular the trial penalty, to the medieval use of torture.[7] Confessions that once were secured by rack and screw are now even more efficiently obtained by terrible threats of increased punishment on any defendant foolish enough to demand their trial rights. This cannot continue to be allowed. Just as medieval methods of torture were subjected to—and displaced by—legal regulation, so too should the modern-day equivalent. Each and every jurisdiction needs to begin a serious conversation about what an acceptable sentencing differential might look like in an effort to identify the critical point at which a sentencing differential morphs from a reasonable acknowledgment of a defendant's acceptance of responsibility into a coercive tool to extract a confession.

I note here that there was widespread agreement (although perhaps not unanimity) among members of the task force that some sentencing differential was acceptable. Indeed, it strikes me that this concession is inescapable. This is true because, all things being equal, a defendant rationally should always prefer a trial to a guilty plea on the ground that the chance of acquittal—no matter how small—makes trial a marginally better bet than taking a plea if the plea will result in the same punishment (but will relinquish the chance of acquittal). A system of plea bargaining is not rational unless there is some benefit to both parties for using it. Prosecutors benefit from guilty pleas by minimizing their resource costs and by ensuring that the people they charge will receive some guaranteed punishment. While resource savings are a real consideration in cases where defendants pay a lawyer to represent them, the vast majority (usually estimated at around 80 percent) of criminal defendants are indigent and therefore do not pay out of pocket for their defense. These defendants gain nothing if their state-appointed lawyers find ways to minimize their resource costs. Under our current practice, the system makes it worth their while to agree to a guilty plea because of the "plea discount" they

6. Albert W. Alschuler, *The Trial Judge's Role in Plea Bargaining, Part I*, 76 Colum. L. Rev. 1059, 1146 (1976).

7. John H. Langbein, *Torture and Plea Bargaining*, 46 U. Chi. L. Rev. 3 (1978).

receive for agreeing to lighten the State's load. This discount appears necessary to any system of plea bargaining since it would otherwise be irrational for a defendant to give up the valuable chance of acquittal by voluntarily entering a guilty plea.

This logic counsels for a modest differential—one that compensates defendants who agree to plead guilty but that doesn't make the alternative of proceeding to trial so onerous that it undermines the defendant's rational ability to exercise their trial right. The incentive system that currently exists, in contrast, prevents most defendants from making a rational choice at all. When faced with the threat of prison rather than probation, or extra years—and often decades—of prison time after trial, defendants accurately perceive their right to trial as a meaningless fiction.

And the current system is even worse than it seems. While many innocent defendants may be coerced into taking a plea simply to avoid a worst-case scenario, some innocent defendants—rightly believing that pleading guilty to something they did not do would be a manifest injustice—refuse the deal (even if taking such a deal is the "rational" thing to do) and go to trial. Those that do and lose then face a double whammy: not only are they wrongfully convicted, but they are also punished far more harshly because of the trial penalty than those who are actually guilty and who took the pleas offered them.

In justifying the current extreme sentencing differentials that characterize modern plea practice, it is asserted that those who get slammed with harsh trial penalties at least had a choice, but that assumption is also not always true. If prosecutors don't offer a deal, then under our current system there is often no benefit in pleading guilty. Such defendants thus may have no real alternative but to go to trial, not because they are innocent or because they especially want to have their day in court, but rather because simply entering an open plea in exchange for nothing is even worse. These defendants may be selected for trial by prosecutors not because the cases are close, the evidence is weak, or questions of culpability are most in need of careful scrutiny by a fact finder but for just the opposite reasons. The evidence is rock solid, the culpability of the defendant is crystal clear, and there is simply no chance that a jury will acquit. The prosecutor loves to (occasionally) try such cases because the prosecutor is certain to win, which helps prop up their "batting average." But the unlucky defendants singled out for such pro forma trials nonetheless suffer the almost certain fate of the enhanced penalties that follow conviction at trial. In a criminal legal system where more than 90 percent of all cases are resolved through guilty pleas, the handful of cases that do go to trial are therefore made up in some substantial part of innocent defendants who buck rationality to demand a trial and patently guilty defendants who don't particularly want a trial but are given no reason to avoid one.

These are the dynamics that the current trial penalty system creates and that make legal regulation of the trial penalty imperative. The goals of trial penalty reform, therefore, are twofold. First, jurisdictions must identify a sentencing differential that is reasonable, that is, one that provides a modest incentive to defendants who know they are guilty and who are unlikely to prevail at trial to accept responsibility for their conduct. Second, jurisdictions must develop reliable mechanisms to enforce it. The proposals to require that plea offers be in writing and filed with the court, and that judges determine plea and sentence outcomes prior to trial, are intended to address the latter. As to the former, the differential chosen should be small enough to prompt defendants whose cases are close to exercise their constitutionally guaranteed trial right. A discount of approximately 33 percent has been accepted by many thoughtful policymakers as a reasonable differential. Such a discount is employed in England and Wales.[8] It is also the approximate discount awarded under the U.S. Sentencing Guidelines for acceptance of responsibility. Whether or not 33 percent is the "right" discount, however, is a matter that can be resolved only through experience. Practicality might demand a somewhat larger differential—perhaps 50 percent—if a 33 percent discount induces so few guilty pleas that the trial system is thrown into crisis. Practicality also might admit a smaller discount if current preferences for resolving cases by plea persist. In any event, the differential chosen must be small enough to encourage more defendants to contest their cases in court and thereby reverse the trend of the vanishing trial. In addition, the availability of the discount should not hinge on the discretion of the prosecutor. It should be available in all cases to ensure that trials are reserved only for cases in which guilt is truly contested.

Implementation of these goals is made marginally easier by the fact that the impacts can be readily measured. Successful reform of the trial penalty would result in a smaller percentage of criminal convictions from guilty pleas and a larger number of trials. Improvement in the selection of cases for trial would result in more closely contested cases that go to trial, and thus we should expect a higher overall acquittal rate. More trials, and more acquittals, would be the mark of a healthier criminal legal system and should be the target of reform efforts.

Standardization of Plea Agreements and Waivers

A standard feature of today's lawless plea bargaining system is the absence of any restrictions on what prosecutors can demand in exchange for guilty pleas. Terms vary from jurisdiction to jurisdiction and often from defendant to defendant. There is not yet any national consensus on the types of rights that a defendant may properly be required to waive to obtain the benefits of a plea bargain. Examples of aggressive demands are legion. Defendants are regularly asked to waive their rights to appeal, to seek collateral review, to challenge the ineffective assistance of their own lawyers, to forgo discovery, or to raise issues regarding the State's unconstitutional conduct, including its failure to produce exculpatory Brady material. They often must waive their right to appeal a sentence, even if the sentencing court clearly erred. The list goes on. The rights sought to be waived vary markedly from jurisdiction to jurisdiction. Waivers held valid in some places have been held to violate constitutional rights or ethical rules in others. The U.S. Department of Justice under President Biden only recently agreed to end the practice of demanding that defendants relinquish their right to seek compassionate release as a price of a bargain.[9]

---

8. *See* Brian D. Johnson, *Trials and Tribulations: The Trial Tax and the Process of Punishment*, 48 Crime & Just. 313, 323 (2019) (noting that England and Wales have enacted a "standard 33 percent sentence plea discount").

9. *See* Carrie Johnson, *Justice Department Ends Limiting Compassionate Release in Plea Deals after NPR Story*, NPR (Mar. 11, 2022), https://www.npr.org/2022/03/11/1086140965/justice-department-ends-limiting-compassionate-release-in-plea-deals-after-npr-s.

Practices also vary regarding the consequences of litigating a case. In some jurisdictions, defendants who fail to enter an early plea might, as a matter of office policy, face harsher charges as a consequence. This was the practice in at least one prosecutor's office in California. As discussed in a case called *Riggs v. Fairman*,[10] the Riverside County district attorney's office treated potential Three Strikes cases differently for plea bargaining purposes than it treated all other cases. In potential Three Strikes cases, the office's pre–preliminary hearing plea offers "typically were the best offers ever to be made to the defendant."[11] In cases where the initial offer was declined, the office often "added into a superseding information charges that had not been alleged in the original complaint."[12] In effect, if a defendant had the temerity to decline a plea offer prior to the preliminary hearing, not only would that offer be gone forever, but also a new indictment containing potentially dramatically enhanced charges might be filed. This is precisely what happened to Michael Riggs, who was charged with petty theft after stealing a bottle of vitamins. Riggs's lawyer failed to appreciate the potential Three Strikes liability that his client faced and therefore advised him to decline the five-year offer that had been extended. Prosecutors then filed a superseding information charging Riggs as a Three Strikes offender, which increased the sentence he faced upon conviction to 25 years to life, and refused to reinstate the earlier plea offer. Riggs went to trial and received the 25-years-to-life sentence.[13]

The Riggs case helpfully illustrates that guilt or innocence is not the only matter at issue in plea bargaining. Riggs had little hope of winning at trial—there was security footage of him taking the vitamins. But he might have rightfully disagreed with the prosecutor that this conduct deserved a five-year prison sentence. No doubt his refusal of the offer was motivated by a desire to negotiate a less onerous sentence or to allow the trial court to make a more favorable sentencing decision.[14] The prosecutors' superseding information charging a harsh mandatory minimum sentence short-circuited that logic.

The bargaining practices of the Riverside DA are far from unusual.[15] In many offices, plea offers get worse if the defendant refuses to plead guilty at arraignment or files motions for discovery or seeks to suppress evidence. These practices effectively penalize defendants and their lawyers for investigating the facts and the law in their

10. Riggs v. Fairman, 399 F.3d 1179 (9th Cir. 2005).

11. *Id.* at 1191 (Bea, J., dissenting).

12. Riggs v. Fairman, 178 F. Supp. 2d 1141, 1144–45 (C.D. Cal. 2001), *aff'd*, 399 F.3d 1179 (9th Cir. 2005).

13. Ultimately, Riggs's conviction and sentence were vacated after a successful habeas petition based on ineffective assistance of counsel and further litigation regarding the appropriate remedy. *See* Riggs v. Fairman, 399 F.3d 1179, 1181 (9th Cir. 2005).

14. Riggs's trial lawyer failed to properly counsel him about his exposure to a Three Strikes charge, which courts subsequently found to constitute constitutionally ineffective assistance of counsel in violation of the Sixth Amendment. *See id.* at 1183.

15. Indeed, the Arizona ACLU has filed suit against the Maricopa County DA because of the routine use of such tactics in the Maricopa County Early Disposition Courts. As the ACLU has explained, Maricopa County "prosecutors have an explicit policy of threatening a 'substantially harsher' plea offer unless people give up their right to a trial or a preliminary hearing." As a result of this policy, defendants, "including those who may be innocent, are coerced into pleading guilty before a judge even has the chance to determine if prosecutors have sufficient evidence to continue going after someone." *Luckey v. Adel*, ACLU (July 7, 2021), https://www.acluaz.org/en/cases/luckey-v-adel.

cases and for making considered strategic decisions based on a full understanding of their legal situation. And in cases like Riggs's, they also prevent defendants from even engaging in an honest discussion about appropriate consequences or calling in a judge to adjudicate the dispute in a neutral manner.

Plea offers sometimes contain incentives of dubious merit. Deals might include promises to withhold prosecution of a family member if the defendant pleads guilty. Codefendants might be informed that they all must agree to plead guilty or no one gets a deal, even if some members of the group may have stronger legal defenses than others. There is significant evidence that plea deals that require cooperation are particularly problematic. While inducements to avoid charges may be a useful—and perhaps invaluable—tool for prosecutors in some otherwise unsolvable cases, they also provide dangerous incentives to some people to falsely accuse others to obtain the benefits of a bargain. The National Registry of Exonerations is replete with innocent individuals who were convicted based on false accusations brought by individuals promised leniency (or no prosecution at all) if they testified against others at trial.[16]

Whether or not some or all of these various practices should be allowed is beyond the scope of this chapter. At minimum, however, each of these practices should be the subject of careful scrutiny by the relevant legal actors in each jurisdiction. Ideally, a consensus would develop regarding the propriety of some of these practices, the rejection of others, and the parameters that should constrain them. The legal community needs to make reasoned decisions about which rights are subject to waiver as part of a plea deal and which should be nonwaivable. Whether a plea offer should get worse over time or based on efforts to litigate a case is a hard question. But certainly, the consequences of investigating and litigating a case should not vary on a case-by-case basis. Legal regulation is needed to ensure uniform treatment of all defendants and to protect the basic function of the criminal legal system to make accurate and morally justifiable factual and legal findings. Finally, policymakers need to revisit the formal and informal ways that a system of discretionary charging and plea bargaining can be used to induce cooperation. Protections are needed to safeguard innocent people from false accusations, and limits on the type of rewards that prosecutors can bestow on cooperators are essential to prevent cooperation bargaining from providing an end run around limitations on the trial penalty.

Ending Inherently Coercive Plea Bargaining Tactics: Time-Served and Death-Avoidance Pleas

There is one last topic I wish to explore in this chapter: the use of two inherently coercive tactics to induce guilty pleas. The tactics are as common as they are controversial. The first is the use of the time-served plea. There are many features of the plea

16. Barry Williams's case provides an illustrative example. Williams was wrongfully convicted of murder in part based on the false testimony of an alleged eyewitness. The eyewitness, who was facing robbery charges in his own case, testified against Williams to escape the robbery charge. The witness, John Gardner, eventually recanted his trial testimony. In his recantation, he said that another man committed the crime and explained that the prosecutor "basically told me that either Barry was going to do time for the murder or I was going to do time for the robbery." The prosecutor and his trial team then coached Gardner on what to say on the witness stand. Nat'l Registry of Exonerations, *Barry Williams* (Apr. 22, 2021), https://www.law.umich.edu/special/exoneration/Pages/casedetail.aspx?caseid=5946.

bargaining system that are designed to put pressure on defendants to relinquish their right to trial, but few are as effective as the time-served plea. Time-served pleas take advantage of the universal human desire to minimize immediate pain and reduce or eliminate uncertainty. They ask a currently incarcerated individual to trade their right to contest charges for immediate release. Such offers are almost always irresistible. After all, where the choice is freedom now versus remaining locked up for weeks or months until a trial, with no guarantee of victory, even a defendant's knowledge of their innocence may not be powerful enough to overcome the promise of immediate release. A guilty plea under such conditions should clearly be viewed as involuntary. It has no independent value as a marker of acceptance of responsibility or of the legal or factual accuracy of the conviction. More than anything, time-served pleas suggest that pretrial detention is being used to exert coercive pressure on defendants to plead guilty. The authorized purposes of pretrial detention are to ensure that a defendant appears at trial and to protect the community from persons deemed to be too dangerous to release. The prosecutor's offer of a time-served plea directly negates the latter rationale, indicating the prosecutor's acknowledgment that the defendant does not, in fact, represent a threat to the community. Admittedly, a time-served offer is logically consistent with the former justification—after all, if pretrial detention is justified by a rational fear that the defendant would fail to appear for trial, the waiver of trial (and agreement to plead guilty) eliminates that continued need. But it is simply too easy, and too convenient, to rationalize time-served pleas on this basis.

Indeed, the fact that a prosecutor is willing to release a defendant in a criminal case based on a guilty plea and a time-served sentence suggests that pretrial detention is being used as a de facto punishment rather than a procedural safeguard. It indicates that the prosecutor deems the defendant's pretrial detention an adequate punishment, and the interests of justice satisfied, with no need for further judicially imposed sanctions. And if the point of the exercise was not to impose any additional punishment on the defendant but rather merely to get a formal entry of conviction on the defendant's permanent criminal record, there was never much need for pretrial detention to ensure this outcome. If the defendant had failed to appear at trial, then at minimum a warrant would have been issued that would serve substantially the same purpose in terms of establishing a defendant's criminal record. Depending on the law of the jurisdiction, a conviction might also be obtained via trial in absentia or through default judgment. In any event, the criminal record–keeping function of conviction would be similarly satisfied.

One of the most innovative proposals to emerge from the task force's deliberations, therefore, is the recommendation that in cases in which the prosecutor is prepared to offer a time-served plea offer, pretrial detention should cease.[17] Given that pretrial detention is an inappropriate source of bargaining leverage and that its use for this purpose exceeds the narrow grounds that otherwise exempt pretrial detention from the due process requirements inherent to a system of justice founded on the presumption of innocence, such limitations make perfect sense. As the task force recommendations reflect, all jurisdictions should adopt a "release-first" bargaining policy. That is, if the state is prepared to make a time-served plea offer, or indeed any offer that doesn't

17. ABA Crim. Just. Section, 2023 Plea Bargain Task Force Report 12, https://www.americanbar.org/content/dam/aba/publications/criminaljustice/plea-bargain-tf-report.pdf.

anticipate continued incarceration or detention, the making of the offer itself should trigger release. Only then might a defendant be able to fairly assess the advisability of waiving the right to contest the charges.

The second inherently coercive practice that needs to be ended is one that is common in death penalty states: using the threat of capital punishment to induce defendants in capital cases to plead guilty. The decision to seek and impose a death sentence is the most solemn matter that our legal system imposes on prosecutors, judges, and jurors. It is a wrenching determination that must be based on the totality of the facts and circumstances, and it can be made only after the fact finder has considered all the mitigating evidence that a defendant can adduce. While the aggravating factors (if any) that counsel for imposition of a capital sentence are contestable, there is no doubt that refusal to plead guilty should not be one of them.

The threat of a death sentence is exceedingly coercive, and desperation triggered by the prosecutor's threat to seek a death sentence is a notorious cause of wrongful guilty pleas. The National Registry of Exonerations contains dozens of accounts of innocent individuals who pleaded guilty to avoid a threatened death sentence. These individuals won exonerations only after years of wrongful imprisonment, and only because they were lucky enough to discover new evidence that clearly established their innocence. Many more innocent defendants no doubt have spent decades in prison without any prospect of exoneration simply because no new evidence happened to turn up.

It may be convenient and economical for states to use the death penalty to induce capital defendants to plead guilty. Capital trials are expensive and resource intensive. But the threat of a death sentence is as close to a literal "gun to the head" type of bargaining tactic as can be imagined. Not all capital defendants who are offered a guilty plea to avoid a death sentence are guilty. The tactic sweeps up innocent and guilty alike in its overbearing power. Moreover, in cases where prosecutors have made a plea offer that takes a death sentence off the table in exchange for a guilty plea, prosecutors have already signaled a belief that justice can be done with a sentence less than death.

Finally, there are considerations of community participation in the decision-making process that deserve some weight. It would not be correct to say that capital punishment decisions are the lone province of the jury. Plainly the discretion to pursue a capital charge is the prosecutor's in the first instance. But the decision should be subject to review—both administrative and judicial—and never solely the product of one person's unquestioned impulse. Indeed, capital punishment procedures incorporate a penalty phase to ensure that there is unanimous support from a jury. Using death sentences as a bargaining chip at the margins deprives a representative jury of its constitutional function to weigh aggravating and mitigating circumstances and undertake the moral dialogue central to such grave moral choices. For this reason too, decisions to seek a death sentence should be completely decoupled from a defendant's insistence on exercising their right to trial or willingness to enter a guilty plea.

In contemplating how these arrangements could be practically implemented, we are brought back to the first requirement of plea formalization. All offers must be in writing and filed in the trial court prior to any guilty plea proceeding, with enough advance warning to ensure that a defendant has time to consult with friends, family, and an attorney and make a truly voluntary decision about whether to enter a plea, knowing the concrete consequences of accepting the plea and the worst-case consequences of declining the plea and going to trial. For defendants who are being held in pretrial detention, an offer that includes immediate release would itself trigger release. For defendants charged with a capital offense, an offer that would take the death penalty off the table would trigger the dismissal of the capital charge.

There will always be pressure to look for ways around more stringent bargaining limits, perhaps through the development of tacit norms such that prosecutors would make plea offers only after defense counsel, or a defendant, signals agreement to plead guilty on the offered terms. Defeating such end runs will require vigilance, a creative spirit, and a commitment by all stakeholders in the system to abide by new norms. Safeguards would need to be in place to protect defendants' right to decline to plead guilty in such cases. To prevent the development of back-channel bargaining, courts might need to get involved. Perhaps some fraction—say 10 percent—of proposed plea cases should be channeled to trial by the judge regardless of a defendant's preference for a plea. Such a mechanism might weaken the development of expectations about the consequences of plea offers as a matter of course.

Although this chapter began with an explanation of why voluntary guilty pleas remain essential to our criminal legal system, what I am proposing here would, in a quite powerful sense, fundamentally alter—and some might say end—the practice of plea bargaining. After all, if sentencing differentials are limited, if time-served offers can't be used to extract guilty pleas, if the trial penalty is truly abolished, what is left to bargain about? Indeed, that is precisely the point. Plea "bargaining" is, almost by definition, dispute resolution without law. By formalizing the process by which the terms of guilty pleas are fixed, we would fundamentally reset the system's objectives. In such a world, the decision confronting prosecutors would not be "What offer can I make that would make this case go away?" but rather "What outcome in this case would satisfy the dictates of justice?"

There would be other collateral benefits of such a change. A fixed trial penalty/plea discount would select cases for trial on the correct basis: those cases where the prosecution's evidence is weakest, or the defendant's chances of acquittal are greatest, would be the ones most likely to go to trial. The slam-dunk cases would almost always be resolved by plea, since the defendant would know there would be virtually no shot at acquittal and the benefits of even a modest plea discount would be clear. Knowing that defendants would be inclined to go to trial if they had reason to believe that the prosecutor's case was weak, prosecutors might feel compelled to do a better job of screening cases up front. With more cases going to trial, all parties might feel obligated to more thoroughly research the facts and the law, since they would know that the odds that their case might be put to the test have increased. Standardized waiver provisions would help protect the integrity of the trial process by ensuring that essential procedural rights that protect innocent defendants and ensure a fundamentally fair process are not transformed into bargaining chips. Certainly, and if nothing else, requiring all plea offers to be in writing and filed in court would dramatically enhance our understanding of guilty plea practices, providing a deep well of data that could be used to increase our understanding of the day-to-day workings of the criminal legal system that, for better or worse, constitutes the criminal justice system we actually have.

CHAPTER 10

Three Cures for Coercive Plea Bargaining

Clark Neily

The Bill of Rights devotes more words to the procedure for resolving criminal charges than any other subject, and for good reason. The Founders understood perfectly well that of all government powers, the one most likely to be abused is the enforcement of criminal law. And they recognized that the potential for abuse is exacerbated by the fact that the government wears two hats in the context of a criminal prosecution: accuser and adjudicator. This explains their decision to put ordinary citizens at the very heart of the criminal justice system and to imbue that system with a strong preference for false acquittals over false convictions, famously expressed in the maxim that it is "better that ten guilty persons escape, than that one innocent suffer."[1] For this reason, the Task Force Report starts with a principle dedicated to the revival of the jury trial. Indeed, Principle 1 reads: "A vibrant and active docket of criminal trials and pre- and post-trial litigation is essential to promote transparency, accountability, justice and legitimacy in the criminal justice system." As this chapter will explore, reviving the jury trial requires combating the impermissible coercion during plea bargaining that regularly discourages defendants from exercising their right to trial. This chapter lays out achievable and practical reforms that can do just that.

There is perhaps no greater affront to the foundational principles of the adversarial adjudicative process than modern plea bargaining, which stands for the proposition that there is an alternative mechanism for resolving criminal charges that is quicker, easier, and far less expensive than the one prescribed by the Constitution, yet equally reliable and free from any major problems or pathologies. Unfortunately, this is false. The truth is that inducing people to condemn themselves—particularly in mass numbers—is an inherently illiberal practice that inevitably employs coercion to ensure that those who operate the machinery of confession can deliver the numbers expected of them. Thus, despite recognizing that "it is critical that the moral force of the criminal law not be diluted by a standard of proof that leaves people in doubt about whether innocent men

1. 4 William Blackstone, Commentaries *352.

are being condemned,"[2] the Supreme Court has upheld a variety of palpably coercive plea practices—including threatening recalcitrant defendants with life in prison or even the death penalty—while lower courts have embraced such appalling tactics as threatening to indict a defendant's family members in order to exert plea leverage.[3]

As shocking as those practices may seem to the uninitiated, they are inevitable in a system that depends on the vast majority of defendants to commit the fundamentally irrational act of exchanging the possibility of acquittal and freedom for the certainty of conviction and punishment. But more than a century of plea practice in this country demonstrates that nearly anyone can be induced to relinquish a thing of value—including the constitutional right to a jury trial—if the cost of refusing is high enough. That is the iron law of American-style plea bargaining, and it is starkly reflected in the fact that in 2021, 98.3 percent of all federal convictions were obtained through guilty pleas.[4] And while the precise amount of coercion in the plea process is debatable, its presence is not. As the report notes in Principle 5, there is indisputable evidence that innocent people regularly plead guilty to crimes they did not commit, and there is good reason to believe that those cases represent merely the tip of the false-plea iceberg.[5] The report makes clear that in order to reform modern plea practice, we must recognize that "in the current system, innocent people sometimes plead guilty to crimes they did not commit."[6]

The incontrovertible reality of false pleas stands in sharp contrast to the Supreme Court's recognition that it is "important in our free society that every individual going about his ordinary affairs have confidence that his government cannot adjudge him guilty of a criminal offense without convincing a proper factfinder of his guilt with the utmost certainty."[7] But persistent indifference to the use of coercion to induce guilty pleas renders this sentiment more aspirational than descriptive of the current criminal justice system. Fortunately, however, as with so many of the system's pathologies, the primary obstacles to change are complacency and a lack of commitment to constitutional values, both of which can be overcome.

The specific reforms proposed next reflect three basic insights about plea bargaining. First, plea bargaining is here to stay, so the focus should be on improving rather than trying to eliminate it; second, when a decision is made to abandon established safety protocols like the criminal-adjudication procedures set forth in the Bill of Rights, the risk of doing so should be borne by all involved rather than just the defendant; and third, designing a truly fair plea process requires stepping behind the "veil of ignorance" to ensure a result that could be rationally chosen by someone who does not know

2. *In re* Winship, 397 U.S. 358, 364 (1970).

3. *See, e.g.*, Bordenkircher v. Hayes, 434 U.S. 357 (1978) (threatening life sentence to induce plea); Brady v. United States, 397 U.S. 742 (1970) (capital punishment); United States v. Seng Chen Yong, 926 F.3d 582, 591 (9th Cir. 2019) (family members).

4. U.S. Sent'g Comm'n, Overview of Federal Criminal Cases 8 (Apr. 2022). Information regarding plea rates at the state level is less precise but similar. *See, e.g.*, Ram Subramanian et al., *In the Shadows: A Review of the Research on Plea Bargaining* 1, Vera Inst. of Just. (Sept. 2020), https://www.vera.org/downloads/publications/in-the-shadows-plea-bargaining.pdf.

5. *See, e.g.*, Jed S. Rakoff, *Why Innocent People Plead Guilty*, N.Y. Rev. Books, Nov. 20, 2014.

6. ABA Crim. Just. Section, 2023 Plea Bargain Task Force Report 10, https://www.americanbar.org/content/dam/aba/publications/criminaljustice/plea-bargain-tf-report.pdf.

7. *In re Winship*, 397 U.S. at 364.

whether they will encounter the system as a prosecutor, a defendant, or a victim. But first it makes sense to dispel any doubts about whether efforts to induce defendants to plead guilty ever cross the line from permissibly motivating to unconstitutionally coercive. They certainly do, and the judiciary's collective indifference to that fact can neither change nor legitimate it.

Although some coercion is inherent in any interaction between the State and a defendant, the task force was most concerned about excessive coercion that can overbear the will of a rational defendant to reject a plea and proceed to trial. Principles 2, 3, and 4 are all dedicated to acknowledging and rooting out this impermissible coercion. The most powerful evidence of such coercion is the fact that innocent people have been induced to plead guilty to crimes they did not commit. There is simply no plausible explanation for why that would happen other than the application by prosecutors of sufficient pressure to overcome the will of a rational defendant. Innocent people pleading guilty certainly represents a floor for what constitutes impermissible coercion, however difficult it may be to define that concept with any precision at other points along the spectrum between voluntary and involuntary.[8]

Of the 375 exonerations by DNA evidence to date, 44 (11.7 percent) were the result of convictions from false guilty pleas.[9] This is consistent with the National Registry of Exonerations, which reports that, among the registry's first 1,600 exonerations, 13 percent involved false guilty pleas.[10] Thus, there is abundant, undisputed evidence that defendants in the U.S. criminal justice system regularly plead guilty to crimes they did not commit.[11] And while it is difficult to estimate with any precision the total number of false guilty pleas, documented exonerations surely represent merely the tip of the false-plea iceberg because "innocent defendants who plead guilty have an exceptionally hard time convincing anybody of their innocence, or even getting a hearing. Judges, prosecutors, police officers, journalists, friends, lawyers, even innocence organizations are all less likely to believe in the innocence of a defendant who pleads guilty."[12]

The fact that innocent people plead guilty to crimes they did not commit is hardly surprising given the powerful levers that prosecutors can—and routinely do—bring to bear in seeking to induce what they refer to euphemistically as "cooperation." These potentially coercive levers fall into three broad categories: increasing the defendant's exposure to punishment if they go to trial and lose; making the defendant suffer for exercising their right to trial whether they win or lose; and increasing the defendant's chances of being convicted at trial by impairing their ability to mount a vigorous defense.

---

8. *See, e.g.*, Samantha Luna, *Defining Coercion: An Application in Interrogation and Plea Negotiation Contexts*, 28 PSYCH. PUB. POL'Y & L. 240 (2022) (noting the difficulty of defining "coercion" in the plea bargaining context and proposing a model).

9. Innocence Project, *DNA Exonerations in the United States (1989–2020)*, https://innocenceproject.org/dna-exonerations-in-the-united-states/ (last visited Feb. 16, 2024).

10. Nat'l Registry of Exonerations, *The First 1,600 Exonerations* 2 (2015), https://www.law.umich.edu/special/exoneration/Documents/1600_Exonerations.pdf (last visited Feb. 16, 2024).

11. *See, e.g.*, Rakoff, *supra* note 5.

12. Nat'l Registry of Exonerations, *Innocents Who Plead Guilty* 1 (Nov. 24, 2015), https://bit.ly/2VJrXRc.

Increased Exposure to Punishment

The most common mechanism for inducing guilty pleas is the so-called trial penalty, defined as "the substantial difference between the sentence offered prior to trial versus the sentence a defendant receives after a trial."[13] Trial penalties can be generated through a variety of techniques well known to prosecutors, including vertical and horizontal overcharging (that is, bringing a more serious charge than the conduct truly warrants or charging several different offenses for the same act); triggering mandatory minimum sentences, including by charging the defendant as a habitual offender or with the use of a firearm in conjunction with the base offense; bringing conspiracy charges against bit players in a group scheme so they have the same exposure as the kingpins; and threatening to seek a sentence on the basis of uncharged or even acquitted conduct, which, astonishing as it may seem, remains perfectly legal in the United States but apparently nowhere else.[14] And while it is impossible to quantify the magnitude of the trial penalty with precision, a 2018 report by the National Association of Criminal Defense Lawyers indicates that the average sentence imposed after a trial is more than three times longer than the average sentence arising from a guilty plea.[15]

But it would be a mistake to focus on the average amount of the trial penalty because all that conveys is a rough sense of the typical defendant's level of risk aversion. The relevant question isn't how much pressure prosecutors typically exert by threatening a longer sentence but how much pressure they can exert as they ratchet up the pressure to overcome the will of a recalcitrant defendant who refuses to plead guilty. And the answer to that question is clear: so long as they don't employ physical torture or otherwise break the law, there is no limit to the amount of pressure a prosecutor may bring to bear to induce a plea. Thus, the Supreme Court has found that threatening a defendant with the death penalty if he goes to trial was not unduly coercive,[16] nor was threatening a defendant with a life sentence if he refused a five-year plea offer.[17] And indeed massive differentials like these remain a common feature of the system, as reflected, for example, in the Varsity Blues college admissions investigation where prosecutors routinely made plea offers ranging from weeks to months while threatening to add conspiracy charges carrying 20 years or more against defendants who refused to "'take responsibility for their conduct early on.'"[18]

---

13. Nat'l Ass'n of Crim. Def. Laws., *The Trial Penalty: The Sixth Amendment Right to Trial on the Verge of Extinction and How to Save It* 11 (July 10, 2018), https://www.nacdl.org/Document/TrialPenaltySixthAmendmentRighttoTrialNearExtinct.

14. *See, e.g.*, Judge Nancy Gertner, *Why Innocent People Plead Guilty: An Exchange*, N.Y. Rev. Books (Jan. 8, 2015), https://www.nybooks.com/articles/2015/01/08/why-innocent-plead-guilty-exchange/ (noting that "[n]o other common law country in the world enables the prosecutor to seek a sentence based on criminal conduct never charged . . . or . . . for which a defendant was acquitted").

15. Nat'l Ass'n of Crim. Def. Laws., *supra* note 13, at 15.

16. Brady v. United States, 397 U.S. 742 (1970).

17. Bordenkircher v. Hayes, 434 U.S. 357 (1978).

18. Maria Cramer, *As Charges Mount for Parents in Varsity Blues Case, Some Legal Observers See Prosecutorial Strong-Arming*, Bos. Globe, Oct. 25, 2019 (quoting lead prosecutor, U.S. attorney Andrew Lelling).

Making the Defendant Suffer

Another way to discourage defendants from exercising their right to trial is to ensure they suffer for doing so. The most common example of this is pretrial detention, which results in defendants being confined in jails that are often far more unpleasant than prisons, with little ability to confer with counsel, communicate with friends or relatives, or prevent their lives from falling apart as they lose their jobs, miss car and rent payments, and perhaps even lose custody of their children.[19] Moreover, prosecutors can be highly adept at pushing off trial dates and defeating speedy-trial claims, with the result that those in pretrial detention often have literally no idea how long it will take for the charges against them to be resolved—that is, unless they agree to plead guilty.[20] Not surprisingly, people who are incarcerated while awaiting trial are substantially more likely to plead guilty than people who are free.[21]

Another way to make people suffer for exercising their trial rights is when prosecutors threaten to indict a defendant's family members if the defendant refuses to plead guilty—or promise to refrain from indicting them in exchange for a guilty plea. Conscience-shocking though that tactic may be to many, anecdotal evidence of its use abounds,[22] and the issue has arisen with sufficient frequency that more than half of the federal courts of appeals have weighed in on it, upholding the practice every time.[23]

Impairing the Defense

Another way to make people more amenable to pleading guilty is to undermine the quality of their defense. There are several ways to do this, including by assigning them an overworked and underresourced public defender[24] or by seizing their assets to ensure that they are unable to afford their counsel of choice, as the government was allowed to do in a 2014 Supreme Court case called *Kaley v. United States*.[25] Other sandbagging

19. *See, e.g.*, Shima Baradaran Baughman, *Costs of Pretrial Detention*, 97 B.U. L. Rev. 1, 4–7, 15–17 (2017).

20. *See, e.g.*, George Joseph & Simon Davis-Cohen, *Internal Documents Reveal How Bronx Prosecutors Are Taught to Slow Down Cases*, The Appeal (Aug. 2, 2018), https://theappeal.org/internal-documents-reveal-how-bronx-prosecutors-are-taught-to-slow-down-cases/.

21. *See, e.g.*, Megan T. Stevenson, *Distortion of Justice: How the Inability to Pay Bail Affects Case Outcomes*, 34 J. Law, Econ. & Org. 511, 512–13 (2018) (finding that pretrial detention leads to a 13 percent increase in the likelihood of being convicted, which is "largely explained by an increase in the likelihood of pleading guilty among those who would otherwise have been acquitted, diverted, or had their charges dropped").

22. *See, e.g.*, Nat'l Ass'n of Crim. Def. Laws., *supra* note 13 (recounting experience of Viken Keuylian, an exoneree who claims he was pressured into a false guilty plea in part by threats to indict his sister).

23. *See, e.g.*, United States v. Seng Chen Yong, 926 F.3d 582, 591 (9th Cir. 2019) (collecting cases).

24. Peter A. Joy, *Ensuring the Ethical Representation of Clients in the Face of Excessive Caseloads*, 75 Mo. L. Rev. 771, 778 (2010) (noting that "almost every jurisdiction in the United States exceeds" caseload guidelines for public defenders).

25. Kaley v. United States, 571 U.S. 320, 350 (2014) (Roberts, C.J., dissenting) (noting that "few things could do more to undermine the criminal justice system's integrity than to allow the Government to initiate a prosecution and then, at its option, disarm its presumptively innocent opponent by depriving him of his counsel of choice") (internal quotation and citation omitted).

tactics include withholding potentially exculpatory evidence during plea discussions[26] and discouraging witnesses from testifying for the defense—a practice that is technically improper but difficult to detect or to prove.[27]

The fact that prosecutors have used these and other tools to elicit false guilty pleas from innocent defendants is hardly surprising in light of studies that suggest it is far easier to induce false confessions of guilt than commonly supposed. Thus, as demonstrated by Professors Lucian Dervan and Vanessa Edkins, laboratory experiments focusing on false accusations have repeatedly shown that a majority of demonstrably innocent people will agree to less severe punishments to avoid the risk of losing an evidentiary hearing and receiving more severe punishments.[28] In one study, Dervan and Edkins created a simulation in which students were invited to participate in a project that they were told was designed to test individual work versus group work.[29] Using a cooperating student in the room with the test subjects, they managed to get about half the students to cheat by violating certain rules.[30] They then accused *all* the students of cheating and offered leniency to any who agreed to confess.[31] Fully 56 percent of the innocent subjects chose to plead guilty to avoid the harsher punishment that would supposedly be imposed had they unsuccessfully challenged the accusation.[32]

Given these experiments, the hundreds of documented false guilty pleas, and the virtually unlimited power of prosecutors to exert plea pressure, it should perhaps come as no surprise that virtually everyone who has studied the question recognizes that plea bargaining can and does become coercive. To take just one of many examples from judicial opinions, Judge John Gleeson of the U.S. District Court for the Eastern District of New York observed that in order to "coerce guilty pleas . . . prosecutors routinely threaten ultra-harsh, enhanced mandatory sentences that *no one*—not even the prosecutors themselves—thinks are appropriate" and warned that this tactic "coerces guilty pleas and produces sentences so excessively severe they take your breath away."[33]

Remarkably, even some components of the Department of Justice have acknowledged that plea bargaining can become coercive. For example, a 2011 report prepared by the Bureau of Justice Assistance notes that "[p]rosecutors have been found to use threats that *coerce* defendants into accepting pleas to secure a conviction when the

26. *See, e.g.*, Mansfield v. Williamson Cnty., 30 F.4th 276 (5th Cir. 2022) (affirming dismissal of civil rights lawsuit against prosecutors who elicited a false guilty plea from the plaintiff while withholding exculpatory evidence and affirming that criminal defendants have no constitutional right to the production of such evidence during plea discussions).

27. *See generally* Bennett L. Gershman, *Threats and Bullying by Prosecutors*, 46 Loy. U. Chi. L.J. 101, 108 (2014); *see also* Don Samuel, *Prosecutor or Judge Threatening Defense Witnesses*, Casetext (Sept. 1, 2015), https://casetext.com/analysis/witnesses-prosecutor-or-judge-threatening-defense-witnesses (collecting cases).

28. Lucian E. Dervan & Vanessa A. Edkins, *The Innocent Defendant's Dilemma: An Innovative Empirical Study of Plea Bargaining's Innocence Problem*, 103 J. Crim. L. & Criminol. 1, 34 tbl. 1 (2013).

29. *Id.* at 28.

30. *Id.* at 28–30.

31. *Id.* at 30.

32. *Id.* at 34 tbl. 1.

33. United States v. Kupa, 976 F. Supp. 2d 417, 419–20 (E.D.N.Y. 2013).

evidence in a case is insubstantial."[34] Similarly, a 1985 report by another Department of Justice component, the National Institute of Justice, explained that "[w]hile pleas today appear to be more likely to be 'intelligent'" in the sense that defendants were aware of all the consequences, "they have not lost their *coercive character*. The majority (77 percent) of the defendants [surveyed] said they *felt they had to accept the plea bargain*."[35]

Given the undeniable fact that coercion plays a troubling role in modern plea bargaining, the key questions are whether there is any way to ameliorate it, and if there is, then whether doing so should be a high priority. The answer to both questions is plainly yes, and the failure to make any real progress on that front represents a growing challenge to the legitimacy of the criminal justice system. Besides the general indifference of most judges and prosecutors, the primary obstacles appear to be the difficulty of drawing a judicially administrable line between permissible inducements and impermissible coercion, together with the sense of futility that this seems to engender. But in fact, a number of reforms hold real promise and could be readily implemented.

As suggested earlier, effective plea bargaining reform must satisfy two requirements: first, it should ensure that the risk of departing from the centuries-old procedural safeguards that constitute nearly half the Bill of Rights be shared equally by both sides; and second, the rules according to which the plea bargaining process operates must be ones that a rational person would accept as appropriate from behind the proverbial veil of ignorance—that is, without knowing whether they will encounter that process as a prosecutor, a defendant, or the victim of a crime. The current plea bargaining process meets neither of those standards because it saddles defendants with the full risk of departing from constitutionally prescribed adjudicative procedures, and it does so in a way that no rational person would agree to in advance if they believed it was just as likely that they would end up being the prosecuted rather than the prosecutor. Three ways the system could embrace the principles of shared and rational risk are first, by implementing a system of trial lotteries to audit the plea process and determine how often it produces false guilty pleas; second, by requiring a sentinel event review whenever a false guilty plea is identified; and third, by providing jurors with more information than they currently receive and thereby resurrecting the historical practice of jury independence.

Trial Lottery

The crucial first step in addressing coercive plea bargaining is to get a better understanding of how often people are induced to plead guilty to charges on which the government would not have been able to secure a conviction at trial—either because the defendant is in fact innocent or because of some defect in the government's case such as a faulty indictment, failure of proof, misreading of the relevant statute, police or prosecutorial misconduct, or myriad other reasons. It is important to frame the issue this

34. Bureau of Just. Assistance, U.S. Dep't of Just., Plea and Charge Bargaining: Research Summary 2 (Jan. 24, 2011), https://bja.ojp.gov/sites/g/files/xyckuh186/files/media/document/PleaBargainingResearchSummary.pdf.

35. William F. McDonald, Plea Bargaining: Critical Issues and Common Practices 132 (1985) (emphasis added).

way because inducing innocent people into falsely pleading guilty is not the only way that plea bargaining can be abused. Even before the era of modern plea bargaining, Columbia professor Michael Finkelstein noted in 1975 that "pressures to plead guilty have been used to secure convictions that could not otherwise be obtained," and he estimated that "one-third of all defendants pleading guilty in high-rate districts would ultimately have escaped conviction if they had refused to consent."[36] Whether that estimate is accurate matters less than the fact that plea bargaining can be—and unfortunately plainly has been—used to secure convictions in cases that would otherwise have been dismissed due to the government's inability to obtain a conviction via the constitutionally prescribed adjudicative process that includes, among other things, opportunities to challenge the admissibility of evidence, confront witnesses, obtain potentially exculpatory evidence, and remind jurors of the substantial difference between a preponderance-of-the-evidence standard and proof beyond a reasonable doubt.

As described by Professors Brennan-Marquez, Henderson, and Brown in their eponymous article, the basic idea of using trial lotteries to audit the plea process is straightforward.[37] A given court system would select a random sample of cases in which a plea agreement has been reached and send them to trial to see whether the government is able to obtain a conviction. If so, the case proceeds like any other in which a plea agreement has been reached: the defendant pleads guilty, the prosecution fulfills whatever promises it has made, and the defendant is sentenced accordingly. But if the jury acquits, then the charges are dismissed and the defendant goes free. And if the jury is unable to reach a verdict, the prosecution can decide whether to retry the case or dismiss the charges. There are, of course, many details that would have to be worked out in order to implement the proposed pilot program, but the authors make a persuasive case that there are no insurmountable challenges to implementing a trial lottery—only practical ones.

Besides sparing some innocent defendants a false conviction, a key virtue of trial lotteries would be to clarify whether illegitimate guilty pleas (again, defined as a guilty plea in a case where the government would not have been able to obtain a conviction at trial) are vanishingly rare, as some scholars contend,[38] or instead fairly common, as others contend.[39] This in turn would enable judges, prosecutors, and policymakers to decide whether to continue treating coercive plea bargaining as a minor, low-priority issue or to reassess and consider making a real effort to combat it, as this chapter proposes.

---

36. Michael O. Finkelstein, *A Statistical Analysis of Guilty Plea Practices in the Federal Courts*, 89 Harv. L. Rev. 293, 309–10 (1975).

37. Kiel Brennan-Marquez et al., *The Trial Lottery*, 56 Wake Forest L. Rev. 1 (2021).

38. Paul G. Cassell, *Overstating America's Wrongful Conviction Rate? Reassessing the Conventional Wisdom about the Prevalence of Wrongful Convictions*, 60 Ariz. L. Rev. 815, 847 (2018) (suggesting an overall false-conviction rate of 0.016 percent to 0.062 percent).

39. *See, e.g.*, Lucian E. Dervan, *Bargained Justice: Plea Bargaining's Innocence Problem and the* Brady *Safety-Valve*, 2012 Utah L. Rev. 51, 85 (noting that "[a]t least one study has concluded that as many as 27 percent of defendants who plead guilty would not have been convicted at trial" and suggesting a more conservative range of 1.6 to 8 percent); *see also* Rakoff, *supra* note 5 (noting false-plea estimate of 2 to 8 percent and arguing that even 1 percent would represent at least 20,000 people "who are in prison for crimes to which they pleaded guilty but in fact did not commit").

A supplement to the trial-lottery proposal would be to treat false guilty pleas the same way navies have always treated the loss of a ship in peacetime, which is to regard the incident as presumptively career-ending and subject the responsible person—captain or prosecutor, as the case may be—to a board of inquiry at which they may attempt to justify the catastrophe that it was their sacred professional duty to avoid. Prosecutors who prefer not to expose themselves to that risk—whether because they have lingering doubts about the strength of a particular case or because they are just unwilling to risk their career for the sake of efficiency—may simply decline to make a plea offer and take the case to trial instead. This proposal also has the salutary effect of more equitably spreading the inherent risk of jettisoning the exoneration-favoring adjudicative procedure described and prescribed by the Bill of Rights.

Sentinel Event Review

In many fields, including medicine and commercial aviation, it is standard procedure to conduct a "sentinel event review" following certain catastrophic outcomes, such as a plane crash or significant act of malpractice. The point of the review is not so much to assess blame as to identify the root causes of the incident and determine what systemic changes can be made to prevent the same thing from happening again. To its credit, the National Institute of Justice has created a Sentinel Events Initiative to "investigat[e] the feasibility of using a sentinel event review approach to learn from errors in the criminal justice system."[40] Unfortunately, however, there is still no established practice at the federal or state level of conducting sentinel event reviews in the wake of exonerations, including those occasioned by false guilty pleas. As with trial lotteries, there does not appear to be any insurmountable challenge to employing sentinel event reviews as a partial antidote to coercive plea bargaining—and, like trial lotteries, they would doubtless supply a wealth of valuable information about the pathology of false pleas.

Better-Educated and -Informed Juries

The third and final easily adoptable reform would be to provide more information to empaneled jurors so they are better able to perform the government-checking and injustice-preventing roles they played before, during, and for roughly a century after the founding. This could include an explanation of what might happen to the defendant if the jury convicts, the substance of any plea offer, and the power of juries to acquit against the evidence in order to prevent injustice (which is sometimes inappositely referred to as "jury nullification" despite the fact that jurors, unlike judges, have no power to strike down laws).

There are two distinct ways that some or all of this information could be provided to jurors. One is for the judge to do so, and in fact legislation has been proposed in Tennessee that would require a criminal trial judge, upon request of defense counsel, to advise the jury that while they "should" find the defendant guilty if the State proves its case beyond a reasonable doubt, "you may still find that based upon the facts of this case, a

40. Nat'l Inst. of Just., *Sentinel Events Initiative* (Nov. 1, 2017), https://nij.ojp.gov/topics/articles/sentinel-events-initiative.

guilty verdict will yield an unjust result, and you may find the defendant not guilty."[41] With respect to sentencing consequences, Professors Daniel Epps and William Ortman warn that "[w]hile the Constitution guarantees defendants a jury, courts permit prosecutors to coerce defendants using the threat of severe punishment into giving up this right and pleading guilty" and propose as a remedy that "in every criminal case, the judge should disclose the defendant's sentencing exposure to the jury for each count."[42] This practice would undo the federal judiciary's "iron law of jury ignorance"[43] and "enable a virtuous political feedback loop that could make our extraordinarily punitive legal system less severe."[44]

Unfortunately, there appears to be little likelihood that our former-prosecutor-heavy judiciary[45] will embrace the idea of founding-era-informed juries anytime soon, which poses the question of whether there might be some other means of providing information about sentencing, plea bargaining, and the power of conscientious acquittal to jurors even when judges and prosecutors would prefer that they remain ignorant of it. The answer is yes, absolutely, and a surprisingly strong argument can be made that the First Amendment protects some or all of those communications, even to empaneled jurors.

As a thought experiment, imagine that someone produced a jury-explainer video with A-list Hollywood talent, excellent production values, and a compelling narrative that informed viewers about America's dubious distinction as the world's leading jailer of human beings and the plea-driven system of mass adjudication necessary to sustain it. Imagine further that the video urged viewers to welcome jury service instead of trying to avoid it and advised them that, contrary to whatever impression they may be given by representatives of the judiciary or criminal justice system, American jurors have absolute, unreviewable authority to acquit factually guilty defendants in order to prevent injustice and that this power of conscientious acquittal could serve as a powerful antidote to the twin pathologies of overcriminalization and mass incarceration.

Conventional wisdom is that while the First Amendment certainly protects the creation of such a video and its distribution to most audiences, any deliberate effort to share the video with empaneled jurors would constitute criminal jury tampering that is not protected by the right to free expression. But in fact both premises are highly questionable, both because many jury-tampering statutes are phrased in such a way as to exclude at least some of that speech and because it is far from clear that the government's justifications for imposing a prior restraint on distributing the video to empaneled jurors would satisfy the exacting test for content-based restrictions on speech.[46] Moreover, it may not even be necessary to target empaneled jurors in the first place. If the hypothetical video proves sufficiently compelling to go viral—or with sufficiently effective microtargeting of people who are eligible for but have not yet been called for

41. S.B. 833, 112th Gen. Assemb. (Tenn. 2021).

42. Daniel Epps & William Ortman, *The Informed Jury*, 75 Vand. L. Rev. 823, 824–25 (2022).

43. *Id.* at 827.

44. *Id.* at 826.

45. Clark Neily, *Are a Disproportionate Number of Federal Judges Former Government Advocates?*, Cato Inst. (May 27, 2021), https://www.cato.org/study/are-disproportionate-number-federal-judges-former-government-advocates.

46. For a thorough discussion of these issues, see Clark Neily & Jay Schweikert, *Founding-Era Informed Juries and the First Amendment*, 20.2 Ohio St. J. Crim. L. 321 (2023).

jury service—it may become impossible in certain judicial districts to empanel a jury of 12 people who have not seen the video. If so, then the "iron law of jury ignorance" will have been repealed without the assistance of the judiciary and perhaps even over its steadfast objection.

Conclusion

As the Task Force Report makes clear, coercive plea bargaining is a cancer on America's criminal justice system and should be treated as such—with strong medicine, complete resolve, and an unwavering commitment to eradicating it from the body politic. This chapter has provided some reflections on how we might bring to life the principles of the report with real-world solutions that can combat coercive plea bargaining and revive the heart of the American adjudicatory system, the jury trial.

CHAPTER 11

Parting Thoughts

Editors

As the Task Force Report and the preceding chapters illustrate, there is much work to do if the American criminal justice system is to move forward toward a more just, more transparent, and fairer system of pleas. But we are now deep into that work, and a diverse and unified front has emerged to assist in implementing the change that is needed. Change of this magnitude, however, will take time.

Plea bargaining did not come to dominate swiftly. Rather, it rose slowly in the shadows of the criminal justice system, first in sporadic ways during the 1700s and 1800s and then in a surge in the early to mid-1900s before emerging from the shadows in the latter half of the 20th century. Even after its emergence, however, most plea practices and policies, if there were any, remained hidden from review, oversight, or public scrutiny. This long historic rise led us to today's system of justice—one in which 95 percent to 98 percent of convictions come from a plea of guilty, where plea practices vary from jurisdiction to jurisdiction, where the use of staggering sentencing differentials in some cases leads even the innocent to plead guilty, where cases have documented the use of threats against children and spouses to induce pleas of guilty, where impermissible conditions and waivers of rights are often found within the bargains, and where bargaining has exacerbated existing racial discrimination in the criminal justice system. Fundamentally, this also means that today's system of justice is one at direct odds with the Founders' vision of a system of trials and the Constitution's and Bill of Rights' codification of such an aspiration.

Unlike the shadowy rise of plea bargaining, the movement to reform plea bargaining of the last decade has been on display for all to see. Further, the movement has been one in which various actors in the criminal justice system have come together to engage in open dialogue and collaboration to both identify the areas in need of reform and consider thoughtful and effective responses to those challenges. These concepts of collaboration and open dialogue served as the basis for both the ABA Criminal Justice Section Plea Bargain Task Force and this book.

The task force was created with an eye toward bringing together members of the prosecution, defense, judiciary, academy, and advocacy communities to share experiences and insights as we considered paths forward. The opening meeting of the task force began by creating a list of the many ways in which plea bargaining is a benefit to the actors within the system and the system itself. The list was lengthy and illustrated plea bargaining's potential. The group then moved to creating a list of concerns about the way modern plea bargaining operates. This list was also lengthy and, importantly, was created by all who were present and reflected concerns emanating from each corner of the system. This collaborative spirit continued throughout the task force's work as the group met year after year to tackle the list of concerns through deep analysis and careful contemplation of potential responses and the possible consequences that might result from those actions. That process in totality led to the creation of the 14 Principles and the ability to present those principles to the criminal justice community as the unanimous recommendations of a group comprised of stakeholders representing many different interests.

This book further advances the work of the task force by delving more deeply into many of the issues, recommendations, suggestions, and principles contained in the Task Force Report. Plea bargaining itself is a complex topic, and reforming a system that has become so dominant and varied is even more challenging. The work of the movement to reform plea bargaining and the Plea Bargain Task Force will take much time to see results and achieve its objectives. But that journey has now begun in a way not previously seen. That open dialogues across the criminal justice community are occurring, including those that occurred at the task force meetings and within the bounds of this book, is itself a victory for efforts at reform. In the end, the system will have to change more than procedures and policies. The system will have to change the culture of bargains and with that, the culture of the criminal justice system itself.

APPENDIX A

Resolution 502

(Adopted at the Annual Meeting of the ABA House of Delegates)

August 8, 2023

Denver, Colorado

AMERICAN BAR ASSOCIATION

CRIMINAL JUSTICE SECTION

SECTION OF CIVIL RIGHTS AND SOCIAL JUSTICE

REPORT TO THE HOUSE OF DELEGATES

RESOLUTION

RESOLVED, That the American Bar Association adopts the Fourteen Principles contained in the American Bar Association Criminal Justice Section 2023 Plea Bargain Task Force Report, dated August 2023.

2023 Plea Bargain Task Force Report Principles

Principle 1: A vibrant and active docket of criminal trials and pre- and post-trial litigation is essential to promote transparency, accountability, justice, and legitimacy in the criminal justice system.

Principle 2: Guilty pleas should not result from the use of impermissibly coercive incentives or incentives that overbear the will of the defendant.

Principle 3: In general, while some difference between the sentence offered prior to trial and the sentence received after trial is permissible, a substantial difference undermines the integrity of the criminal system and reflects a penalty for exercising one's right to trial. This differential, often referred to as the trial penalty, should be eliminated.

Principle 4: Charges should not be selected or amended with the purpose of creating a sentencing differential, sentencing enhancement, punishment or collateral consequence to induce a defendant to plead guilty or to punish defendants for exercising their rights, including the right to trial.

Principle 5: The criminal justice system should recognize that plea bargaining induces defendants to plead guilty for various reasons, some of which have little or nothing to do with factual and legal guilt. In the current system, innocent people sometimes plead guilty to crimes they did not commit.

Principle 6: A defendant should have a right to qualified counsel in any criminal adjudication before the defendant enters a guilty plea. Counsel should be afforded a meaningful opportunity to satisfy their duty to investigate the case without risk of penalty to their client.

Principle 7: There should be robust and transparent procedures at the plea phase to ensure that the defendant's plea is knowing and voluntary, free from impermissible coercion, and that the defendant understands the consequences of their decision to plead guilty.

Principle 8: The use of bail or pretrial detention to induce guilty pleas should be eliminated.

Principle 9: Defendants should receive all available discovery, including exculpatory materials, prior to entry of a guilty plea, and should have sufficient time to review such discovery before being required to accept or reject a plea offer.

Principle 10: Although guilty pleas necessarily involve the waiver of certain trial rights, there are rights that defendants should never be required to waive in a plea agreement.

Principle 11: An adequate understanding of the collateral consequences that may flow from a guilty plea is necessary to ensure the guilty plea is knowing and voluntary.

Principle 12: Law students, lawyers, and judges should receive training on the use and practice of plea bargaining consistent with the findings and recommendations of the ABA Criminal Justice Section Plea Bargain Task Force Report.

Principle 13: Court systems, sentencing commissions, and other criminal justice stakeholders, including prosecutor offices and public defenders, should collect data about the plea process and each individual plea, including the history of plea offers in a case. Data collection should be used to assess and monitor racial and other biases in the plea process.

Principle 14: At every stage of the criminal process, there should be robust oversight by all actors in the criminal system to monitor the plea process for accuracy and integrity, to ensure the system operates consistent with the Principles in this Report, and to promote transparency, accountability, justice, and legitimacy in the criminal system.

Author Biographies

Russell D. Covey (Editor)

Russell Covey is a professor of law at Georgia State University College of Law, teaching criminal law and procedure. He served as cochair of the ABA Plea Bargain Task Force. In addition to publishing many book chapters and articles in his field, Covey is the coeditor of *The Wrongful Convictions Reader* (Carolina Press 2018). He has filed amicus briefs on behalf of the National Association of Criminal Defense Lawyers. Covey's recent work studies police misconduct and the effects of jailhouse informants as causes of wrongful convictions.

Lucian E. Dervan (Editor)

Lucian E. Dervan is a professor of law and Director of Criminal Justice Studies at Belmont University College of Law in Nashville, Tennessee. He created the ABA Plea Bargain Task Force during his time as chair of the ABA Criminal Justice Section in 2018–2019 and went on to serve as cochair of the task force. He is also the founding director of the Plea Bargaining Institute, which serves as the global intellectual home for academics, policymakers, advocacy organizations, and practitioners working in the plea bargaining space to share knowledge and collaborate. His research and writing focus on plea bargaining, white collar crime, and international criminal law. In the plea bargaining field, his research and writing focus on the history of plea bargaining, the constitutionality of plea bargaining, the psychological forces present in the plea bargaining system, and the phenomenon of false pleas of guilty. In addition to his books and articles, he is the founder and author of *The Plea Bargaining Blog*. He is a member of the American Bar Foundation and previously served as a member of the ABA Board of Governors, chair of the ABA Commission on the American Jury, and chair of the ABA Criminal Justice Section. Prior to joining the academy, Dervan served as a law clerk to the Honorable Phyllis A. Kravitch of the U.S. Court of Appeals for the Eleventh Circuit. He also practiced law with King & Spalding LLP and Ford & Harrison LLP.

Thea Johnson (Editor)

Thea Johnson is a professor of law at Rutgers Law School. She served as the reporter for the ABA Plea Bargain Task Force. Her scholarship focuses on the ways that stakeholders manipulate the plea process and stretch ethical boundaries to achieve particular outcomes. She has won several awards for her scholarship, including the 2022 Greg

Lastowka Award for scholarly excellence at Rutgers. Prior to joining Rutgers Law, Johnson was an associate professor of law at the University of Maine School of Law, a Thomas C. Grey Fellow at Stanford Law School, and a public defender in New York City.

Vanessa A. Edkins

Dr. Vanessa Edkins is the Director of Quantitative Research at Gartner, Inc. She is also professor emeritus of psychology at Florida Institute of Technology, where she previously served as the department head of the School of Psychology. She served as a member of the ABA Plea Bargain Task Force. She has published many works, including the book *A System of Pleas: Social Science's Contribution to the Real Legal System*. Her work has been cited in the *Wall Street Journal*, *The Economist*, and congressional testimony. In addition to her publications, Edkins has been a part of the Steering Committee on an NSF Research Coordination Network grant, which examines plea bargaining from multiple fields of study.

Clark Neily

Clark Neily is Senior Vice President for Legal Studies at the Cato Institute. He served as a member of the ABA Plea Bargain Task Force. Neily was a senior attorney and constitutional litigator at the Institute for Justice and director of the institute's Center for Judicial Engagement. He is an adjunct professor at George Mason's Antonin Scalia School of Law. He is also the author of *Terms of Engagement: How Our Courts Should Enforce the Constitution's Promise of Limited Government*.

Norman L. Reimer

Norman L. Reimer is Of Counsel at the New York firm Vladeck, Raskin, & Clark, P.C., where he has resumed his career as a criminal defense attorney and pursues systemic criminal justice reform. For more than a decade, a central focus of his work has been to expose and reform the trial penalty and the coercive plea practices that enable it. Reimer served as the Global CEO of Fair Trials from 2021 to 2022. Fair Trials is a global criminal justice watchdog, fighting for fairness, equality, and justice, that works to expose, challenge, and remedy systemic injustice in criminal processes. Before joining Fair Trials, Reimer served as the executive director of the National Association of Criminal Defense Lawyers (NACDL) from 2006 to 2021. NACDL is the preeminent organization in the United States dedicated to enhancing the capacity of the criminal defense bar to safeguard fundamental rights and promote reforms in furtherance of a fair, rational, humane, and nondiscriminatory criminal legal system. Prior to his time at NACDL, Reimer was a criminal defense lawyer based in New York City for over 20 years, practicing in state and federal court at both the trial and appellate levels and promoting systemic reform through his service as both a leader of the organized bar and the chair of numerous task forces and committees. He is a passionate advocate for the rights of the accused and the need to limit governmental overreach in the enforcement of its criminal laws.

Adnan Sultan

Adnan Sultan is a staff attorney at the Innocence Project, where he works nationwide to litigate post-conviction cases. He served as a member of the ABA Plea Bargain Task Force. Part of his work at the Innocence Project is instructing law students at the Innocence Project clinic at Cardozo School of Law in New York City. Prior to his position at the Innocence Project, Sultan worked as a staff attorney at the Bronx Defenders and was a member of the Bronx Defenders' Forensic Practice Group.

Index

U

V

W